GLOBAL ARMS PRODUCTION

Center for International Affairs
Harvard University

GLOBAL ARMS PRODUCTION: POLICY DILEMMAS FOR THE 1990s

edited by

Ethan B. Kapstein

**John M. Olin Institute for Strategic Studies
Economics and National Security Program
Harvard University
and
Department of Politics
Brandeis University**

UNIVERSITY
PRESS OF
AMERICA

Lanham • New York • London

University Press of America®, Inc.

4720 Boston Way
Lanham, Maryland 20706

3 Henrietta Street
London WC2E 8LU England

Co-published by arrangement with the
Center for International Affairs, Harvard University

The Center for International Affairs provides a forum for the
expression of responsible views. It does not, however, necessarily
agree with them.

Library of Congress Cataloging-in-Publication Data

Global arms production : policy dilemmas for the
1990s / edited by Ethan B. Kapstein.
p.   cm.
At head of title: Center for International Affairs, Harvard University.
Includes bibliographical references and index.
1. Weapons industry—International cooperation.
2. Defense industries—International cooperation.
3. Weapons industry—Government policy.
4. Defense industries—Government policy.
I. Kapstein, Ethan B.
II. Harvard University. Center for International Affairs.
HC79.D4G56   1992   338.4'76234—dc20   91–46128 CIP

ISBN 0–8191–8527–2 (cloth : alk. paper)
ISBN 0–8191–8528–0 (pbk. : alk. paper)

The Center for International Affairs
Executive Committee, 1991-1992

The Center for International Affairs is an autonomous multidisciplinary research institution within Harvard University's Faculty of Arts and Sciences. Founded in 1958, the Center seeks to provide a stimulating environment for a diverse group of scholars and practitioners studying various aspects of international affairs. Its purpose is the development and dissemination of knowledge concerning the essential features and crucial trends of international relations. Major Center research programs include national security affairs; U.S. relations with Europe, Japan, Africa, and other areas of the world; nonviolent sanctions in conflict and defense; and international economic policy. At any given time, over 160 individuals are working at the Center, including faculty members from Harvard and neighboring institutions, practitioners of international affairs, visiting scholars, research associates, postdoctoral fellows, and graduate and undergraduate student associates.

John M. Olin Institute for Strategic Studies
Economics and National Security Program
Study Group on Global Arms Production

Henri Conze, HCI, Paris, France

C. Michael Farr, Air Force Institute of Technology, Dayton, Ohio

Jacques S. Gansler, TASC, Arlington, Virginia

Grant T. Hammond, Air War College, Maxwell Air Force Base, Alabama

Joel J. Johnson, Aerospace Industries Association of America, Washington, D.C.

Ethan B. Kapstein, Project Director, Economics and National Security Program, Harvard University, Cambridge, Massachusetts, and Department of Politics, Brandeis University, Waltham, Massachusetts

William W. Keller, Office of Technology Assessment, U.S. Congress, Washington, D.C.

Richard Kwatnoski, Defense Systems Management College, Fort Belvoir, Virginia

Jack Nunn, Office of Technology Assessment, U.S. Congress, Washington, D.C.

Stanley Sienkiewicz, Department of Commerce, Washington, D.C.

Robert H. Trice, McDonnell Douglas, St. Louis, Missouri

Raymond Vernon, John F. Kennedy School of Government, Harvard University, Cambridge, Massachusetts

CONTENTS

Preface

Why do states collaborate in the production of advanced weaponry? Under what conditions do such collaborative arrangements succeed? What are the implications of armaments collaboration for the international economic and security environments? What will happen in the coming years as new alliances and security arrangements emerge? These are questions that concern policymakers, industry executives, and scholars alike, and that are likely to remain high on policy agendas as the arms trade receives renewed scrutiny.

Arms collaboration is not a new phenomenon, but there is increasing debate--both in the United States and abroad--over the associated costs and benefits. Critics charge that collaborative projects result in proliferation of powerful weapons capabilities, technology give-aways, the creation of defense-industrial competitors, and the loss of domestic jobs. Supporters argue that the very same projects strengthen alliance relations, provide access to new technology, and result in arms sales which might otherwise have been lost to foreign competitors. All these arguments pro and con were presented, for example, during the recent Congressional debate over the FSX, a Japanese jet fighter that would be built using technology and systems integration techniques purchased from the American firm General Dynamics.

From the perspective of microeconomics, it can be argued that collaborative arrangements for the production of complex weapons systems represent a "second-best" solution to the problem of defense acquisition. In the "first-best" world of the neo-classical economist, weapons would be built by countries according to the principles of comparative advantage; as a result, the United States would produce and export the bulk of the major weapons systems. But arms sales, of course, do not follow free-market dictates; government policies generally interfere with market processes. The result is a second-best world, where collaborative arrangements are struck owing to the desire of states to maintain domestic military-industrial capacity on the one hand, while incorporating capital and technology from abroad on the other. As a policy instrument, collaboration seeks to resolve some of the dilemmas associated with seeking national security in a global economy. In short, collaboration may be seen as a form of protectionism.

In practice, however, the success rate of collaborative projects presents a "mixed bag." Over time, either the states that are parties to the agreement, or the firms that are responsible for research, development, and production, have often found it impossible to live with the contractual terms originally set for the weapons project. In fact, the impediments to international collaboration are not difficult to understand; success depends upon persistent state commitment to a weapons project that may take ten years or more to complete, coupled with the ability of the industrial partners involved to execute the tasks assigned to them.

These practical difficulties notwithstanding, it would appear that future trends may continue to favor collaborative ventures. The end of the Cold War has meant a sharp reduction in defense budgets throughout the Western alliance, but at the same time the costs associated with new weapons programs continue to rise. To be sure, some countries may get out of defense production altogether. But those countries which wish to maintain a defense-industrial base will have no choice but to seek partners as they share the economic and technological risks associated with project development. Already, arms collaboration is well-advanced in Western Europe, and many more trans-Atlantic and trans-Pacific projects have been pursued than is commonly believed. At the same time, the industrial firms that actually build weapons have developed a dense network of corporate alliances, joint ventures, and international sourcing arrangements. At the sub-system and component levels, if not always at the level of the final product, the defense industries of the West are intertwined.

The chapters in this book treat arms collaboration from the perspectives of business executives, government officials, and academics grappling with various aspects of this issue-area. Arms collaboration raises serious questions concerning alliance relations, technology transfer, arms control, and international program management. Despite the political and economic complexities associated with collaborative programs, remarkably little of an analytical nature has been written to date which might help business executives and policymakers as they contemplate the costs and benefits associated with this approach to arms transfers. The book was written as a contribution to what we think will be an ongoing debate in this country and abroad over the costs and benefits.

The opening chapers of the book provide three different overviews. In the Introduction, I provide a conceptual framework for analyzing arms collaboration, drawing on the "second-best" perspective. Using NATO's experience from World War II to the present as an example, I trace the growing desire of America's alliance partners to incorporate the most advanced military technology and industrial processes in an effort to improve their domestic defense capabilities. Writing from more policy-oriented perspectives in their chapters, Jacques Gansler and William Keller discuss the conflicts that make collaborative programs so difficult to achieve in practice. Gansler, who has been on both the government and business ends of defense procurement, provides a litany of factors that mitigate against arms collaboration, while arguing at the same time that the current procurement policies of the United States are desperately outmoded. Keller, in contrast, focuses on the international security implications of arms collaboration, and he suggests that such projects may help diffuse lethal technology around the world.

Chapters 3 and 4 bring a geographic focus to the volume. Joel Johnson writes about the many problems that have impeded greater collaboration between the United States and NATO-Europe, which is all the more surprising given the success of collaborative ventures within Western Europe. For his part, Jack Nunn analyzes the sharp debates that have occurred over collaboration with America's fierce economic competitors in the Far East, especially Japan. Again, this competition notwithstanding, Nunn reminds us that there has been a great deal more collaboration between the U.S. and Japan than is often imagined.

Chapters 5 through 8 provide a "hands-on" approach to arms collaboration that should be of particular value to those in industry and government who are actually working on the problem. A seasoned defense executive with substantial experience in Washington, Robert Trice describes from a business point-of-view what makes for success and failure in collaborative programs. Michael Farr, a U.S. Air Force officer who has conducted perhaps the most in-depth analysis to date on success and failure, provides his remedies for success. And in their respective chapters, Grant Hammond and Stan Sienkiewicz analyze two of the most problematic sticking points in the collaborative process: the role of offsets and technology transfer. Collectively, the book provides a uniquely comprehensive examination of international arms collaboration.

It should be emphasized that, beyond providing insights into the weapons marketplace, the story told here has broader implications for our understanding of some of the enduring tensions in the international economy. Throughout the postwar era, the Western allies have sought to create a liberal international economy based on the principles of free trade, currency convertibility, and direct investment flows. The advancement of these objectives, however, has come into conflict with the particular politico-military interests of the alliance partners. Few states in the international system have allowed the division of labor to determine the structure of their high technology and defense-related industries. Viewed heuristically, the issue of arms collaboration can help us to understand why corporate alliances have emerged as an increasingly prominent feature of the global marketplace, since this corporate form addresses national demands for military and economic security, without exclusion from the international economy.

This book is the product of a study group formed under the auspices of the Economics and National Security Program, John M. Olin Institute for Strategic Studies, Harvard University. It evolved following a major conference cosponsored by the program and the Industrial College of the Armed Forces at the National Defense University, which was held in May 1990. The codirectors of the program, Ethan B. Kapstein and Raymond Vernon, thank the authors from government and industry who gave of their hectic schedules to attend (and address) the Washington conference and several study group meetings at Harvard, and to prepare contributions for the book. The program directors also wish to thank the Pew Charitable Trusts for their generous support of this project, and in particular they would like to express their gratitude to Kevin Quigley, Dan McIntyre, and Steve Del Rosso from the Trusts' Public Policy division for their extraordinary assistance at all stages.

Ethan B. Kapstein
Cambridge, Massachusetts

Introduction:
Explaining Arms Collaboration

Ethan B. Kapstein

Ethan B. Kapstein is Assistant Professor of International Relations at Brandeis University, and Co-Director of the Economics and National Security Program at the John M. Olin Institute for Strategic Studies, Harvard University. He wishes to thank Robert Art, Stephen Krasner, Michael Mastanduno, Andrew Moravcsik, Jonathan Tucker, and Raymond Vernon for their comments, and the Pew Charitable Trusts for its support of this project. Portions of this chapter have appeared in *Political Science Quarterly* 106 (Winter 1991/92).

Looking at why and how states collaborate in the production of advanced weaponry raises questions of both theoretical importance and policy relevance. From a theoretical perspective, the issue of inter-state collaboration is among the most prominent concerns of research in international political economy.[1] In the policy realm, the costs and benefits associated with armaments collaboration have been widely debated, as exemplified by the recent controversy over the FSX, a Japanese jet fighter that will be built using technology and systems integration techniques purchased from the American firm General Dynamics.[2]

In this chapter I argue that collaborative arrangements for the production of complex weapons systems represent a "second-best" solution to the problem of arms manufacture. Such arrangements reflect the desire of states to maintain domestic defense-industrial capacity on the one hand, while incorporating capital and technology from abroad on the other. As a policy instrument, collaboration seeks to resolve the underlying tension between nationalistic conceptions of security and the globalization of advanced industries.

This chapter focuses on the evolution of the NATO arms market. The general framework developed here, however, may be profitably extended to studies of other collaborative arrangements, such as those now prominent in Western Europe.[3] Although the present author has not done so, it would also be of value to extend the work to commercial economic ventures in which international collaboration has become widespread.

In practice, not all collaborative arrangements to produce weapons have succeeded. Over time, either the states that are parties to the agreement, or the firms that are responsible for research, development and production, have often
found it impossible to live with the contractual terms originally set for the project. I argue that the impediments to international collaboration are not difficult to understand; success depends upon persistent state commitment to a weapons project that may take ten years or more to complete, coupled with the ability of the industrial partners involved to execute the tasks assigned to them. Beyond providing insights into the weapons marketplace, the story told here has broader implications for our understanding of some of the enduring tensions in the international political economy. Throughout the postwar era, the Western allies have advanced the spread of a liberal international economy based on the principles of free trade, currency convertibility, and direct investment flows.[4] The advancement of these objectives, however, has come into conflict with the particular politico-military interests of the alliance partners. Few states in the international system have allowed the division of labor to determine the structure of their high technology and defense-related industries.[5] Viewed as a heuristic case study, the article raises the hypothesis that corporate alliances will emerge as a prominent feature of the global marketplace, since this corporate form addresses national demands for military and economic security, without exclusion from the international economy.

THE STRUCTURE OF ARMAMENTS PRODUCTION

The world's defense industries sit on the cusp of economics and national security. In nearly all industrial states, and in a growing number of developing countries, public officials have used protectionist measures to maintain and stimulate indigenous defense firms, and to ensure that some military-industrial capability rests on national soil. At the same time, the defense industries, like their high-technology counterparts on the commercial side, have formed complex global networks through joint-ventures, corporate alliances, and offset purchase arrangements. These networks enable defense firms to access foreign markets, technologies, and capital.[6]

National solutions to the problem of acquiring costly, "high-tech" defense goods depend upon the availability of two key resources: technology and money. The matrix diagram presented in Figure 1 provides a static view of state opportunities to acquire defense products; the dynamic element introduced by state and corporate policies over time may be deduced by the diagonal movement (south-west to north-east) from coproduction to codevelopment.

The matrix suggests that when states have both technological and financial resources, they can opt for autonomous solutions to weapons acquisition; the French *Rafale* aircraft program, or the British *Harrier*, provide examples. But few alliance members outside the United States have the ability to mobilize the assets necessary for weapons production, as exemplified by the growing debate in France over the costs associated with the *Rafale* program.[7] Moving to the south-west, when states possess financial resources to invest in an industrial infrastructure but lack technology, they are limited to assembling foreign technology products, or coproduction; the F-16 program in Western Europe and Turkey provides a notable example (this program is described in some detail in the chapter by Robert Trice). When neither financial nor technological resources are available, states must import needed defense goods. Finally, when states have achieved a certain level of technological capability but lack financial resources to develop and market the technology, or when they seek to spread the risks associated with weapons development, they may opt for collaborative codevelopment projects; codevelopment, which requires substantial "up-front" investment in R&D, is at least 50 percent more costly than coproduction.[8] The "Nunn Amendment" weapons programs (named after Senator Sam Nunn), which provide government funds for Western defense industries engaged in codevelopment projects, fit into this latter category; the Nunn amendment is discussed later in the article.

FIGURE 1
STATE STRATEGIES FOR ACQUIRING WEAPONS

Financial Assets

	Y	N
	Y	Autonomy (Rafale)	Codevelop (Nunn Amendment)
Technology Assets		
	N	Coproduce (F-16)	Import

State Acquisition Preferences:
    Autonomy > Codevelop > Coproduce > Import

Below the matrix I provide an ordering of state acquisition preferences. *Ceteris Paribus*, states would always prefer to be autonomous in weapons research, development and production; they are impeded from doing so by their inability to mobilize technological and/or financial assets. Codevelopment and coproduction are "second-best" solutions; they enable the state to maintain a domestic defense-industrial base and to share the financial and technical risks of weapons development with alliance partners. Reliance on imports, while economically cost-effective, is the least desirable political option, as attested to empirically by the large number of alliance states that have sought, at a minimum, coproduction agreements (including such small states as Belgium and the Netherlands), and the growing number of states in the developing world that are engaged in defense production.[9]

State preferences in the defense industry are clearly at odds with "free market" dictates. Public officials have rejected competition and comparative advantage as the basis for military industrialization, even within the NATO orbit, and they have been unwilling to permit indigenous defense capabilities to vanish. As Keohane and Nye felicitously argue, statesmen often seek to avoid the "efficiency trap" as they fashion policy alternatives; they recognize the political need for "second-best," non-market solutions.[10]

Despite the propensity of states that lack sufficient internal resources to engage in collaboration, weapons codevelopment programs (as exemplified by the Nunn amendment) have proven difficult to execute in practice. Codevelopment requires that firms divide the labor involved in a weapons project and produce their share of the project on time and within a specified budget. It further requires a state-level commitment to procure the jointly-produced weapons system. It may take ten years or more, however, to go from basic research and development to prototype construction.[11] Over this prolonged time-frame, economic and strategic variables may change; firms may be unable to "deliver the goods" while changes in state strategy can end the commitment to a given weapons-system. The possibilities for unraveling, of course, are multiplied as the numbers of states and firms involved in a project increase. These changes in strategy and capability can undermine the rationale for a collaborative project, or make it less attractive to public officials. Thus, while collaborative programs enjoy a compelling logic, success remains elusive.

To summarize the argument, collaborative programs for building weapons represent a "second-best" solution to the problem of military procurement. The first-best solution of free trade and competition has been rejected by states which seek to protect and maintain indigenous defense capacity. However, in spite of the (second-best) logic of these new corporate arrangements, severe impediments to successful codevelopment exist at both the firm and state levels.

CHANGE IN THE ALLIANCE ARMS MARKET

Since its inception in 1949, the North Atlantic Treaty Organization (NATO) has sought to transform its national collection of troops and weapons into a united force capable of coalition warfare. The terms of that transformation, however, have changed with shifts in the relative capabilities of the alliance partners. During the early postwar years, NATO's effort to create an arsenal characterized by the rationalization, standardization, and interoperability (RSI) of weapons systems was based on European imports of U.S. defense goods. Such imports were often financed through the Foreign Military Sales (FMS) assistance program. But as Western Europe recovered from the war and rebuilt its domestic arms industries, this approach to RSI was no longer acceptable.

The growing capabilities of European defense firms are mirrored in the data on U.S. arms exports to its NATO partners. Following the early postwar boom, weapons sales dropped precipitously from a high-water mark of $15 billion in 1953 to a level of only $3 billion in 1962 (see Table 1).[12] In response to these market developments, the Kennedy Administration launched a new program entitled "Win the Game in Europe by Managing Problems, Organizing Sales Effort." An aggressive U.S. sales campaign—as opposed to unilateral military aid—became the basis for NATO acquisition policy.[13]

In order to win sales in an increasingly competitive market, U.S. firms promised coproduction (but not codevelopment) of weapons systems with their European counterparts. During the first years of this effort, the Hawk (1958), Sidewinder (1959), and Bullpup (1962) missiles, the F-104G fighter (1960), the Mark 44 torpedo (1960), and the M-72 Light anti-tank weapon (1963) were built in collaboration with European manufacturers.[14] As a result of this policy, U.S. dominance in NATO weapons markets was maintained, even as the U.S. was sharing technology and production techniques with potential competitors.

Indeed, the German decision to purchase the Starfighter over a competing French design from Dassault was made at least in part owing to the "generous licensed-production offer" Lockheed made to German industry. Jonathan Tucker argues that "Lockheed was willing to make an aggressive offer because it desperately needed a major contract to ensure its economic survival." The deal included substantial technology transfer and, of course, joint production of the aircraft. In Tucker's words, "the Starfighter program proved to be a windfall for the German aeronautics industry."[15]

TABLE 1
U.S. ARMS EXPORTS TO NATO-EUROPE, 1950-1964
(in thousands of 1986 dollars)

Fiscal Year	NATO-Europe Imports
1950	$470,602
1951	5,326,963
1952	6,934,724
1953	15,316,117
1954	13,532,406
1955	9,133,364
1956	10,327,070
1957	7,873,933
1958	6,589,474
1959	4,657,500
1960	4,822,043
1961	3,083,550
1962	3,035,576
1963	5,471,253
1964	3,355,656

Source: Paul Ferrari et al., *U.S. Arms Exports* (Cambridge, Mass.: Ballinger, 1988), p. 95.

By the time the Starfighter program began to wind-down in the mid-1960s, "West Germany had achieved the capacity to manufacture (but not to develop) high performance aircraft at the same level as the French and British industries."[16] For the French, however, the German decision to produce an American fighter had been a major disappointment. Joint production by France and Germany of a French plane would have gone a long way toward keeping the French aeronautics industry competitive against the United States. This set-back prevented France from achieving the economies of scale deemed necessary to remain an effective competitor, given the rapidly increasing costs associated with weapons research, development, and procurement.

In the face of renewed American competition owing to defense coproduction agreements, Britain and France became increasingly concerned with the problem of maintaining their national aerospace industries. Each country continued to have independent strategic interests outside the NATO orbit, and both viewed a vibrant defense industry as critical to overall technological and industrial development. Accordingly, both countries sought to find partners who would cooperate in the production and procurement of major weapons systems, in order to spread the financial and technical risks and the acquisition costs.

One manifestation of European efforts to maintain autonomous arms capabilities was the British initiative in 1968 to launch Eurogroup, consisting of ten NATO-Europe countries (France, which withdrew from the NATO unified command structure in 1966, did not join Eurogroup, but in 1976 it and the Eurogroup members founded the Independent European Program Group (IEPG) to effect broader European cooperation). Eurogroup "marked the real beginning of a European response to US dominance and the imbalance in transatlantic arms transfers..." While the ten members made some progress in launching cooperative development programs in the absence of France, especially in the area of land armaments, French participation since 1976 has greatly extended the range and scope of collaborative programs.[17]

Over the past twenty-five years, collaboration has emerged as the principal European response to the dual problem of rising weapons costs and ensuring the maintenance of some *national* defense capabilities in the face of U.S. competition and technical superiority. Although this is not the place to describe in detail European defense teaming—a large literature on this topic already exists—by the late 1960s collaboration had become widespread, and involved a variety of weapons systems, as shown in Table 2.[18] Consistent with strategic trade theory, European governments used subsidization of research and development, discrimination in procurement policies, and provision of capital to defense contractors on favorable terms, as techniques for expanding the market for "national champions."[19]

TABLE 2
SELECTED EUROPEAN COLLABORATIVE ARMS PROJECTS

Project	System	Start Date	Countries
Jaguar	Aircraft	1965	GB, France
Lynx	Helicopter	1967	GB, France
Tornado	Aircraft	1968	GB, FRG, Italy
Alpha Jet	Aircraft	1969	France, FRG
Otomat	Missile	1969	France, Italy
RITA	Communications	1973	France, Belgium

Sources: Tucker, "Shifting Advantage" (see n. 9); Kolodziej, *Making and Marketing Arms* (see n. 26); Hartley, *NATO Arms Cooperation* (see n. 14).

From the perspective of NATO's collective security, the proliferation of armaments programs in the United States and Western Europe had both positive and negative elements. To be sure, the United States hailed the increase in the West's "defense industrial base" and consequently the enlarged mobilization capacity that would certainly be needed in the event of a prolonged conflict with the Soviet Union. But conversely, the overlap in weapons programs and the lack of NATO standardization resulted in a tremendous waste of financial resources and military inefficiency that could prove fatal on the battlefield. An influential report by Thomas Callaghan of the Center for Strategic and International Studies (CSIS) in 1974 asserted that rationalization and standardization of NATO armaments could lead to alliance-wide acquisition savings of over $10 billion per year.[20]

From the perspective of the U.S. prime defense contractors, the growing sophistication of the European armaments industry spelled declining export markets. This became especially troublesome in the early 1970s, as the Vietnam war was winding down. During the Vietnam conflict, American firms had already lost some third world markets to European competitors owing to the U.S. government's refusal to approve sales of systems that were needed in the war zone, such as the A-4 Skyhawk. Traditionally, the industry had looked to export markets to make-up for part of the cyclical decline in domestic procurement; now, the industry was being squeezed both at home and abroad.[21]

In response to these changes in the NATO marketplace, U.S. Secretary of Defense James Schlesinger launched a new weapons policy initiative in the summer of 1975 that came to be known as the "two-way street." This represented an effort to balance the U.S./NATO-Europe trade balance through innovative weapons procurement arrangements, while maintaining open markets for U.S. defense contractors. According to consultant Thomas Callaghan, Schlesinger *"harbored many reservations about...a cartelized Europe..."* (my emphasis). By July the "two-way street" had been adopted by Congress in the Culver-Nunn Amendment (the first Nunn amendment), which "declared it to be *national* policy that weapons and equipment...shall be standardized or at least interoperable with the equipment of its NATO allies..."[22] Schlesinger told Congress that the objectives of the two-way street were to: (1) enhance NATO standardization; (2) encourage American *and* European technological and industrial strength; (3) encourage *independent, competitive* national weapons programs; (4) increase U.S. purchases of European military hardware; and (5) increase European purchases of U.S. hardware on the basis of coproduction.[23]

At the same time as the two-way street was being declared official policy, it was being translated into practice by American and European defense firms. In the summer of 1975 General Dynamics (GD) and four European Participating Governments (EPGs—Belgium, Denmark, the Netherlands, and Norway) announced the "deal of the century"; coproduction of the F-16 lightweight fighter aircraft that had been recently adopted by the U.S. Air Force. The F-16 program gave the EPGs access to F-16 advanced technology, the construction of two assembly lines in Europe (in Belgium and the Netherlands), an opening to American and foreign defense markets through offset arrangements, and numerous benefits to European subcontractors. According to a prominent GD official, the coproduction deal led to "a number of innovative international business arrangements, which...include direct and indirect offsets, development of foreign suppliers, creation of joint ventures, and licensed production..."[24]

The F-16 program effectively segmented NATO's jet aircraft market into three groups: the EPGs that purchased the plane; the French, who remained autonomous; and the major Eurogroup countries (Britain, West Germany, and Italy) that pursued the development of a multi-role combat aircraft (MRCA), named Tornado. Cynical European observers deemed that this is exactly what the United States wanted to do: to divide and conquer. By engaging at least some NATO countries in attractive coproduction deals, the U.S. could weaken major competitors and maintain its Western European market share.[25]

The F-16 came to be seen, in the eyes of many European industrialists and public officials (particularly in France), as a Trojan horse wheeled in under the banner of the two-way street.[26] To be sure, the United States had purchased the French-designed ROLAND missile, but even this program raised suspicions; it appeared that the American licensees, Hughes and Boeing, sought to improve the French model and then export the redesigned missile back to NATO countries (ultimately the U.S. cancelled the ROLAND program). It soon became apparent to American officials that their approach to the two-way street—based on competitive R&D and licensing arrangements—had failed to provide the basis for an enduring NATO armaments policy.[27]

On February 2, 1976, France joined the Eurogroup members in their collaborative activities, forming the Independent European Programme Group (IEPG). This "marked the beginning of strong French participation in continuing Western European efforts to cooperate closely in arms procurement and production." The objectives of IEPG were to strengthen European armaments industries; increase American purchases of European equipment; and promote standardization of equipment among the IEPG member states.[28] The creation of the IEPG demonstrated a European commitment to the maintenance of *national* defense industries based on *collaborative* as opposed to *competitive* defense projects.[29]

With the founding of the IEPG, the American hegemon recognized that its preferred NATO armaments policy—based on competitive R&D and competitive procurement—faced mortal opposition in Europe. In the words of a French public official, the U.S. approach to RSI was "dead in the water."[30] The Europeans were now capable of producing a wide-array of weapons, even if these systems were generally based on second-generation technology. For American firms, growing European capabilities meant that business based on off-the-shelf exports and licensed coproduction was coming to an end; in 1982, arms sales to NATO-Europe totalled only $2.1 billion.[31] Western Europe had, indeed, engaged in significant "profit shifting" away from American defense firms since the end of World War II.

But European efforts to develop innovative defense technology were less successful. Given the size of the U.S. domestic procurement market, the experience of American defense contractors in the manufacture of "high technology" defense products, and the scale of U.S. defense spending, it was unlikely that European firms would be able to develop comparable advanced technology and compete with their American counterparts for NATO-wide contracts (including U.S. defense contracts) at any time in the near future.[32] The United States far-outstripped NATO-Europe in the area of defense R&D; in 1984 the "big three" of Western Europe (Britain, France, and West Germany) spent $6.5 billion on defense research, whereas the U.S. invested $29.3 billion.[33] If Western European firms were to participate in the larger NATO weapons market, they would have to find some way to participate in the development of leading-edge defense technology.

COLLABORATION AS POLICY

In 1983 the president of the Center for Strategic and International Studies, David Abshire, was appointed by President Reagan to the post of U.S. Permanent Representative to the North Atlantic Council.[34] Abshire came to government with strong views regarding alliance industrial cooperation; ten years earlier, he had supported the writing of the "Callaghan Report," which had generated widespread interest in the problem of NATO RSI, and in 1976 he had established the CSIS Transatlantic Policy Panel, composed of leading American and European public officials (including Senator Sam Nunn) and business executives, many of whom came from defense firms. Abshire, in short, was at the hub of a transnational policy network dedicated to enhancing arms cooperation within the NATO orbit.[35]

Once in Brussels, the new representative went to work building political support for armaments cooperation. But rather than separate the defense industrial issues from broader political-military ones, he purposely melded them. His strategy was to address the issue of RSI in the context of the contemporary debate over NATO's conventional force structure. The U.S. Mission produced an analysis that pointed to Warsaw Pact superiority in conventional forces (CSIS, incidentally, was involved at this time in a major study of the NATO/Warsaw Pact conventional balance), and concluded that "given limited resources to achieve improved conventional defense, a key mechanism had to be significantly enhanced armaments cooperation."[36]

Abshire called for a NATO "resources strategy" that would be an intrinsic part of the west's "grand strategy." The objective of this resources strategy would be to make more efficient use of the "West's superior resources to bear on the problem of improving conventional forces at affordable costs...It demands improved industrial and armaments cooperation across the Atlantic..."[37] Under Abshire's leadership, RSI was transformed from an acquisition problem into a strategic imperative.

Nonetheless, Abshire recognized the need for "economic" analysis in support of his conclusion that armaments cooperation was a good thing. In this regard, consultant Thomas Callaghan played a vital role. In an article that proved to be widely influential, he warned of "the structural disarmament of NATO." NATO nations, he said, were squeezed between rising weapons costs on the one hand and decreasing procurement dollars on the other. As a result of these trends, the member states would find themselves at a growing disadvantage to the Warsaw Pact's superior conventional forces. NATO efficiency was further reduced by the ragtag collection of systems that weren't interoperable. The only way to solve this problem was to promote *collaborative* research and development and *collaborative* procurement.[38]

Senator Sam Nunn found the Callaghan prognosis correct, and alarming. He recalled:

> I talked many times with defense consultant Tom Callaghan...I read his articles. I talked with David Abshire...and Dennis Kloske (a Department of Defense official) and they brought the idea (of the Nunn Amendment) up to me. I liked it. I thought it was a very good idea so I came back and got to work on it.[39]

The Callaghan approach to arms collaboration was also attractive because it played upon a growing problem in defense budgeting, namely, the costs associated with basic research. A modern weapons system, like the Advanced Tactical Fighter (ATF), could absorb hundreds of millions of dollars in "paper studies" before prototypes were even built.[40] R&D in the defense area was expensive and highly risky; the chances that a given scientific investigation would translate into a weapon that was ultimately procured by the armed forces was slim.[41] During the 1950s, the "up-front" R&D costs associated with weapons acquisition comprised only five percent of the cost of the system; by the 1980s this had risen to over fifty percent.[42]   Accordingly, public officials and defense industry executives were seeking new ways to spread the financial and technical risks associated with the weapons acquisition process. In short, Callaghan's analysis made an alliance virtue out of economic necessity. For the U.S. defense industry, however, collaboration based on codevelopment with NATO-Europe involved a Faustian bargain; it was an exchange of technology for market access. One industry organization stated that the interest in a NATO RSI policy based on codevelopment reflected "a buyers' market where purchasers can demand concessions...For the U.S., though, the stakes can be high—market access in exchange for development and production work and, often, technology."[43] Indeed, in a 1983 report the Defense Science Board, a Pentagon advisory group composed of defense industry executives, had warned that codevelopment projects involved a "trade-off...between the strengthened alliance that increased technology sharing may help establish and the inevitably increased competition for U.S. industry that it will also create."[44] For the firms, codevelopment was a second-best solution to the problem of marketing arms; their preference would have been to perform R&D autonomously and then export or coproduce end-items.[45] But industry recognized that the second-best solution helped it to overcome two important problems: first, access to European markets; second, growing R&D costs. This incipient industrial interest was articulated by Nunn in an interview with *Jane's Defence Weekly*. Nunn stated that industry "liked the idea" of cooperative research and development. Given the up-front costs of performing defense R&D, they welcomed the creation of a new pool of research funds. Knowing that firms wished to remain active in European markets, he reported that executives wanted to get "involved" in arms cooperation "at the R&D stage, at the very outset of development so the system could grow up in an environment of cooperation from the beginning."[46]

   In March 1985, Dennis Kloske, the DOD's special advisor for armaments, prepared a concept paper entitled "Creation of a Funding

Source for US Participation in NATO Co-Development Programs."
Kloske argued that the establishment of a "general fund" upon which
the services could draw to support NATO cooperative programs
would have several significant advantages in meeting the Pentagon's
political and economic objectives. These objectives included
encouragement of armaments cooperation, easing of financial burdens
on the US for weapons development, standardization of weapons, and
a desire "to keep American industry involved with European
counterparts during Europe's industrial 'realignment' and period of
introspection."[47]

On May 22, 1985, Senator Sam Nunn introduced an amendment
to the Fiscal Year 1986 Department of Defense Authorization Act,
which was cosponsored by a bipartisan group of senators including
William Roth, John Warner, John Glenn and Barry Goldwater. This
amendment encouraged arms collaboration between the United States
and its NATO allies through collaborative research and development
programs. According to one journalist who has followed the Nunn
Amendment since its inception:

> The term 'NATO cooperative research and development
> projects' was specifically defined...It refers to a project
> involving joint participation by the United States and one or
> more other member nations of NATO...to carry out a joint
> research and development program...These programs are
> required to fall into one of the following categories...(a) to
> develop new conventional defense equipment and munitions;
> or (b) to modify existing military equipment to meet United
> States military requirements.[48]

Secretary of Defense Casper Weinberger signaled his
commitment to the Nunn Amendment in a letter to the service
secretaries dated June 6, 1985. He urged the secretaries to ensure
that acquisition programs be designed with broad NATO objectives,
including armaments cooperation, in mind. Historically, the services

had procured weapons based on their narrow self-interest, and indeed *inter-service* procurement had been no more successful than *international* collaboration![49]   The Nunn Amendment would only succeed if the services cooperated with their NATO counterparts.[50]

The Nunn Amendment represented a major shift in U.S. preferences in the area of NATO arms procurement. For a decade, U.S. policy had been based on the concept of *competitive* research and development (R&D) among member states, and *competitive* procurement of end-items.[51] Competition in weapons production and procurement would promote an economically efficient alliance division of labor in the building of weaponry; in the language of economic theory, it was a "first best" policy.[52]   With the Nunn Amendment, the United States adopted a new approach to NATO rationalization, standardization, and interoperability. It now encouraged *collaborative* programs among alliance member states, from the research and development stages to the ultimate procurement and fielding of systems.

The Nunn amendment provided several incentives to American defense firms to ensure their participation. First, it offered a pool of research funds for cash-starved defense industries, so long as they collaborated in weapons R&D. Second, by promoting collaboration, the amendment helped maintain access for U.S. defense firms to the European market, advanced RSI, and it encouraged the spread of economic and technological risks inherent in weapons development. Finally, by subsidizing research, it reduced the up-front expenditures that companies must commit to a new weapons program. In sum, the amendment appeared to serve prominent state and industry objectives.

IMPLEMENTING COOPERATIVE PROGRAMS

Following the enactment of the Nunn amendment, and congressional appropriations of $100 million for NATO cooperative R&D projects, Deputy Secretary of Defense William Taft directed the military services to nominate prospective systems for funding. The DOD implementation process was outlined by armaments advisor Dennis Kloske in a memorandum of June 1986.[53] Under Kloske's guidance,

> two criteria have evolved in determining the suitability of a project for Nunn Amendment funding: the project must address a priority military requirement identified by one of the...major NATO commanders...in addition, the nominating military service must be prepared to fund the project after the permissible two years of Nunn Amendment funding.[54]

These two criteria reflect the department's concern that "dog programs" (projects of marginal value to the armed forces) not be offered for funding. The services must provide a military justification for each project they nominate, and they must be willing to finance the program after the two-year Nunn Amendment "seed money" is gone. Once these two criteria are met, the DOD then signs Memoranda of Understanding (MOU) with the NATO allies involved in joint weapons development.

The U.S. armed forces identified four candidates for Nunn funding in FY86, while the IEPG in Europe proposed six weapons programs. Four of these ten programs ultimately received funding: a precision guided munitions (pgm) project; the NATO frigate; a friend or foe identification system; and a system involving target acquisition.[55]

During the initial two years of its existence, the Amendment generated, in the words of Senator Nunn, tremendous "excitement" on both sides of the Atlantic.[56] By 1989, the United States had launched twenty-seven programs involving cooperative research and development. As of June 1989, the Pentagon was projecting an investment of $3 billion in these programs over the five year period FY90-FY95; the NATO-Europe contribution was expected to be almost double that amount.[57]

But by the autumn of 1989, the feeling of optimism regarding cooperative programs was collapsing. Suddenly, NATO members were "cancelling billions of dollars in weapons-standardization programs because of simultaneous declines in perceptions of the Soviet threat and in Western defense budgets." Britain, France and Italy withdrew from the most visible Nunn project, the NATO frigate, while the United States and Britain quit an air-to-ground missile program. From the intra-European perspective, the most significant cancellation was Germany's decision to leave the ASRAAM (advanced short-range air-to-air missile) project; cooperation, a German defense official proclaimed, was "not an end in itself..."[58] With the end of the Cold War, NATO leaders perceived the resurgence of "old go-it-alone habits."[59]

But the cancellation of several Nunn amendment programs should not be associated solely with strategic factors at the systemic level. Variables at the level of the firm would also lead us to predict that many if not most collaborative programs would be cancelled.[60] In Figure 2, I suggest that cancellation will likely result from changes in state military strategy on the one hand, and/or alterations in firm capabilities on the other.

On the X-axis I have placed changes in firm capabilities, while on the Y-axis I have placed changes in state policy. The matrix suggests that programs can only succeed when firms execute their assigned tasks, and when states continue their commitment to a weapons system. The matrix, of course, is not intended to provide a complete account of program success and failure, but only to introduce two of the major independent variables.[61] Further, the outcomes of "cancel" and "maintain" are parsimonious; programs can also be cut-back, stretched-out, or altered. Nonetheless, the matrix suggests that the development and fielding of a collaborative weapons system will only succeed when firm capabilities are maintained and state strategic interests are constant over time.

FIGURE 2
THE RISK OF CANCELLATION IN COLLABORATIVE PROGRAMS

Change in Firm Capabilities

		Y	N
	Y	Cancel	Cancel
CHANGE IN STATE		MSOW*	NATO Frigate
STRATEGY	N	Cancel	Maintain
		Project X**	NAAWS***

*Modular Standoff Weapon
**A Secret NATO Program about which further information is unavailable
***NATO Anti-Air Warfare System
Source: Adapted from Farr, "Management of International Cooperative Programs"
(see n. 60).

A detailed DOD-sponsored study of six collaborative programs
supports the hypothesis that both state and firm-level factors are
responsible for success. The "more successful" programs were those
in which state requirements were maintained over the life of the
program, and the industrial partners were able to reach mutually
beneficial risk-sharing agreements. An example of a successful
program is provided by the NATO Anti-Air Warfare System
(NAAWS), which has responded to a long-standing NATO need of
identifying friends and foes in air combat situations. The failed
programs, such as the NATO Frigate, most often resulted from a
change in state-level military requirements. The inability of industry
to "staff" a program adequately and meet cost and performance
schedules has been, according to the DOD study, a secondary factor,
but it does explain—again according to the study—the cancellation of
a secret NATO program, Project X, about which I have no further
information. When neither a state nor a firm-level commitment exists
for a program, cancellation must result.[62]

Strategically, changed views of the Soviet threat have clearly influenced NATO armaments directors. The prospect of a wide-ranging Conventional Forces in Europe (CFE) treaty raises questions about the scope and type of conventional weapons that will remain in Western Europe, greatly complicating the acquisition ʼprocess. Further, shrinking defense appropriations in NATO member states are forcing defense ministers to prioritize programs according to their military and *domestic* economic contributions. In the United States, the decline in defense spending has coincided with increasing anxiety over the condition of the "defense industrial base." Protectionist efforts to restore the base—using such tools as the "Buy American" act and the Defense Production Act of 1950—clash with cooperative programs. Indeed, Congress is becoming polarized between the internationalists like Nunn on the one hand and the fortress Americans like Representative Mary Rose Oakar on the other.[63]

Regarding the firms involved in codevelopment, there is evidence that several programs have simply been poorly implemented and managed. In many cases, the firms have not delivered their share of the promised goods. According to one transnational defense industry lobbying group, "no new administrative procedures have been established to govern this (cooperative) process."[64] As suggested at the outset, firms must meet their contractual obligation in a collaborative agreement if the weapons program is to succeed.

In sum, there are severe impediments to the successful fielding of collaborative weapons. Indeed, arms collaboration provides a case study of a policy that may be appealing as an idea, but that in practice is very difficult to execute. Given that successful collaboration depends on firms and states having a consistent commitment to a long-term project, one can predict that only a small percentage of joint projects will ever be acquired by NATO's armed forces.

CONCLUSIONS AND PROSPECTS

The NATO arms market has witnessed significant change since the organization's inception in 1949. At that time, Western Europe was in shambles, and U.S. foreign policy focused on economic recovery. By procuring weapons for the allies offshore—from European suppliers—the U.S. hoped to reinvigorate both the European economy and the postwar rearmament effort.

The Europeans would have sought to rebuild their indigenous arms industries in any case. Given independent foreign policy interests, and the perceived economic importance of defense-related industries, European leaders were determined to invest in this sector. By the 1960s, they had largely succeeded with rehabilitation, as Europe and America were competing for weapons sales in third markets.

The initial U.S. response to these rising capabilities was to promote a "two-way street" through competitive research and development and competitive procurement. The government also encouraged firms to coproduce weapons under licensing arrangements. The (American) state's goal was to maintain alliance cohesion and promote NATO RSI; at the same time, American firms wanted to retain a share of the European arms market.

A competitive strategy, of course, played to the alliance leader's comparative advantage in the production of most advanced weapons systems. But the allies proved unwilling to allow the international division of labor to shape their defense sector. They created the Eurogroup and the IEPG, and through increasing collaboration among continental producers, and protectionist procurement policies, the Europeans managed to stave off American imports and further develop their prowess in the manufacture of complex weapons systems. Today, in the words of Dennis Kloske, "it is very clear that many nations within the Western world want to retain, advance, or develop an advanced (weapons) capability." They view defense industries—and aerospace firms in particular—"in terms of national prestige, in terms of technology competitiveness, in terms of export competitiveness."[65]

The Nunn Amendment represents the most recent U.S. response to weapons acquisition in the NATO orbit. By promising cooperation with its allies, the U.S. has offered advanced military technology in return for continued access to the European market. In short, a Faustian bargain has been struck.

Beyond providing an examination of the NATO arms market, this chapter has sought to shed light on some of the enduring tensions in the postwar international political economy. States in the Western alliance (and elsewhere) continue to wrestle with the dilemma posed by the obligation of ensuring national security on the one hand, while promoting economic efficiency and growth on the other. Since first-best economic solutions (competition and free trade) are unlikely to attract widespread political support when it comes to high-technology and defense-related industries, public officials and firms face the prospect of remaining mired in the world of the second-best.

NOTES

1. For a classic article on collaboration, see Ernst Haas, "Why Collaborate? Issue-Linkage and International Regimes," *World Politics* 32 (April 1980), pp. 357-405. For a recent treatment of theoretical issues, see Robert Keohane, *After Hegemony* (Princeton: Princeton University Press, 1984).

2. For a review of the political debate over armaments collaboration, see Office of Technology Assessment, *Arming the Allies* (Washington, D.C.: Government Printing Office, 1990), and *Global Arms Trade* (Washington, D.C.: Government Printing Office, 1991).

3. See Jonathan Tucker, "Partners and Rivals: A Model of International Collaboration in Defense Technology," *International Organization* 45 (Winter 1991).

4. See, for example, Robert Gilpin, *The Political Economy of International Relations* (Princeton: Princeton University Press, 1987).

5. See Phillip Taylor, "Weapons Standardization in NATO: Collaborative Security or Economic Competition?" *International Organization* 36 (Winter 1982), pp. 95-112.

6. See Theodore Moran, "The Globalization of America's Defense Industries," *International Security* (Summer 1990); see also Ethan B. Kapstein, "Losing Control: National Security and the Global Economy," *The National Interest* (Winter 1989/90), pp.85-90.

7. See, for example, "Dassault: Le Plan Serge," *Le Nouvel Economiste*, July 15, 1988, pp. 28-34.

8. Jacques Gansler, *Affording Defense* (Cambridge, Mass.: MIT Press, 1989), p. 215.

9. On state preferences see Jonathan Tucker, "Shifting Advantage: A Game-Theoretic Model of International Collaboration in Advanced Technology" (Ph.D. diss., Massachusetts Institute of Technology, 1990); on the growing number of weapons producers, see SIPRI, *SIPRI Yearbook 1989* (Oxford: Oxford University Press, 1988).

10. Joseph Nye and Robert Keohane, "International Interdependence and Integration," in Fred Greenstein and Nelson Polsby, eds., *Handbook of Political Science*, vol. 6 (Andover, Mass.: Addison-Wesley, 1975), p. 400.

11. Ibid.

12. Paul Ferrari, et.al., *U.S. Arms Exports* (Cambridge, Mass.: Ballinger, 1988), p. 95.

13. Taylor, "Weapons Standardization," p. 99.

14. Keith Hartley, *NATO Arms Cooperation* (London: Allen&Unwin, 1983), p. 34.

15. Tucker, "Shifting Advantage," p. 148.

16. Ibid., p. 151.

17. See Paul Hammond, et.al., *The Reluctant Supplier* (Cambridge, Mass.: Oelgeschlager, Gunn & Hain, 1983), pp. 210-219.

18. On the politics, see Tucker, "Shifting Advantage"; Mary Jo Morris, *Multinational Teaming in the Defense Industry* (MIT-Japan Science and Technology Program, 1989); William Walker and Philip Gummet, "Britain and the European Armaments Market," *International Affairs* 65 (Summer 1989), pp. 419-442; and Pauline Creasey and Simon May, eds., *The European Arms Market and Procurement Cooperation* (London: Macmillan, 1988).

19. Taylor, "Weapons Standardization," p. 100.

20. See Gardiner Tucker, *Toward Rationalizing Allied Weapons Production* (Paris: The Atlantic Institute, 1976); Thomas A. Callaghan, Jr., *U.S./European Economic Cooperation in Military and Civil Technologies* (Washington, D.C.: Center for Strategic and International Studies, August 1974).

21. See Andrew Pierre, *The Global Politics of Arms Sales* (Princeton: Princeton University Press, 1982).

22. Callaghan, *Pooling Allied and American Resources*, p. 125.

23. Adapted from Tucker, "Shifting Advantage," pp. 21-22.

24. R.H. Trice, "International Cooperation in Military Aircraft Programs," Paper presented to the Workshop on International Arms Collaboration, Harvard University, November 8, 1989.

25. Virginia Lopez, *The U.S. Aerospace Industry and the Trend Toward Internationalization* (Washington, D.C.: Aerospace Research Center, March 1988), p. 54.

26. On the French reception to the F-16, see Edward Kolodziej, *Making and Marketing Arms* (Princeton: Princeton University Press, 1987), pp. 337-338; and Hammond, *Reluctant Supplier*, pp. 218-219.

27. Daniel K. Malone, *Roland: A Case for or Against NATO Standardization* (Washington, D.C.: National Defense University Press, May 1980); Interview with Sam Nunn, *Jane's Defence Weekly*, April 11, 1987, p. 641; Michael Klare, *American Arms Supermarket* (Austin, Tex.: University of Texas Press, 1984), pp. 170-172.

28. Hammond, *Reluctant Supplier*, p. 212.

29. Kolodziej, *Making and Marketing Arms*, p. 164.

30. Quoted in David M. Abshire, "Arms Cooperation in NATO," *Armed Forces Journal International* (December 1985), p. 67.

31. U.S. Arms Control and Disarmament Agency, *World Military Expenditures and Arms Transfers: 1988* (Washington, D.C.: Government Printing Office, 1989), p. 122.

32. See Andrew Moravcsik, "1992 and the Future of the European Armaments Industry," Working Paper OIWP-90-001, John M. Olin Institute for Strategic Studies, Harvard University, November 1989.

33. Francois Heisbourg, "Public Policy and the Creation of a European Arms Market," in Creasey and May, *European Arms Market*, p. 68.

34. In addition to the cited documents, this section is based on interviews with U.S. public officials and defense industry executives.

35. Abshire, "Arms Cooperation in NATO."

36. Ibid.

37. See David M. Abshire, "Refitting NATO Strategy for the Future," *Wall Street Journal*, September 12, 1984, p. 33; Abshire, "European Security--Old Realities, New Ideas," *The Atlantic Community Quarterly* (Summer 1985), pp. 131-142; Abshire, "Challenges to NATO in the 1990s," *The Atlantic Community Quarterly* (Fall 1987), pp. 278-287.

38. Thomas A. Callaghan, Jr., "The Structural Disarmament of NATO," *NATO Review* (June 1984), pp. 1-6.

39. Interview with Sam Nunn, *Jane's Defence Weekly*, April 11, 1987, p. 641.

40. Richard Stevenson, "New Jet Fighter: Risks are High," *New York Times*, December 27, 1989, p. D1.

41. Jacques Gansler, *Affording Defense* (Cambridge, Mass.: MIT Press, 1989), pp. 215-238.

42. Ibid., p. 215.

43. Quoted in Office of Management and Budget, *Offsets in Military Exports*, December 1988, p. 3.

44. Defense Science Board, *Industry-to-Industry International Armaments Cooperation: Phase 1-NATO Europe*, June 1983.

45. This analysis has been corroborated through interviews with executives from the prime U.S. defense contractors.

46. Interview with Sam Nunn, *Jane's Defence Weekly*.

47. Dennis Kloske, "Creation of a Funding Source for US Participation in NATO Codevelopment Programs," March 1985, mimeographed.

48. David J. Kuckelman, "NATO Finally Tries Cooperation," *Defense and Foreign Affairs* (December 1987), p. 10.

49. Jacques Gansler, "International Arms Collaboration," address to the workshop on International Arms Collaboration, Harvard University, November 8, 1989.

50. Casper Weinberger, Memorandum to Service Secretaries, June 6, 1985, mimeographed.

51. See Phillip Taylor, "Weapons Standardization in NATO: Collaborative Security or Economic Competition?," *International Organization* 36 (Winter 1982), pp. 95-112.

52. Anne Hessing Cahn and Joseph Kurzel, "Arms Trade in the 1980s," in Cahn, et.al., *Controlling Future Arms Trade* (New York: McGraw-Hill, 1977), p. 72.

53. Kuckelman, "NATO Finally Tries Cooperation," p. 11.

54. Frank Cevasco, "The Initiative in Action," *Jane's Defence Weekly*, April 11, 1987, pp. 655-656.

55. For details, see Frank Cevasco, "The Initiative in Action," *Jane's Defence Weekly*, April 11, 1987, pp. 655-656; see also Robin Beard, "New NATO

Approaches to Improved Armaments Cooperation," *NATO's Sixteen Nations* (November 1986), pp. 26-32.

56. Interview with Senator Sam Nunn, *Jane's Defence Weekly*, p. 642.

57. James Compton, "Statement on Armaments Cooperation," Committee on Armed Services, United States Senate, June 14, 1989, mimeographed.

58. Giovanni de Briganti, "Germany Questions Cooperative Programs," *Defense News*, October 2, 1989, p. 1.

59. Peter Almond, "NATO Nations Cut Joint Projects," *Washington Times*, October 16, 1989, p. 1; see also John Morrocco, "Tight Budgets, Design Conflicts Undercut NATO Weapons Projects," *Aviation Week and Space Technology*, September 25, 1989, pp. 18-19.

60. For a study that seeks to explain success and failure in Nunn Amendment programs, see C. Michael Farr, "The Management of International Cooperative Projects," Defense Systems Management College, Washington, D.C., December 1989, mimeographed.

61. Ibid.

62. Ibid.

63. See Center for Strategic and International Studies, *Deterrence in Decay* (Washington, D.C., 1989); for a review of the congressional debate, see Ethan B. Kapstein, "Losing Control: National Security and the Global Economy," *The National Interest* (Winter 1989/90).

64. American League for Exports and Security Assistance, "Implementing NATO Armaments Cooperation: An Industry Perspective," February 24, 1988, mimeographed.

65. Dennis Kloske, Statement to the Senate Armed Services Committee, April 11, 1988, in U.S. Congress. Senate, *Department of Defense Authorization for Appropriations for Fiscal Year 1989* (Washington, D.C.: Government Printing Office, 1988), p. 843.

1
Collaboration, Internationalization, and Security

Jacques S. Gansler

Dr. Gansler is Senior Vice President of TASC. He is a former Deputy Assistant Secretary of Defense, a former electronics industry executive, and the author of *Affording Defense* (MIT Press, 1989) and *The Defense Industry* (MIT Press, 1980). Since 1984 he has also been a Visiting Scholar at the Kennedy School of Government, Harvard University.

Traditionally, the desire to have a self-sufficient defense industrial base has been a major factor in a nation's security posture—particularly in terms of the weapon systems that represent state-of-the-art and associated components technology. However, in recent years, even the United States has found it more and more difficult to remain autarkic in its defense industry. Industry after industry has become international in structure and conduct, and other nations have begun to take a technological leadership position in various critical, defense-related areas—with Europe and Japan often replacing the United States as the world's leader. As future U.S. defense budgets dramatically decline (the result of the worldwide geopolitical "revolution of 1989" and America's fiscal deficits from the 1980s), it has become increasingly difficult to maintain the historically-desired condition of defense industry self-sufficiency—or even of assured access to supplies (a minimum requirement for independence of political action). The result is that defense industrial base planners have begun to think globally and to ask themselves "if these are our allies in wartime, why should we not buy from them in peacetime—and be able to depend on them for crisis needs?"

However, a dilemma arises, due to the no longer monolithic nature of "the threat." When all defense planning was focused on the Soviet Bloc, it was easy to derive who was "friend or foe" for any likely conflict. But in today's environment, future guarantees of "assured access" to industry and technology are much less predictable due to the great uncertainties associated with future Third World and regional conflicts.

Additionally, the required national security access may be greatly influenced by economic competitiveness conditions; particularly, when "critical defense technologies" are often the identical technologies being used in the commercial world (e.g., electronics and advanced materials), and when one's military allies may well be one's economic competitors. This issue becomes further complicated when viewed from the industrial perspective. Many (if not most) U.S. private-sector defense industrial operations are divisions or subsidiaries of large, multinational firms—who tend to think globally (in terms of sales and profit optimization), rather than nationally (in terms of either their original geographic location or the nationality of their primary owners). Thus, the dilemma is a three-cornered one: *first*, nations may be competing economically in one set of alignments; *second,* nations may be competing militarily in perhaps different, but time-varying, alignments; and, *third*, overlaid on this, is the growing globalization of industry, where a firm's interests may no longer represent, or even necessarily be concurrent with, the interests of a given nation. Frequently, the national government's needs conflict with the desires of home-based corporations. (Ironically, often public policy makers in the U.S. have assumed that these firms were "theirs;" especially when they were dealing with a defense division of the firm.)

Thus, establishing public policy on issues such as technology transfer, foreign ownership, control of arms exports, etc. becomes extremely complex and difficult—since it means *simultaneously* dealing with all three aspects of the dilemma; and this complexity means that each issue must be treated on an individual case basis. Unfortunately, most nations—particularly the U.S.—lack one organizational structure or public policies to be able to handle this three-cornered dilemma.

Finally, *multinational weapons programs introduce still additional complexity.* The declining defense budgets and the globalization of industry and technology have begun to make collaborative efforts between nations in the development and production of new weapon systems look more and more attractive. This, of course, is not a new phenomenon. For many years, nations have been attempting to take advantage of the potential gains that collaboration can offer, i.e., (1) mutual military advantage, (2) mutual defense budget savings (of either R&D or production), and (3) achievement of national long-term economic objectives (critical skills employment, industrial development, "technology transfer," etc.).[1] Unfortunately (as will be discussed later), these objectives have been rarely achieved since other, contradictory, objectives have tended to dominate the historic collaborative efforts.

Nonetheless, nations and corporations are clearly moving in the direction of greater and greater international interdependence. Thus, public policy will have to shift in order to address these "second best" alternatives. The challenge, of course, is to develop a strategy for collaboration which recognizes each nation's security needs yet acknowledges the desires for globalization of each of the participating defense industrial operations. That challenge is the one to which we must now turn.

To address the public policy dilemma among the needs of national security (both military and economic), industrial globalization, and international arms collaboration in the future development and procurement of weapon systems, it will be necessary for policy makers to dramatically change their traditional ways of thinking. Some areas are obvious. For example, future world power (both economic and military) will increasingly be a function of a nation's ability to rapidly develop and deploy advanced product and process technologies. Additionally, it is clear that when only some of the nations have a "national technology strategy," then the principles of laissez-faire will likely work to the disadvantage of those countries without a technology strategy.

Perhaps the nation that will have the greatest difficulty accepting the need for change is the United States. Traditionally, as the leading economic and military power, the U.S. has been able to assume a basically autarkic position.   However, the U.S. is becoming increasingly dependent on both foreign capital and foreign technology. This dependency extends to essential military equipment as well as to critical portions of the overall U.S. economy.   In general, globalization is both inevitable and desirable; however, in areas of critical technologies, for either defense or industrial competitiveness, this foreign dependency is becoming a growing security concern.

DEFENSE ACQUISITION: THE NEED FOR CHANGE

The hardest thing for a nation to accept is that traditional policy paradigms have lost their relevance. For example, the following seven traditional U.S. assumptions are being increasingly questioned:

- The nation can no longer *assume* that economic and security public policy issues can be *separately* treated.

- The nation can no longer *assume* a *self-contained* (domestic) defense industry.

- The nation can no longer *assume* that government is *not involved* in international industrial competitiveness.

- The nation can no longer *assume* a U.S. technological *leadership* in *military*-relevant technologies.

- The nation can no longer *assume* an *available* U.S. skilled labor force.

- The nation can no longer *assume* that what is in a U.S. corporation's interest is *necessarily* in the nation's interest.

- The nation can no longer *assume* that critical defense technologies and critical civilian technologies are *different*; areas such as advanced electronics, new structural materials, supercomputers and advanced manufacturing equipment *are critical to both.*

Thus, *new national policies are required to address these changed realities.* The old policies are simply not sufficiently relevant to the new environment. The objective of this new set of policies must be to assure that in areas such as trade policy, tax policy, education, financial markets, government R&D investments, defense procurement practices, and the many other ways in which government affects industry "structure, conduct, and performance," the nation takes actions designed to allow, and even give incentives to those market operations which will result in actions that simultaneously strengthen both national security and national industrial competitiveness. Today, most developed countries, with the glaring exception of the U.S., recognize this dual-purpose need and are (with varying levels of success) taking action accordingly. By contrast, current U.S. government policies actually result in: high costs of capital, poor education of future workers, short-term investment incentives, uncompetitive international trade practices, high cost and low quality goods (especially in defense-related products), and a general government/industry relationship which has the two sides in constant opposition rather than working together toward a common set of long-term national goals.

As long as the U.S. was the undisputed economic and military leader of the world, it could afford to essentially ignore the coming realities. Today, however, the economic, military, and political changes around the world can no longer be ignored. Steps must be taken to change U.S. policies to match the needs of today's realities and *to use public policy—including national security procurement policy and resource decisions—to help, rather than continue to retard, America's industrial strength.* Such actions will help the nation, the industries doing business in the country, and the nation's trading partners.

The U.S. must begin to make these basic changes in the defense industry. This is a totally controlled sector of the economy, i.e., a single government buyer, 100 percent regulated by the government, etc. Most other nations have long recognized the importance of their defense industries and, in fact, have government organizations responsible for assuring the health, viability, innovativeness, responsiveness, etc. of their defense industrial base. No such organization (or organizations) exists within the United States and, certainly, the establishment of one is necessary, though not sufficient in and of itself. The second, and perhaps most critical, step for the United States is to recognize that *it is absolutely essential for the U.S. Department of Defense to dramatically change, over the next five years, the whole way it does its business.* The changes must include: the weapon's requirements process, the budget process, the design and development process, the procurement process, and the government's approach to the defense industrial base.

At best, these critical changes will be challenging and difficult. At worst, impossible. Yet they must be made. To see why, we must view the current problems from five different, but overlapping, perspectives: first, in terms of the effects of the changed geopolitical and military environment on equipment selection; second, the implications of the precipitous decline in the defense budget; third, from the viewpoint of what is obtained for the money, spent on the design, development, and procurement of defense equipment; fourth, from the current condition and projected future of the defense industrial base (both on a domestic and international basis); and fifth, from the viewpoint of the present and potential impacts of defense procurements on international industrial competitiveness (for the U.S. and its allies).

Briefly consider each of these five perspectives. At the geopolitical level, the focus must shift from the single-minded concentration on large-scale nuclear or conventional conflicts with the Soviet Union to a far wider range of much more unpredictable, but extremely violent, "regional" conflicts (as Saddam Hussein has clearly demonstrated). Unfortunately, with the recent and rapid worldwide proliferation of sophisticated military equipment (e.g., ballistic and cruise missiles; chemical and nuclear warheads; advanced anti-aircraft missiles; silent, non-nuclear submarines; communications and intelligence satellites; etc.), many "third-world" countries represent a serious threat to U.S. interests, a threat that does not respond to traditional (rational) deterrents and one for which current doctrine, tactics, force structure, equipment, and support structure are not adequately prepared. These contingencies require the rapid development of new and different military equipment. (They are not simply subsets of the historical, central-European scenario.) But, meeting the demands presented by this set of new equipment needs will be made far more difficult by the second of the dramatic changes—namely, the defense budget decline.

With the collapse of the Warsaw Pact and the growing economic and ethnic problems in the Soviet Union, the "top-line" of the U.S. defense budget is going to be significantly reduced over the next few years. However, this budget reduction is likely to be far greater for the weapons acquisition account. To preserve the viability of the all-volunteer forces, the military have been arguing for only "gradual" reductions in manpower; thus, demanding an increasing share of a declining budget for "manpower, operations, and maintenance." Similarly, there is a general recognition that areas such as "worldwide intelligence gathering" and "maintenance of a strong technology base" are essential—each, again, requiring an increased share of the declining budget. As a result, there will be little money left over for the development and procurement of new weapon systems—including many that have already begun development but will have to be either greatly slowed down or terminated. The few available acquisition dollars will go primarily for subsystem modernization of existing weapon platforms (planes, ships, and tanks) and the remainder will be used to develop and procure small quantities of selected "golden bullets" (equipment that promises order-of-magnitude improvement in force effectiveness for fighting these "likely" regional and "special operations" conflicts). However, even these few new weapons will have to be much cheaper and fielded much more rapidly. Which brings us to the third of the historic trends.

From the equipment perspective, the U.S. has been able, over the last 30 years, to design, develop, procure, and support the *best performing* weapon systems in the world. From generation to generation, the performance of U.S. weapons has been dramatically improving (at something like 5% per year);[2] however, this improved performance has been matched by *continuously increased unit procurement cost*. From generation to generation, unit costs have increased, in constant dollars and constant quantity, from 5 to 7% per year.[3] As a result, each now costs hundreds of millions of dollars and single ships are measured in the billions. This cost growth has been accompanied by an increasingly longer acquisition cycle, which now averages over 8 years of development and, in some cases, extends to more than 12 years.[4] Clearly, such long cycles are neither affordable nor compatible with modern electronic technology (which is often obsolete in 6 months). Finally, since the DOD has not been able to keep up with the quality improvements that have taken place in the commercial world,[5] weapon's support costs continue to grow. In summary, the DOD ends up fielding weapon systems that are too expensive, take too long, and don't work adequately.

Additionally, the rising unit cost of equipment has resulted in continuously buying fewer and fewer weapon systems. The aircraft example is a well known one: in the 1950s the U.S. bought over

2,000 fighter planes per year; in the 1960s approximately 600 per year; in the 1970s approximately 300 per year; and in the 1980s, after doubling the defense budget, the DOD was able to stay at 300 aircraft per year.[6] The trend is clear and, without drastic changes, Norm Augustine's projection of this data to one aircraft per year, in the year 2054, will probably be a reality.[7] It will, of course, be an outstanding performing aircraft; but the quantity impacts are totally unacceptable. Something must be done to reverse these cost, schedule, and quality trends! We *must* learn to develop and deploy low cost, high quality, high performance weapon systems, with only a few years of product realization time; perhaps, 2 to 4 years (depending upon the product) from proven technology to fielded weapons.

Next, from the defense industrial base perspective, we see increasing inefficiency at the prime contractor level—plants are large and under-utilized; firms carry heavy debt; profits are significantly declining; price-to-earnings multiples are very low; and, obviously, as the budget begins to decline, the defense industry is in a state of fear and panic. These are all signs of an economically "sick" industry.[8] The industry reaction, to date, includes: "downsizing"; domestic "industrial teaming" (to "share the risks"); attempts at diversification into other government business (e.g., NASA); international "industrial partnering" (in a wide variety of forms—from selling the company, to joint ventures, and "teaming"); and a mad rush to replace domestic sales with international sales. Of course, these paths are not mutually exclusive, and combinations of these alternatives are frequently being pursued.

At the equally-critical lower tiers of the defense industry, a shift away from defense has already begun—whenever firms have a choice—and the DOD has found *a growing dependence on foreign sources* (often sole sources) for an increasing number of critical defense components, subsystems, and manufacturing equipment.[9] Thus, the underpinnings of modern U.S. weapon systems are increasingly coming from offshore—since cost, performance, quality, or availability are better elsewhere. Obviously, there is a growing political cry for the U.S. to "take corrective actions." But the cost of autarchy (especially with the existing, highly-specialized, low-volume, high-cost, domestic defense industry) would be so prohibitive that, if the U.S. attempted to support a totally self-contained defense industry, it would require most of the available DOD dollars just to support the industry itself. Thus, the perverse result would be that the nation could no longer afford to buy any additional weapon systems.

Finally, from the "national industrial competitiveness" perspective, the United States has clearly been falling behind its European and Japanese allies in many critical defense technologies—as studies by both the Commerce and Defense Departments (and many others) have demonstrated.[10] In fact, perception polls increasingly show that the general public considers "economic security" a greater threat to the long-term interests of the nation than "military security". And yet, because of the almost total separation of U.S. defense investments from the commercial market, the $38 billion a year of defense R&D (which supports approximately one out of every three U.S. scientists and engineers) and the additional $130 billion a year of defense procurement and capital equipment expenditures (on state-of-the-art technology) are not being utilized to help in the international competitiveness race. In the past, the U.S. could afford to have public policy address military and economic issues independently; but today, from technological and security viewpoints, the issues are becoming increasingly intertwined. Wherever there is overlap, the nation can no longer afford the luxury of separately addressing public policy in the military and civilian spheres. Again, critical changes are required.

To address these growing problems in the defense acquisition arena (which exist in most of the developed countries, but are most glaringly obvious in the United States), it is necessary to establish a "vision" of what the nation's future defense industrial base should be; assess this vision against today's realities; and then take appropriate and achievable action to guide the nation in the desired direction. Within this framework, it is neither desirable nor practical for all U.S. defense industries to be domestic and protected; rather, only a few "critical" industries need to be considered. Thus, the first step is to drastically limit the criteria for "criticality," with only a few industrial subsectors able to fit through the "filters," and with the international structure of the remaining ones determined by market forces.[11]

Within these constraints, then, the six "desired" characteristics of the defense industrial base should be:

1. Domestic—for "critical defense technologies;"

2. State-of-the-art (in order to achieve "technological superiority");

3. Capable of short "new product realization" cycles;

4. High quality and low cost;

5. Capable of rapid production surge in selected equipment areas (to meet changing crisis demands); and

6. Profitable (for investment needs).

A glaring difference exists today between these desired characteristics and the reality of the U.S. defense industrial base—at both the prime contractor and lower tier levels. Specifically, we find (in addition to the weapon equipment schedule, cost, and quality problems and the defense industry financial problems all noted above):

- The U.S. is no longer the leader in many critical defense technologies;

- a sole-source dependency on off-shore suppliers for many critical weapon system components;

- a growing number of international industrial "joint ventures," both at home and abroad;

- a growing dependency, for defense industry survival, on foreign military sales;

- world-wide excess capacity in military equipment production (and significant superpower sales of existing inventories, thus, further flooding the market);

- growing foreign purchases of U.S.-based defense plants;

- growing foreign economic sponsorship of leading-edge, high-technology, U.S. component suppliers and U.S. university, proprietary research;

- increasing government regulation of the defense industry (with the associated, growing inefficiencies);

- increasing difficulty of obtaining the skilled workforce of factory workers, scientists, and engineers (throughout U.S. industry and in the defense industry specifically); and

- almost total inability to rapidly increase production output ("surge") when required for crisis demands—often taking years to obtain the required specialized military parts to build added numbers of weapon systems.

The gross differences between the "desired characteristics" of the future U.S. defense industrial base and the reality of today's current conditions mean that, clearly, "something must be done." The U.S.

defense industry must be dramatically restructured. Within the existing capitalistic, free-enterprise, democratic society, the nation has, essentially, four basic choices:

1. Maintain segregated, defense-only, domestic industrial sectors.

2. Allow the international market to "freely" operate (through industrial agreements and political activities).

3. Cultivate an internationally-integrated, defense-only, structure with our Allies.

4. Cultivate integrated civil/military sectors (wherever appropriate).

Clearly, these four options are not mutually exclusive; and, equally clearly, the "solution" for one industrial sector may be very different than that for another (essentially requiring a sector-by-sector selection). Nonetheless, there are some general comments which can be made about these four options. The first, i.e., maintaining a segregated, defense-only, domestic industry (at least at the prime contractor level), is essentially the option historically pursued by the United States; however, not explicitly, as it is done in many other countries. In recent years, the U.S. has been developing a more and more unique set of DOD procurement practices which has resulted in a highly specialized and highly subsidized defense industrial base—at all levels of the industry. Because of unique and inefficient defense procurement requirements, increasingly more and more companies (with both military and commercial activities) have been separating and segregating their defense operations from their commercial operations. Nonetheless, this may still be a necessary option for a few—highly selected—critical and military-unique sectors of defense, such as nuclear weapons. However, segregation is basically an unaffordable option for the vast majority of military equipment, since it means simultaneously supporting the complete industry and buying the weapons; and this combination is not affordable with the very few dollars that will be available. Additionally, this small, specialized, subsidized defense sector would certainly not be capable of maintaining the extra capacity required for rapid increases in production in periods of crisis (a military requirement that will be growing in importance as the peacetime budget declines and the standing military forces are reduced).

Turning to the second of the options (namely, allowing "free" market forces to operate), we find frequent industrial and political conflicts with the desired, future defense industry characteristics. On the industrial side, the aims of a corporation to achieve their profit maximization on a global basis may conflict with the needs of the nation to achieve its defense on an assured access (or controlled) basis. On the political side, there is frequently a conflict (even within a given country) between the forces arguing for "jobs in my district or state" and the needs of the nation to procure weapon systems efficiently and effectively. The conditions of defense activities—a single buyer, a regulated market, and only a few suppliers (at best) in each sector—are simply not amenable to normal, free market operations. Thus, while the forces of oligopolistic competition can often be used very effectively—by a smart, monopsonistic buyer—to achieve long-term, supply objectives (of a competitive, innovative, responsive, efficient, and profitable domestic defense industry), traditional "free" market forces—with their total dependence on industrial (corporate) objectives and the free play of domestic politics—are simply not likely to achieve a nation's security objectives. In fact, in today's global market, they may frequently even have adverse security implications.

Thus, the most attractive alternatives for the U.S. and most other developed nations of the world are the remaining two options, or some combination thereof, ie., either a small, efficient, internationally-integrated (alliance-based), defense-only structure and/or a highly competitive (efficient and effective) integrated civil/military structure. Unfortunately (given the historic conditions of the defense industry) neither of these two options will be easy to achieve. Additionally, without dramatic changes in the traditional way in which defense business has been done, selecting either (or both) of these options is likely to result in a totally ineffective, or even harmful, conclusion. Nonetheless, since these are the two most attractive long-term options, we must explore each of them in depth, to understand the specific obstacles that must be overcome and the specific changes that are required in order to efficiently and effectively achieve these alternatives in the twenty-first century.

INTERNATIONAL ARMS COLLABORATION: PROBLEMS AND PROSPECTS

First, consider the international arms collaboration option—especially, for selected, defense-unique sectors. Unfortunately, there has been only a limited amount of research in this area; however, a review of prior and current U.S. multi-national codevelopment programs, as well as the "lessons learned" from a variety of forms of collaborative efforts—such as European multi-national programs, U.S. multi-service programs, and U.S. industrial "teaming" programs—indicate that three key points regarding codevelopment and coproduction programs must be emphasized in future collaborative efforts. These are:

1. The traditional management approaches used on these programs have been *unsuccessful* in achieving the promised economic advantages (which usually were the primary rationale for the codevelopment programs). Thus, new approaches are required.

2. The international industrial structure has changed dramatically in recent years; yet, government codevelopment policies have not been revised. Thus, in light of today's realities, such

revisions are essential.

3.   In the future, for budgetary and other reasons, the number of multi-national codevelopment programs is likely to grow. Additionally, each case is likely to be a unique situation regarding the countries involved, the companies involved, the relative technology status, etc. Unfortunately, the U.S. government is currently not structured to efficiently and effectively address these cases. Thus, organizational and procedural restructurings are clearly required.

Briefly consider each of these three points. First, and perhaps most important, is the question of whether or not the objectives of a codevelopment program are, in fact, achieved.   Historically, codevelopment and/or coproduction programs have been initiated on the basis of a variety of arguments. Often, military considerations have been used (e.g., interoperability and/or equipment commonality); while, frequently, political/social arguments (e.g., local employment, "burden-sharing," "cementing alliances," and assistance in "third world democratic advancements") are really an underlying rationale. However, the economic benefit expected to be achieved was the dominant rationale, or at least the one identified in almost all cases investigated. These benefits fall into essentially four categories:

1. **R&D savings**: large U.S. and European R&D budgets are expended on tactical weapon systems which are highly redundant. Thus, there should be a potentially significant R&D savings to each of the countries participating in the collaborative program.

2. **Faster developments**: new weapon system developments are incredibly expensive; yet, they should not be stretched out in an attempt to reduce yearly costs. Therefore, simultaneous investments by multiple countries should allow adequate annual dollars in order to achieve far faster developments.

3. **Production savings**: since the quantities of weapons being built are usually quite small, large economies (of both scale and of specialization) should be achieved by combining the production procurements of each of the participants (thus, costing each far less than it would have on their own).

4. **Technology transfer**: in some technologies the U.S. is ahead and in others their allies are, so both should be able to spend less by exchanging (transferring) technologies—while still protecting them from mutual potential adversaries.

Unfortunately, the data of essentially all historic cases studied indicate that *the total costs and production times associated with joint programs have been greater* than anticipated or than if done by a single country. Clearly, the *potential* for savings exists; but, in reality, program execution problems have largely prevented the realization of these economies.

The importance, for future management considerations, and the controversial nature of this statement (that the projected economic benefits of codevelopment/coproduction have largely not—historically—been realized), make it necessary to briefly review some of the references used in reaching this conclusion. First, consider historic, joint U.S. and NATO-Europe programs. Perhaps the best known of these is the F-16 multi-national program. This effort was highly successful in achieving not only the military and political objectives for all countries concerned, but also the technology transfer objectives for many of the European countries; however, the U.S. costs were greater than they would have been had the U.S. done this program alone.[12] Also, European costs were significantly higher than they would have been had they purchased the aircraft directly from the U.S.. The European costs were expected to be higher since the objective, clearly stated, was to achieve the transfer of U.S. industrial technology; but the fact that the U.S. costs also were higher was a surprise, particularly for this larger quantity buy. Additional examples of adverse results are found in programs transferring European developments to the U.S.. The Roland Missile Program was a classic example. The U.S. tried to "redesign and improve" the missile, but ultimately failed to put it into production. In general, as a U.S. program manager of a multi-national program commented, "the difficulty of running a multi-national program is proportional to $\sqrt{n}$, where n is the number of countries involved."[13] The poor track record on these multi-national programs reflects this management complexity.

A second set of data on the difficulty of collaborative development is gained by studying the actual experience of European countries in joint military development programs. An analysis[14] of the European experience with multi-national projects, such as the joint French and German development of the Transall aircraft, found that:

- there were disagreements over requirements and specifications;

- the project was overly politicized, creating program instability;

- there was no unified government and industrial management structure; and

- both partners ignored the theoretical cost benefits of collaboration.

The multiple "requirements" tended to drive the joint effort to "the *highest* common denominator" and the result was a far higher-cost system than either country needed or would have designed were they separately trying to satisfy their military requirements. Additionally, the program had a more than 100 percent schedule slippage in its "initial operational capability." A more recent study, comparing European single country programs with European multiple country programs (particularly the Tornado and Jaguar), found that, on average, the single country program development schedule was more than a year faster than the multiple country developments; and that, again, the anticipated economies were not realized.

A third set of "collaborative program" data comes from studies of U.S. multi-service programs. Here, the problems of getting the U.S. Army, Navy, and/or Air Force to work jointly on the development of a weapon system are similar to the same difficulties encountered when trying to get two or more nations to work together. A General Accounting Office study of multi-service programs stated that they define a successful joint program as "one which has brought about a substantial harmonization in fielded systems, satisfied participating services, and realized actual savings." The GAO concluded that "by these measures, *no successes have been achieved so far.*"[15] A more extensive study of multi-service programs was undertaken by the Joint Logistics Commanders in 1984.[16] After analyzing 80 joint programs and 50 single service programs, and interviewing many of the program managers, as well as senior officials, in the Department of Defense, they found that:

- two-thirds of the joint programs studied were initiated outside of the military services ("topdown"), primarily by the Office of the Secretary of Defense or the Congress; and that these were largely "sporadic and unstructured". They found that the rational for introducing the multi-service program was, in approximately 90 percent of the cases, based on anticipated cost savings; and yet they found that in no case was a formal cost benefit analysis done; and that, again, in no case was the "estimated" cost savings documented;

- there were a significant number of withdrawals or terminations from the joint programs;

- cost and schedule growths were *far greater* for joint than single-service programs. In fact, they found that the R&D cost growth was 3 1/2 times as large, the production cost growth was over 2 times as large, and the schedule slippage was 2 1/2 times as large;

- the causes of the poor schedule and cost performance results (on the multiservice programs) were: greater funding turbulence, difficulties of resolving technical requirements, difficulties of staffing the organizations, different priorities, lack of commitments on one part or the other, and significantly different business practices;

- the absence of an active and disciplined selection and commitment process for the multiservice programs;

- the joint programs normally require more personnel than typical single-service programs—due to the increased coordination activities—but that this increase was frequently not supplied;

- major issues involving responsibility, authority, or interservice relationships must be resolved in the charter or they will haunt the program throughout its life;

- multi-service, as well as multi-national, programs experienced considerable difficulty in resolving different requirements, and usually found that these escalated to the "highest common denominator"—thus necessitating the design of an expensive system; and

- extreme difficulties existed in trying to run a multi-service program—due to the significantly "different ways of doing business" between the services. (Here, one might have expected the difficulties to be even greater between nations than between U.S. services e.g. different budget cycles, organization philosophies, testing procedures, etc.).

The last set of data on collaborative efforts considers U.S. industrial "teaming" on development programs. This arrangement has some of the same characteristics as multi-national codevelopments; but, here the issue is whether the *government* gets a cheaper, better, faster product than it would have had a single firm been used for the development. This approach (of two defense prime contractors jointly sharing the development program) is not a common approach; however, it has been used in a growing number of recent projects where corporations wanted to reduce their risk and/or where the government's objective was to later split the development team and have the two firms compete in production. However, again the empirical data show that the collaborative effort has had adverse affects on costs and schedules. One recent example of this approach was the development "teaming" on the airborne self-protection jammer (ASPJ), in which former defense-sector rivals Westinghouse and ITT were joint developers. During the development program, the production estimates on this equipment more than doubled and the development itself was completed two and one-half years late.

It is the integrated effect of looking at all of these four categories of prior collaborative efforts that leads to the conclusion that, in those cases studied, "the desired economic benefits for the Government, have not been achieved." Yet, it is clear that the potential for the economic benefits definitely exist. From these case studies, we can conclude that in order to realize the *potential* economies on future collaborative programs, the following six management principles must be applied:

1. The many different military requirements of each country must be *fiscally constrained*. In the initial design phase each performance or design requirement must be traded off

against a pre-established "unit production cost" for the
weapon system (when it later goes into production). Only
through this technique will one be able to avoid the historic
experience of simply designing an expensive system, based
upon "adding up" all of the different sets of requirements
(i.e., combining them to their "highest common
denominator").

2. The schedule and funding for the multi-national program
   must be fixed, and decisions related to the management of
   the program *delegated* to a *single* (joint) program office.
   In this way, rapid choices can be made as each new
   problem arises during the program's development.

3. The cost savings "expected" from the program must be
   explicitly defined at the start of the effort and then
   quantitatively tracked throughout the development program.

4. The international industrial structure for the particular
   program must be arranged so that the *economic* objectives
   are achieved—rather than allowing the objectives to be
   driven by other national desires.

5. *Production planning* must start at the beginning of the
   development phase and continue throughout the
   development effort. (For economies to be realized, it
   cannot be done "later".)

6. Most important, only those programs on which the above
   criteria can be agreed upon, in *advance*, should be
   initiated. Without such agreement, in writing, they are
   doomed to failure.

Now we will shift to the second of the broad changes that the U.S. must make before entering into future codevelopment programs; namely, the need for the policies in the collaborative area to recognize the *realities* of today's international economic environment—something which they, in fact, do not currently do. Unfortunately, these "realities" are something that many U.S. policy makers would much rather deny since, in many case, they are contrary to historic beliefs and practices. Specifically, four such "realities" are:

1. Policies must recognize the growing and desirable "dual-use" (civil and military) applicability of product and process technologies.

2. Policies must recognize the growing and desirable strong interrelationship (hopefully integration) between design and manufacturing (known as "concurrent" or "simultaneous" engineering).

3. Policies must recognize that "world class" U.S. and foreign firms are international ("global"), with important offshore locations for U.S. firms and foreign ownership of critical, domestically-based firms.

4. Policies must recognize that today, and more so in the future, the U.S. will not "lead" in all technologies, including those essential to defense.

Revising the procurement policies of the United States and its alliance partners to accept the existing, and growing, realities of the international industrial environment will obviously be difficult; but it is clearly essential.

Finally, the third major change for future collaborative efforts requires the U.S. to recognize the difficulties presented by these "realities," and the fact that on any individual codevelopment program there will be a variety of unique situations—with regard to the countries involved, the products involved, the technologies involved, the relative status of each country in those technologies, and, particularly, the international and domestic politics involved. Therefore, it will be necessary to treat each example on a "case by case" basis; however, there will be a growing number of these cases, and it will be essential to be able to treat them in a coordinated, yet rapid, fashion. Thus, the U.S. (and its allies) must develop and implement the organizational and procedural changes required in order to expeditiously and yet effectively treat each of these individual, collaborative programs.   Such organizations and procedures do not now exist in the U.S. (nor in varying degrees, in many other countries) and it must become a high government priority to develop them.

To summarize this option, it is clear that if the changes suggested above can be realized on future codevelopment programs, the U.S. and its allies can and should participate far more in such efforts; and would realize the potential advantages associated with them. However, making these changes will be very difficult and will require strong government leadership.

CIVIL-MILITARY INTEGRATION

The fourth of the broad "future defense industry" public policy options available to the U.S. and its Allies—and the one to which more and more people have been turning, because of its economic attractiveness—requires nations to draw from their civilian industrial base the military equipment, subsystems, and components which can be built to satisfy its military needs.   In the U.S. case, the Department of Defense must shift procurement policies dramatically in order to become a "world-class buyer;" one who competes with other world-class buyers (including those in the commercial sector) for high quality and low cost goods, and is a largely *integrated* (civil/military) overall industrial base. Ideally, an industrial base which, for the critical technologies needed by the DOD, is competitive on a world-class basis and yet *domestically located.* As noted above, there will be some industrial sectors which are military-unique (e.g., nuclear weapons); but, for the vast majority of critical defense sectors, the DOD needs—for low cost and high quality equipment yet with assured access to advanced technology—will be satisfied by a U.S. industrial base which supplies world-class goods *simultaneously* to both the civil and military economies.

For this to happen, the Department of Defense must shift from its current, sole focus on weapon's performance to placing equal emphasis on quality, cost, and schedule in specifying the "requirements" and the design characteristics of both the products and manufacturing processes that it procures. This means shifting the weapon's acquisition process focus to areas such as simultaneous engineering, design-to-cost, rapid product realization, and a paperless acquisition and logistics system (utilizing computer-aided acquisition and logistics system techniques for a totally computerized government and industrial operation and using *commercial,* not military, specifications and standards).

The DOD must recognize—which it has not done to date—the two dramatic changes in technology that took place in the 1980s. These changes allow and, in fact, should encourage the integration of civil and military sectors. First, the rapid improvement in quality and performance of commercial equipment, especially electronics. Today, new cars have a computer chip hard-mounted to the engine block, which receives temperatures, vibrations, shocks, etc. equal to those of "mil. specs."; yet, these "ruggedized" commercial chips are much lower in cost, higher in reliability, and two years more advanced in performance than their military equivalents. The Packard Commission[17] and two Defense Science Board Task Forces (in 1986[18] and 1989[19]) have recommended that the DOD modify its practices, so that it can buy these ruggedized commercial parts—but, to date, there has been little progress.

The second major, recent technological advance (which also should encourage greater civil/military integration) is in the manufacturing technology area. Today, "flexible manufacturing technology" allows *low volume, multiproduct* production to be done as efficiently as high-volume, mass production; thus, with multiproduct integration of production operations, the DOD could realize dramatic overhead cost reductions on small-volume defense work. (Perhaps with both defense products and commercial products coming off the same lines—even where the products are different, but the production process for making them is similar.)[20] Yet, here again, the DOD has been slow to capitalize on this new technology. Clearly, in both the product and process areas, the DOD must take advantage of the potential offered by such technology changes.

The three forms of civil and military integration recommended are: (1) "R&D integration," (2) "factory integration," and (3) "buying commercial." Each area presents some problems and requires changes for its implementation. First, consider "R&D integration." The "requirements" for new defense products—particularly those at the lower tiers, such as new electronics, new computers, new software, new machine tools, new structural materials, etc.—should be derived from the *combination* of both future military needs and future civil needs. This will allow the DOD to draw its new products from a domestic industrial base which has the high volume and high quality associated with commercial goods and, yet, the high performance historically associated with military goods. It is important to emphasize here that the technologies required for future weapon systems and those required for future international competitiveness (i.e., electronics, computers, new materials, machine tools, etc.) are *identical*—as confirmed by an overlay of the recent DOD's "critical defense technologies" list[21] and the Department of Commerce's critical "emerging technologies"[22] list. Thus, shifting towards "dual-use" technologies must be a major consideration in future DOD weapon systems R&D. Similarly, new military R&D products must be specified in terms of *commercial* specs and standards, and—most important—must be procured by using *commercial* buying practices.

The second form of integration is "on the factory floor." Here, the engineering teams and the manufacturing teams not only must be integrated themselves (in order to achieve "simultaneous engineering") but the civil and military products that are going through the factory must be designed and built by the same people and on the same machines in order to achieve the overhead absorption that results from high volume; the "technology transfer" that comes from the same people working on multiple products; and the labor stability (and therefore productivity) that comes from the often countercyclical civil and military markets. This "factory integration" means that, for example, an electronics factory would be building military and commercial products on the same line. It also means that government practices, such as process and accounting standards, auditing, inspection, etc., will have to be changed in order to allow and encourage this dual operation on the factory floor.

Factory integration would have the added strategic advantage of meeting the defense requirement for a rapid surge of military equipment for crisis demands—a growing need, which clearly is going to be required in the future, but for which the type and amount is unpredictable. With an integrated factory, commercial product lines could be rapidly "converted" into military product lines. It should be emphasized that it is the "flexible manufacturing technology" which allows an integrated factory to rapidly shift from one product to another, with high efficiency on both. DOD design and buying practices, as well as defense procurement and accounting laws and regulations, must change for such integration to be achieved.

The third form of integration of the civil and military sectors is perhaps the most obvious; namely, that *the DOD must learn how to buy commercial products.* This means changing their specifications and standards, changing their procurement practices, changing their cost accounting standards, changing their auditing practices, etc. The way to approach this issue is to identify each of the barriers and, one by one, remove them.[23] Clearly, the Office of the Secretary of Defense must take the lead in this area; but Congress must also be willing to go along with the needed changes.

As desirable as these three forms of civil/military integration appear, and in spite of every Congressman, White House official, and DOD executive—whenever they get the chance—giving speeches advocating such integration, the reality is that, in recent years, there has been increased legislation and regulation which create disincentives to integration and, in fact, gives incentive to separation. Thus, the result has been increased separation between the civil and military sectors—the exact opposite of what is needed. Instead, the government should not only identify and aggressively remove the existing barriers to integration but replace them with incentives for industry to achieve the needed future integration. To accomplish this, the issue must receive a high priority and high-level leadership—which, today, it is not receiving. However, it is the only way to simultaneously address the nation's broad military and economic needs.

It is interesting to observe that Japan's explicitly-stated "defense industrial strategy" is based on the principle of an *integrated* civil and military industry. Nakasoni published[24] this strategy when he was Minister of Defense years ago, then implemented it as Prime Minister, and, even today, the Japanese continue to implement it as they build up their defense industrial base. Similarly, in Europe there has recently been a dramatic shift towards civil/military integration; emphasizing government R&D funding for "dual-use" technologies. The United States has no choice. If the nation intends to maintain a *domestic*, innovative, responsive, competitive industrial base, this base must be capable of satisfying both military and civil needs.

Nonetheless, a DOD shift towards greater civil/military integration, represents a basic "cultural shift." Thus, the change will be extremely difficult to achieve, particularly given today's separation of the sectors and the (continuing) unique DOD way of doing business. Still, it is the direction that the nation must take, and one that, in fact, the U.S. has slowly begun to shift toward.

The recognition of the international nature of most corporations; the corresponding likelihood of increased collaborative, multi-national weapons development efforts; and the requirement and likelihood that nations will shift, more and more, toward an integration of their civil and military industrial bases mandate a corresponding change in the policies and procedures that are used (both in U.S. and allied nations) in connection with issues such as: international technology transfer, controls on foreign ownership of defense plants; proliferation controls on advanced weapon systems; and, overriding all of these, the need for "assured access" by a nation to its defense engineering and production capabilities (regardless of their location). Establishing "new rules" within individual countries, among allied countries, and between the allies and their former, or even potential, adversaries is critical—and must be addressed in the near term. As older organizations (such as COCOM) rapidly adjust to the changing world's geopolitical and technological shifts, it will be necessary for new policies, procedures, and organizations to be quickly put in place, in order to fill the void.

CONCLUSIONS

Today there is clearly a public policy challenge for the United States as well as its Allies. Not only has the world changed dramatically in the last few years (in a geopolitical sense), but there is a corresponding need for an equally dramatic change in the way a nation does its defense business. Yet, to date, this needed shift is happening (at best) extremely slowly and reluctantly. If we are to shift to a "new way of doing business" in which globalization of industry, co-development of weapon systems, and civil/military integration of technology become the norms (in the weapons acquisition arena), then total changes in organizations, policies, procedures, specifications, weapons requirements, etc. are required. But, due to the anticipated institutional inertia, these changes will only occur with determined and sustained leadership.

Each country must establish and clearly define a "vision" of what form of a defense industrial base it intends to have for the twenty-first century, and then take the needed actions (sector by sector) to achieve it. The globalized nature of industry and technology, as well as the complex geopolitical linkages among nations, will frequently mandate that such actions be taken in consort with other governments in order to balance the conflicting objectives among them. The results of these efforts will clearly affect each nation's future economic posture, its security posture, and its international industrial competitiveness posture. Thus, in many ways, making these needed changes efficiently and effectively is critical to a nation's future; yet, there is enormous resistance to such changes from vested interests. However, it is clear that nations must begin to face up to these issues immediately. Strategies, policies, organizations, international forums, and, most important, leadership are required to initiate the needed steps. The time to do so is now!

NOTES

1. In the FY 1990 report of the American Secretary of Defense to the Congress, he cites five specific objectives of cooperation: (1) reduces needless duplication of R&D efforts, (2) prudently shares the best available technology, (3) promotes commonality and interoperability, (4) provides incentives for our allies to invest in force modernization and burdensharing, and (5) achieves economies of scale throughout the acquisition and logistics cycles.

2. J. S. Gansler and C. Henning, "European Acquisition and the U.S.," *Defense Diplomacy* 7 (June 1989), based on TASCFORM methodology, funded by DOD for over a decade.

3. Air Force Systems Command, "Affordable Acquisition Approach (A3)," Andrews Air Force Base, February 1980; summarized in J.S. Gansler, *Affording Defense* (Cambridge, Mass.: MIT Press, 1989), p. 173.

4. Gansler, *Affording Defense*, p. 173.

5. For example, see the Defense Science Board, *Use of Commercial Components in Military Equipment*, Summer Study, Washington, D.C., 1986.

6. Gansler, *Affording Defense*, p. 170-171.

7. Norman R. Augustine, *Augustine's Laws* (New York: American Institute of Aeronautics and Astronautics, 1982), p. 52.

8. See Gansler, *Affording Defense*, Chapter 8 for a full discussion of these problems.

9. Gansler, *Affording Defense*, pp. 270-271.

10. The Department of Defense, *Critical Technologies Plan*, for the Committee on Armed Services United States Congress, 15 March 1990; and Technology Administration, U.S. Department of Commerce, *Emerging Technologies: A Survey of Technical and Economic Opportunities*, pp. ix-xii and p. 13.

11. For a list of the measures of "criticality" that could be used see the Defense Science Board, *Technology and Technology Transfer*, Washington, D.C., Summer Study 1990.

12. M. Rich et al., *Multinational Co-production of Military Aerospace Systems*, Rand Corporation Report R2861-AF, October, 1981.

13. Discussion with General James Abrahamson when he was program manager of the F-16 program.

14. M.A. Lorell, *Multinational Development of Large Aircraft: The European Experience*, Rand Report R-2596-DR&E, July 1980.

15. General Accounting Office, *Joint Major System Acquisition: An Allusive Strategy*, Washington, D.C., May 1983.

16. Joint Logistics Commanders, *Joint Program Study*, Washington, D.C., June 1984. (Note: The analytic support for this effort was provided by TASC.)

17. President's Blue Ribbon Commission on Defense Management, *A Quest for Excellence*, Final Report to the President, Washington, D.C., June 1986.

18. Defense Science Board, *Use of Commercial Components in Military Equipment*, Summer Study, Washington, D.C., 1986.

19. Defense Science Board, *Use of Commercial Components in Military Equipment*, Washington, D.C., June 1989.

20. Note that the Soviet Union built tanks and railroad cars in the same plant because the production process was very similar for the two products.

21. The Department of Defense, *Critical Technologies Plan*, for the Committees on Armed Services United States Congress, Washington, D.C., March 15, 1990.

22. Technology Administration, U.S. Department of Commerce, *Emerging Technologies: A Survey of Technical and Economic Opportunities*, Washington, D.C., 1990, pp. ix-xii and p. 13.

23. A detailed analysis of these barriers and specific suggestions for their removal is contained in J. Bingaman, J. Gansler, and R. Kupperman, *Integrating Commercial and Military Technologies for National Strength: An Action Agenda*, Center for Strategic and International Studies, Washington, D.C., March 1991.

24. Originally published as "Basic Policy for Development and Production of Defense Equipment," July 1970. See *Defense and Foreign Affairs*, July 1983, p. 25.

2
Global Defense Business:
A Policy Context for the 1990s

William W. Keller

The author is a senior analyst and project director for the Office of Technology Assessment, United States Congress. This paper draws on research conducted by the Office of Technology Assessment (OTA) and on the OTA report, *Global Arms Trade*, OTA-ISC-460 (Washington, D.C.: Government Printing Office, June 1991). The author would like to acknowledge the invaluable criticism and assistance provided by Todd M. La Porte. Carol V. Evans, Lionel S. Johns, Ethan B. Kapstein, and Alan Shaw read the manuscript at several different stages and made helpful suggestions for revision. The views expressed in this chapter are those of the author, and do not necessarily reflect those of the Office of Technology Assessment.

The war in the Persian Gulf graphically demonstrated the consequences of extensive international commerce in powerful advanced conventional weapons. At the same time, the end of the Cold War and the accompanying decline in defense spending have both weakened the political foundation for continuing arms transfers and enhanced the economic motivations for international arms sales. Worldwide, the defense industries face deep recession (and probable permanent adjustment to much lower levels of production) brought on by a general erosion of demand and continued strong overcapacity of production.

Governments take widely differing approaches to the arms trade. Some help their defense companies seek export markets to compensate for insufficient domestic procurement budgets. Some nations view arms sales as an important source of export revenue, a way to spread development costs for new weapons, and a source of domestic employment. Some seek to enhance their stature as regional or international powers by building up a capable defense industry. One country, Japan, has prohibited the export of arms as a matter of public policy.

Traditionally, the U.S. Government has viewed arms sales and transfers primarily as instruments of foreign policy—to exert regional influence, to strengthen alliances, and to oppose the expansion of communist power. In the past 2 years, some government officials have become concerned over the likely loss of important elements of the U.S. defense industry as companies adjust to dramatic declines in domestic procurement; they have become more sympathetic to the desire of defense companies to increase export sales.[1] International sales, however, proliferate advanced weapons and often involve collaborative production arrangements with far-reaching consequences.

This situation poses a major national policy dilemma—how to balance the use of arms exports as instruments of foreign policy; pressure by companies for greater access to foreign markets; the need to stem a dangerous worldwide arms buildup; and the increasing proliferation of both defense equipment and defense industries. This chapter explores the form and dynamics of the international defense industry, the intricacies of technology transfer and equipment sales, and the implications for U.S. policy.

U.S. POLICY TOWARDS ARMS TRANSFERS

Several factors suggest that U.S. policy on arms exports and collaboration[2] in military technology is outmoded and no longer adequate:

1. The winding down of the Cold War is exerting an immediate and powerful downward pressure on defense expenditures in the West as governments implement budget cuts and force reductions associated with decreased East-West tensions;

2. The emergence of new centers of advanced defense industry and technology is accelerating the proliferation of modern weapons (and increasing overcapacity in worldwide weapons production); and

3. Western nations have helped arm Iraq, the rest of the Middle East, and other regions with little concern or oversight about the near- or far-term consequences.

The end of the cold war has radically transformed the structure of international relations and the environment for international defense business. As the Persian Gulf War and nationalist struggles throughout the former sphere of Soviet influence attest, it is still too early to fill in the outlines of the emerging world order. Nevertheless, the threat of Soviet expansionism is greatly reduced, the possibility of a Warsaw Pact invasion of Western Europe has been eliminated, and the Soviet Union appears to be following a policy of restraint in arms exports. Accordingly, the defense equipment requirements of the United States and the European Allies are diminishing significantly. Moreover, a principal reason why the United States transferred weapons and defense technology to allied and friendly nations—to counter communist influence—has been reduced.

The winding down of East-West antagonisms, however, has left profound uncertainty as to the nature and extent of future military threats to the United States, its allies, and its foreign political and economic interests. Military confrontation could come from a variety of heavily armed nations that, like Iraq, oppose U.S. interests and forces in places and for reasons that cannot be easily anticipated. It

FIGURE 1—MAJOR ARMS EXPORTERS, 1968-1987
(constant 1988 dollars, billions)

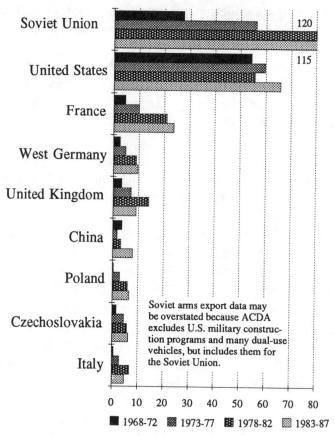

Source: Office of Technology Assessment (OTA)

might conceivably come from reconstituted elements of the Soviet empire. In a multi-polar world the threat of *sporadic militarism* will be reinforced and magnified by the availability of potent weapons and the knowledge of how to make and use them.

Another major factor affecting policy is the proliferation of the defense industries around the world. The arms production and export capabilities of a number of states have expanded—in the United

States, Europe, the Middle East, the Indian subcontinent, South America, and the Western Pacific (see Figure 1). Increasingly, defense trade combines sales of finished defense systems with transfer of the underlying technologies and industrial infrastructure necessary for indigenous production (see Figures 2 and 3). These two subjects—arms sales and technology transfer—are examined in tandem throughout this chapter.

FIGURE 2—WORLDWIDE LICENSED PRODUCTION OF MAJOR CONVENTIONAL WEAPONS SYSTEMS
by Country Issuing License, 1960-1988

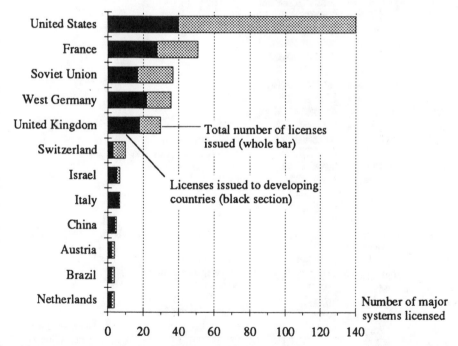

10 other countries issuing fewer than 4 licenses not shown.   Source: OTA

Defense companies in Europe produce equipment for export markets that is often as good as and sometimes better than that exported by the United States.[3] European governments often conduct extensive diplomacy in support of arms sales. In the past, this has

FIGURE 3—WORLDWIDE LICENSED PRODUCTION OF MAJOR CONVENTIONAL WEAPONS SYSTEMS
by Country Receiving License, 1960-1988*

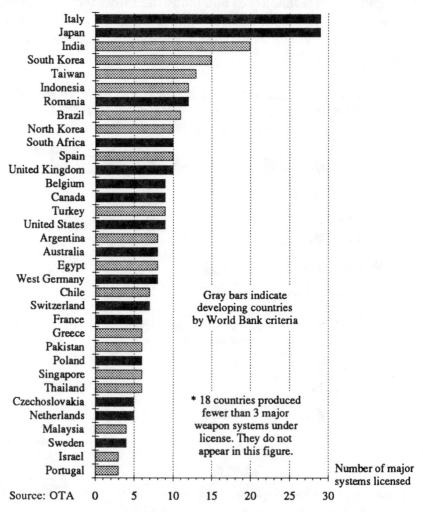

Gray bars indicate developing countries by World Bank criteria

* 18 countries produced fewer than 3 major weapon systems under license. They do not appear in this figure.

Number of major systems licensed

Source: OTA

provided strong competition for U.S. arms exporters, especially in the Middle East, but also in the Western Pacific. Since 1986, however, U.S. arms exports have increased to a ten-year high, while NATO Europe arms exports have fallen. In 1988, the last year for which complete data are available, the United States exported $14.3 billion in arms as compared to $4.1 billion for NATO Europe combined.[4] If this trend continues, it may place the United States in a position to exert profound influence on the course of weapons proliferation. On one hand, the United States may choose to press its present advantage, attempting to increase arms exports to the limits of existing markets. On the other hand, as the principal arms exporter in the West, the United States might decide to exercise its leadership and propose to its Allies ways and means of reducing commerce in modern conventional weapons.

For reasons of national security, nations are willing to underwrite the costs of indigenous development and production of weapons, even in the face of worldwide overcapacity in the defense industries. But most nations cannot buy enough domestically produced defense

FIGURE 4—MAJOR ARMS IMPORTERS, 1983-1988
(constant 1988 dollars, billions)

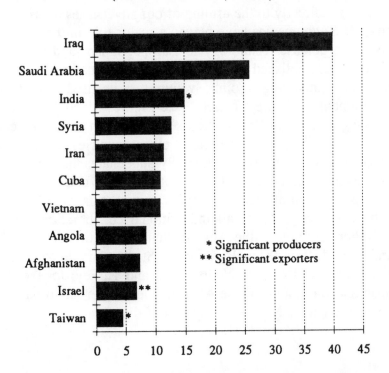

Source: OTA

material to keep unit costs tolerably low. With the exception of the United States and Japan, procurement officials and company executives believe they must produce weapons for export markets in order to fund the next generation of weapons systems. In 1984, for example, Brazil exported 90 percent of its defense production, Italy exported 65 percent, and Israel, France, Spain, and the U.K. exported over 40 percent of defense items produced.[5] This has contributed to a large flow of advanced weapons to developing countries like Iraq, Saudi Arabia, India, Syria, Iran, and others (see Figure 4). Only Japan has been willing and able to subsidize enormous costs for limited production runs of sophisticated defense equipment. Operating under a U.S.-imposed constitution and a highly protective U.S. security umbrella, Japan is the only advanced industrial nation to renounce unilaterally the export of weapons and the projection of military power in international affairs.

The proliferation of the ability to produce modern arms (emanating principally from the United States and Europe) has led directly and indirectly to the arming of our adversaries as well as our friends. U.S. companies have played a major role in the transfer of sophisticated defense technology to Europe, Japan, and elsewhere.[6] This was accomplished largely through international industrial cooperation including joint ventures, licensed production, codevelopment, and direct offsets[7] (see Figures 5 and 6). Figure 5 shows the growth of worldwide licensed production of major weapons systems, including those licensed to other countries by the United States. However, Figure 5 substantially understates the magnitude of technology transfer because it does not count the codevelopment or licensed production of separate parts or components, which probably constitutes the majority of all international collaboration. Among many other examples, the United States has transferred highly advanced production technology for the Stinger missile to Germany, Belgium, Greece, Italy, the Netherlands, and Turkey; for the Patriot to Japan and Italy; and for the AIM-9L Sidewinder air-to-air missile to Japan, Germany, Norway, Italy, and Taiwan.

FIGURE 5—ESTIMATED WORLDWIDE LICENSED PRODUCTION OF
MAJOR CONVENTIONAL WEAPONS SYSTEMS, 1960-1988

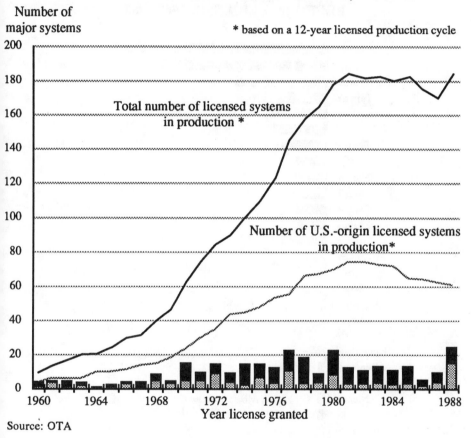

Number of
major systems   * based on a 12-year licensed production cycle

Source: OTA

U.S. and European defense firms not only sell hardware, but
have also helped to build up the defense industries of newly
industrialized countries. This is often accomplished through complex
foreign sales agreements in which the buyer nation might purchase,
for example, a few copies of an advanced fighter or tank, assemble
a second batch under license, and manufacture the rest indigenously
(also under license) to the extent that its industrial base can absorb
and produce the technologies in question. U.S. firms may compete

**FIGURE 6—LICENSED PRODUCTION OF U.S. MAJOR
CONVENTIONAL WEAPONS SYSTEMS, BY COUNTRY
RECEIVING LICENSE, 1960-1988**

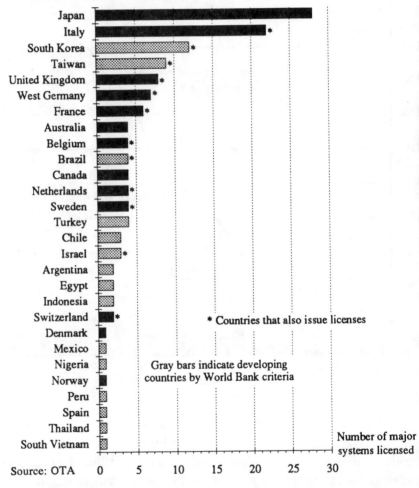

Source: OTA

among themselves or with their European counterparts to make such
a sale. A major sale can become a contest between two or more U.S.
companies to see which is willing to sell the most defense technology
at the lowest price.

The proposed transfer of advanced U.S. fighter technology to South Korea, the Korean Fighter Plane, is a case in point. In 1989, South Korea agreed to buy 120 twin engine FA/18 fighter aircraft from McDonnell Douglas for $5 billion, with 12 planes to be purchased off-the-shelf, 36 assembled from U.S.-built kits, and 72 produced under license in Korea. But by 1991, the price had risen to $6.2 billion, and the Koreans were demanding sophisticated radar, software, and composite materials technologies that the company was reluctant to release. After nearly 2 years, South Korea broke off negotiations and decided to buy the General Dynamics (GD) F-16 fighter instead. GD's ability to offer the F-16 at a lower price and add even more technology, an advanced radar, and air-to-air missiles were decisive factors.[8]

The United States and Europe routinely transfer a great deal of advanced defense technology to less developed nations. In 1988, for example, India, Egypt, Indonesia, South Korea, Taiwan, and Brazil were producing 43 different major weapons under international licensing agreements.[9] Several of these nations have attained significant defense industrial capacity and have entered the arms export business. Between 1978 and 1988, the arms exported by Israel, Brazil, Spain, and South Korea amounted to $16 billion.[10]

The multiplicity of sources (both advanced and developed) has produced a buyers' market in which a range of modern defense equipment is generally available to anyone who can pay for them. As a consequence, the use of arms transfers—or their denial—as instruments of foreign policy has been substantially degraded. At the same time, unilateral U.S. attempts to restrain the arms trade will likely fail because the buyer nation can find alternative sources with competitive defense equipment (see Table 1).

A final factor influencing policy is that many U.S. defense companies are in financial trouble. Decreased procurement budgets and the rapidly escalating cost of weapons systems have combined to threaten the long-term economic viability of many defense companies as presently constituted. In the past 3 years, a handful of U.S. firms

**TABLE 1—SELECTED WEAPONS EXPORTED BY THE UNITED
STATES, SOVIET UNION, AND NATO EUROPE**

Weapons Systems	United States	Soviet Union	NATO Europe
Main battle tanks	M1 Abrams	T-80, T-72	Leopard 2 (Germany) Challenger (U.K.)
	M60	T-64	Leopard 1 (Germany) Chieftain (U.K.) AMX-30B2 (France) Vickers Mk 3 (U.K.) OTO Melara OF-40 (Italy)
Fighter/attack aircraft	F-16	MiG-29	Mirage F-1 (France)
	F-15	Su-27	Mirage 2000 (France)
		Su-24	Tornado (U.K., Germany, Italy)
Missiles Air-to-air	AIM-9M Sidewinder	AA-2 Atoll	AA-8 Aphid R550 Magic (France)
	AIM-9M Sparrow	AA-7 Apex	R530 (France) Aspide (Italy) Sky Flash (U.K.)
Ship-to-ship	RGM-84A Harpoon		SS-M-StyxExocet (France) Sea Eagle (U.K.) Sea Skua (U.K.) Penguin (Norway)
Anti-tank	BGM-71D TOW-2	AT-4 Spigot AT-5 Spandrel	Milan (France) Eryx (France) HOT (France) Cobra (Germany) Swingfire (U.K.)

Source: OTA

have collectively written off over $3.5 billion in R&D investments.[11]
The impact of decreased defense business—large lay-offs and
production cut-backs—has and will continue to be felt in congressional
districts across the nation.

As part of their plans for adjusting to a declining U.S. defense budget, many U.S. defense companies are increasing their emphasis on international business. This is being pursued through selling advanced conventional weapons to foreign governments, and increasingly, transferring defense technology to foreign companies through licensed production of U.S. equipment and joint development of new weapons systems. The international operations of U.S. defense companies expanded throughout the 1970s and 80s, and extensive trade and defense industrial linkages were established around the globe. This process is now being accelerated by a downturn in domestic defense spending and by the threat of competition from Europe and several developing nations for foreign defense sales.

Expanding international business may increase profits for individual U.S. companies, but for the U.S. defense industry in the aggregate the benefits are not so clear cut. International defense industrial collaboration creates competition for U.S. companies both in foreign markets and at home. Highly capable foreign defense firms, moreover, seek strategic business alliances and subcontracting relationships with American companies as a means of penetrating the U.S. market, which is by far the largest and most lucrative in the world. Some have acquired U.S. defense firms; more often, they demand a share of the production of U.S. weapons systems and transfer of manufacturing technology as conditions of importing U.S. equipment. Increasingly, international collaboration transfers defense technology to other countries and results in more foreign-made defense components being imported to the United States.

Many U.S. defense executives argue that they do not bargain away their best technology. This allows them to maintain an edge over the competition for the next sale, and assures that the United States will also enjoy a military advantage in the event U.S. troops have to face U.S.-made weapons, or those derived from U.S. designs, in combat. But the problem of proliferation is somewhat more complex. Advanced weapons systems—both old and new—emanate from many different sources, and tend to fuel regional instabilities. Although they have not been in production for many years, F-4 aircraft, M-60 tanks, Cobra helicopters, Scud ballistic missiles, and MiG-23 fighters (to name a few) are powerful weapons and can produce dramatic military, political, and psychological pressures when transferred to regions where they have not previously been deployed.

The Persian Gulf War heightened the short-term business prospects for a few U.S. defense companies; however, in part because the United States did not lose major equipment, the war will not reverse the downturn in defense business of the late 1980s or even significantly mitigate it. Defense recession comes at a time when the industry is plagued with overcapacity worldwide. The breakup of the Warsaw Pact, coupled with increasingly cordial East-West relations, makes it very likely that this recession may in fact be a fundamental adjustment to lower levels of defense production across the board.

The United States has never viewed arms transfers primarily as a sector in international trade. Indeed, a substantial amount of equipment and training is transferred through various grant programs. In addition, the Foreign Military Sales (FMS) program is structured to place foreign policy goals above economic considerations. In an FMS sale, the recipient country makes a formal request to the United States for security assistance, the State Department evaluates the request (and may or may not authorize it) from a policy standpoint, and the Department of Defense implements it.[12] In most cases, the U.S. Government then buys the equipment from U.S. companies and transfers it at cost (plus a 3-percent administrative fee) to the recipient nation.

In recent years, however, a distinctly economic component has entered U.S. international military sales policies. In a departure from long-standing practice, high-ranking officers of the United States Army and Air Force have advocated foreign sales of U.S. equipment.[13] In addition, direct commercial sales (DCS), in which a U.S. company delivers arms directly to a foreign corporation or government, have expanded significantly.[14] In a direct sale, a U.S. company and a foreign government (or firm) reach an agreement and then apply for the requisite permissions and export licenses. Compared to an FMS sale, profits from DCS sales are often higher, accountability to the U.S. Government is less, and the overall relevance to U.S. foreign policy goals is usually smaller and less direct. Between 1983 and 1988, delivery of arms under DCS agreements rose by a factor of 8 to reach $8 billion per year.[15]

International arms business, in which the United States is first among several prominent suppliers, is building up a dangerously armed world. In the Middle East, arms imported to the region have raised the stakes associated with political instability and have figured prominently in the calculations of militant religious regimes and regional strong men. As the Islamic revolution in Iran demonstrated, once transferred, modern weapons can outlast the governments they were intended to support. As the war with Iraq has shown, arms may outlast the good will of the leaders to whom they were supplied.

If the goal is to stem proliferation of advanced conventional weapons and defense technology, multilateral restraint by Europe, the Soviet Union, and the United States is a prerequisite. Because these three account for about 80 percent of all arms exports (and a higher percentage of advanced material), an agreement to restrain exports could have far-reaching implications.[16] In the context of a "new world order," conventional arms control is clearly an alternative to a continuing arms bazaar, especially to the Middle East. Without the stimulus of a polarizing U.S.-Soviet military confrontation, the continuance of arms proliferation to developing nations has lost much of its military and political justification. Considering its recent role in the Persian Gulf crisis, the United Nations may be the appropriate vehicle to pursue multilateral restraint of defense exports.

U.S. arms exports have become increasingly contentious in the past several years.[17] The FSX fighter codevelopment with Japan, the denied sale of F-15E fighter-bombers to Saudi Arabia, and the 1990 proposal to sell over $21 billion of assorted equipment to the Saudis are well-known examples. Compared to just a few years ago, the stakes are higher and have expanded to include large amounts of money (and jobs), the future health of U.S. defense companies, the transfer of technology with military and commercial applications, the arming of potential future adversaries, and the proliferation of possibly destabilizing military might.

WHY SHOULD POLICYMAKERS CARE?

As the defense industries of the world become more capable, the problem of proliferation increases because no single nation (or group of nations to date) can control the ultimate distribution of advanced weapons and the technologies necessary to build them.

The acquisition of weapons and military technology can and does change the balance of power among nations. By exporting large quantities of potent weapons, the advanced industrial states continue to build up the ability of potentially renegade or terrorist nations to make trouble—to threaten the use of force and to invade weaker nations. The Iraqi invasion of Kuwait is the most recent example; if advanced weaponry continues to proliferate at present rates, it is not likely to be the last. Even though the U.S.-led coalition defeated the Iraqi military with unprecedented efficiency and few losses, transferring potent weapons to foreign militaries makes it more difficult for the United States to reduce the size and cost of its military and still protect American interests abroad.

The Persian Gulf War also demonstrated the destructive capability of modern conventional weapons; in less than 2 months, coalition forces devastated the physical infrastructure of Iraq and killed tens of thousands of Iraqi soldiers. This toll in destruction of life and human suffering may only be the beginning. Even with vastly less hardware, Iraq's leadership may still devastate the Kurdish and Shiite Moslem populations (and other internal challenges).

Increasing proliferation of sophisticated weapons and technological know-how has injected new elements of uncertainty and risk into international relations. The United States and other major exporters are gradually losing control of the weapons transferred as well as the technology and industry necessary to produce and support them. There can be no assurance that weapons the United States and its allies make available to friends today will not be used against U.S. troops tomorrow. As the Iraqi situation has presaged, arms trade and collaboration will increasingly influence the environment in which foreign policy decisions are made. If other nations had not armed Iraq, the United States might have avoided the need to use force in the Persian Gulf.

Advanced weaponry and defense technology may not always be used for the purposes intended or stay in the hands of the regime to which they were sold. In the Middle East, the United States alone sent about $11 billion in military hardware to Iran between 1969 and 1979 and trained over 11,000 Iranian military officers.[18] The weapons failed in their purpose, i.e., to enhance the stability of a friendly and moderate regime in the region, and were later used to wage war against Iraq. The Soviets, the French, and several developing nations supplied the Iraqis with a vast arsenal (see Figure 7 and Table 2), in order to balance against the new Iranian threat. Those weapons, and U.S. weapons captured from the Kuwaitis,[19] were then available for use against coalition forces in the Arabian Peninsula. Future proposals for defense industrial cooperation between U.S. and European firms will have to be evaluated in light of these circumstances, as well as the comparative permissiveness of European arms export policies.

Increasingly, international business arrangements lead to foreign penetration of the U.S. defense market. Typically, a U.S. company (acting as the prime contractor) subcontracts a portion of a defense system to a foreign company. Many foreign defense firms have established strong marketing presences in the Washington metropolitan area to monitor the U.S. defense market and cement

FIGURE 7—ARMS TRANSFERS TO IRAQ BY COUNTRY
1984-1988
(current dollars)

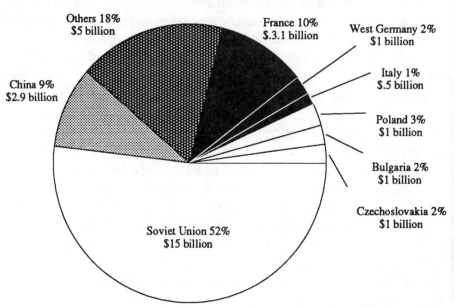

Others 18%
$5 billion

France 10%
$.3.1 billion

West Germany 2%
$1 billion

China 9%
$2.9 billion

Italy 1%
$.5 billion

Poland 3%
$1 billion

Bulgaria 2%
$1 billion

Czechoslovakia 2%
$1 billion

Soviet Union 52%
$15 billion

Source: OTA   The United States transferred no arms to Iraq during this period

business ties with U.S. defense contractors. In addition, an increasing number of European companies are acquiring U.S. defense firms through foreign direct investment, essentially buying their way into the U.S. market. The U.S. Congress has given these activities increasing scrutiny in recent years.

Arms transfers also constitute a major element in the continuing struggle between Congress and the Executive over how much influence Congress can and should exert over foreign policy. The Executive continues to view and use arms exports as a vital and powerful instrument in the conduct of foreign relations, and Congress continues to assent, sometimes reluctantly, using its regulatory and oversight powers to sway and circumscribe the foreign policy agenda of the President.

TABLE 2—DEVELOPING NATIONS'ARMS EXPORTS TO IRAQ
1982-1989

Brazil	66 Astros-II SS-30 multiple rocket launchers 20 Astros Guidance fire control radoars 200 EE-9 Cascavel armored cars 300 EE-3 Jacara scout cars
China	4 B-6 bombers (copy of Soviet Tu-16) 72 Hai Ying-2 ship-to-ship missiles (arming B-6 bombers) 700 T-59 main battle tanks 600 T-69 main battle tanks 650 Type 531 armored personnel carriers 720 Type 59/1 130mm towed guns 128 C-601 anti-ship missiles
Egypt	70 F-7 fighter aircraft (Chinese version of MiG-21) 80 EMB-312 Tucano trainers (built under Brazilian license) 150 BM-21 122mm multiple rocket system 100 Sakr-30 122mm multiple rocket launchers 90 D-130 122mm towed guns 96 D-30 122mm towed howitzer

Source: Office of Technology Assessment, from data in Stockholm International Peace Research Institute, SIPRI Yearbooks, 1970 through 1990, *World Armaments and Disarmament.*

ISSUES AND OPTIONS FOR DECISIONMAKERS

Historical Perspective

The topic of conventional arms exports and controls has a long history, and the relevant legislation and associated government programs are extraordinarily complex. Before turning to a discussion of the issues and policy options raised in this chapter, a brief sketch of congressional and executive branch interactions over security assistance and conventional arms control is presented.

Since the passage of the Foreign Military Sales Act of 1968, Congress has exerted strong oversight and has imposed numerous controls on the military assistance activities of the United States. These have included downgrading or eliminating the Military Assistance Advisory Groups at U.S. embassies, earmarking up to 99 percent of foreign military financing funds for particular countries, and restricting third-party transfers of U.S. weapons under the Arms Export Control Act of 1976, the International Security Assistance Act of 1977, and subsequent regulations.

In addition to extensive reporting requirements and regulation of arms exports, Congress has at times mandated outright prohibition of security assistance to countries such as Turkey, Pakistan, and Iraq. It has also instituted an elaborate notification process enabling it to block a proposed sale under exceptional circumstances. These and other requirements reflect its determination to retain responsibilities in foreign policy and maintain its power to regulate commerce with foreign nations derived from article I, section 8 of the Constitution.[20]

Nevertheless, Congress has often been a reluctant partner in the U.S. foreign military sales program.[21] As a result, the executive branch has exercised considerable latitude in the definition and conduct of arms sales and the transfer of defense technology. This is evident from the extreme change of policy from the Carter to the Reagan administrations.[22] President Jimmy Carter saw arms transfer "as an exceptional foreign policy implement, to be used only in instances where it can be clearly demonstrated that the transfer contributes to promote our security and the security of our close friends."[23] Four years later President Reagan took the opposite approach. Arms transfers would be "an essential element of [U.S.] global defense posture and an indispensable component of its foreign policy."[24]

Although President Bush proposed in May 1991 that major suppliers nations exercise "collective self-restraint" in arms sales to the Middle East,[25] the Bush administration has consistently acted to support foreign sales of U.S. defense equipment. It has directed U.S. embassy personnel to increase the level of assistance provided to U.S. defense companies,[26] created the Center for Defense Trade within the State Department, and proposed a "defense GATT" that would allow free and open trade in arms and defense technology within the NATO Alliance, and with other U.S. allies.[27]   In March 1991, the Administration proposed that the Export-Import Bank guarantee up to $1 billion in commercial loans to members of NATO, Australia, Japan, and Israel to purchase defense equipment from U.S. contractors.[28]

The Bush administration has also used weapons transfers liberally in support of its Persian Gulf policies. It has proposed the sale of over $26 billion in U.S. weapons to a variety of countries in the Middle East.[29]   In his address to a joint session of Congress following the end of the Persian Gulf War, the President pressed Congress for greater latitude in arms transfers.[30]

There is, then, a continuing tension not only between Congress and the Executive concerning arms transfers, but also between the policy of arming our allies and the desire to prohibit the export of advanced weapons and technology to potentially hostile or irresponsible nations. The recent Persian Gulf experience will most likely increase these tensions.   Despite long-term congressional misgivings and widely divergent approaches by different Presidents, the knowledge and industrial infrastructure necessary to build advanced weaponry is proliferating beyond our control.

THE SPREAD OF DEFENSE TECHNOLOGY AND DEFENSE INDUSTRY

The first three issues presented below address the question: To what extent should U.S. policy restrict or permit the transfer of U.S. defense technology to foreign nations? Licensed production (and other forms of international collaboration) is generally increasing worldwide, and U.S. companies account for a large share of the defense technology being transferred in the West.[31] The implications for the United States of increasing collaboration, however, depend on the defense policies and level of industrial development of the different partner nations. Accordingly, this policy discussion addresses three separate cases: Japan, the advanced European defense producers, and certain developing nations.

Issue 1: Transferring Defense Technology to Developing Nations

The developing nations depend far more heavily on transferred defense technology than do Japan and the Western European states. For countries such as South Korea, Brazil, India, Taiwan, Indonesia, Singapore, and Australia, licensed production is a major vehicle for the promotion and building up of indigenous defense industrial capabilities. While licensed production of components is far more common, these nations have also undertaken extensive production of major weapons systems in this way. India has produced 20 major weapon systems under license; South Korea, 15; Taiwan, 13; Indonesia, 12; Brazil, 11: North Korea and Spain, 10 each; Turkey, 9; and Argentina and Egypt, 8 each.[32]

Increasingly, U.S. industry transfers defense technology to a wide range of developing nations on an ad hoc basis in the absence of consistent policy direction. U.S. decisionmakers face a clear policy choice: whether or not (or to what extent) to permit U.S. companies to build up the defense production capabilities of the developing world. The principal considerations on which policy in this area might be based are discussed below.

Licensed production and other forms of international collaboration in defense technology are critical to building the defense industries of developing countries. Many of these countries have very weak R&D capability in defense technology; and the advanced technology and R&D resources they do possess are often dedicated to commercial efforts. Defense companies in South Korea, for example, typically depend on the government's Agency for Defense Development (ADD) for most of their R&D, and ADD itself has very limited R&D facilities and programs. The long-term strategy of the Korean government is to draw U.S. defense companies into cooperative production and R&D relationships so that Korean firms can learn from their more advanced partners.[33]

In the absence of significant foreign assistance, the indigenous defense industrial capability of most of the developing nations would cease to expand, and might even collapse. While there is some evidence that the developing nations are beginning to transfer defense technology among themselves, they are still largely unable to produce the technology or absorb the costs associated with indigenous *development* of modern weaponry. Because domestic demand is so limited, most must find export markets to reduce the units costs. For this reason, U.S. restrictions on third party sales of U.S. weapons produced under license is a major issue for developing countries. They face the same problems of overcapacity and high development costs that have plagued the advanced producers—only for them, the problems are more acute.

Industrial linkages between U.S. defense companies and weapons producers in the developing world have expanded in recent years. Frequently, these are built into the structure of arms sales. What used to be straight-forward sales of major platforms have now become sales combined with eventual licensed production of all or part of the weapon in question. These kinds of arrangements contribute to globalization of the defense industrial base. Global sourcing may already be making defense production more efficient, but in the long term, it will also tend to displace U.S. defense subcontractors (and U.S. workers) and increase U.S. dependence on foreign-made defense products.

Nations with developing defense industries constitute a significant expansion of worldwide defense production capacity, which is not surprising considering their growing technological and industrial presence in international civilian markets. These countries are now entering the international arms trade or have active strategies to do so. Some, like Brazil and Israel, have already made their presence felt; others, like South Korea, intend to supply a large portion of their own domestic needs as well as those of their allies. Most will likely adopt a dual-use approach to defense technology, i.e., seeking to leverage civilian technology for defense purposes, producing high quality, but not state-of-the-art weapons systems.

The United States is now engaged in and negotiating transfer of advanced defense technology to a variety of developing countries. These include the M1 Abrams tank coproduction with Egypt, the Korean Fighter Plane (a General Dynamics F-16 sale and licensed production arrangement), and the Indigenous Fighter Plane with Taiwan (a twin engine fighter based on F-16, F/A-18, and F-20 technology). While the United States cannot stop these nations from building their defense industries, U.S. policy on transferring defense technology to them will make a very large difference. Of the 15 major weapons systems produced under license by South Korea, for example, 12 were transferred from the United States; and U.S. companies licensed 9 of 13 major foreign systems being produced in Taiwan. It is unlikely that South Korea or Taiwan would have achieved present levels of defense production without significant and sustained assistance from U.S. defense companies (see Table 3).

Some argue that turning off the U.S. spigot would not solve the problem because the defense industrial base is already global and other nations (particularly in Europe) could provide the requested items. Clearly, controls on defense industrial collaboration would not eliminate the flow of defense technology unless coordinated with other advanced defense industrial states.

As the largest and most advanced producer of defense systems in the West, a U.S.-led diplomatic initiative to restrict collaboration might, however, slow the pace of defense industrial and technological dispersion. It would also place the United States in a position to exert diplomatic pressure on its NATO Allies and the Soviet Union. Working together, the NATO countries and the Soviet Union could

TABLE 3—MAJOR U.S. WEAPONS SYSTEMS PRODUCED UNDER LICENSE BY SOUTH KOREA AND TAIWAN

South Korea

F-16 Fighting Falcon fighter (negotiating)
F-5E Tiger-2 fighter
F-5F Tiger-2 fighter
H-76 Eagle helicopter
Model 500MD helicopter
PL-2 light plane trainer
M-101A1 105 mm towed howitzer
M-109-A2 155 self-propelled howitzer
M-114-A1 towed howitzer
CPIC type fast attack craft
LCU-1610 type landing craft
PSMM-5 type fast attack craft

Taiwan

F-5E Tiger-2 fighter
F-5F Tiger-2 fighter
F-5F Tiger-2 trainer
Model 205 UH-1H helicopter
AIM-9J air-to-air missile
AIM-9L air-to-air missile
MIM-23B Hawk land mobile surface-to-air-missile
M-60-H main battle tank
FFG-7 class frigate
PL-1B Chienshou lightplane
Lung Chiang class fast attack craft

Source: Office of Technology Assessment, from data in Stockholm International Peace Research Institute, SIPRI Yearbooks, 1970 through 1990, *World Armaments and Disarmament.*

stem the vast majority, perhaps as much as 90 percent, of technology transferred in international defense trade. A possible approach is discussed below under Issue 4.

Issue 2: Collaboration with Western Europe

The major defense producing nations of Europe—France, Germany, the U.K., and Italy—have long collaborated with one another in the development and production of defense equipment. Some have adopted export-led defense industrial policies, with exports accounting on aggregate for at least one-third of European defense production. European defense companies are eager to exchange technology with U.S. firms, although historically, because U.S. defense technology was far superior, the United States has transferred a great deal more to Europe than it has received. That situation has changed; for purposes of export and collaboration, U.S. and European defense technology and production are now roughly comparable. Many transatlantic subcontracting and joint venture arrangements are now in effect.[34]

Powerful political and economic forces have transformed the security arrangements of Europe and challenged the continued relevance and viability of the NATO Alliance itself. Major changes in Soviet policies, German unification, the Treaty on Conventional Forces in Europe (CFE), break up of the Warsaw Pact, economic integration of the European Community, and the Persian Gulf War have all helped to undermine the basic assumptions that have driven East-West security relations in the post-World War II period. While much is still uncertain, many analysts believe Western Europe will become increasingly self-reliant, eventually approaching security concerns not as individual nations or members of NATO, but from the perspective of an independent, single European pole of defense. Accordingly, differences in U.S. and European defense industrial and arms export practices will figure heavily in calculating the benefits and risks associated with a U.S. policy to permit or restrict the transfer of U.S. defense technology to Western Europe.

In the past, U.S. policies to transfer technology and arms to Europe were motivated largely by security considerations and military preparations associated with the cold war and the threat of a potential Warsaw Pact invasion of Western Europe. Those policies worked.

**TABLE 4—FRENCH WEAPONS TRANSFERRED TO IRAQ
1981-1988**

143	Mirage F-1C	Fighter/interceptor
105	AMX-30 Roland	Antiaircraft vehicle, missile armed
734	AM-39 Exocet	Antiship missiles
708	ARMAT	Antiradar missiles
1,200	AS-30L	Antiship missiles
1,600	HOT	Antitank missiles
4,800	Milan	Antitank missiles
1,050	Roland-2	Surface-to-air missiles
257	R-530	Air-to-air missiles
534	R-550 Magic	Air-to-air missiles

Source: Office of Technology Assessment, from data in Stockholm International
Research Institute, SIPRI Yearbooks, 1970 through 1990, *World Armaments and
Disarmament.*

In the space of a few decades, they helped build sophisticated defense
industries across Western Europe. These policies also contributed to
extreme peacetime overcapacity in the defense industries of the West,
and to intense international competition for sales of advanced
weaponry.

In considering U.S. policy toward transatlantic defense industrial
collaboration and technology transfer, several factors should be
analyzed. Countries with whom the United States has collaborated
extensively in the past may in fact transfer weapons and technology
to nations that oppose U.S. security and economic interests. In the
past, European governments have been willing to export their most
advanced weapons to a wide range of countries. Although they were
not used effectively in the Persian Gulf War, some of the most
sophisticated weapons in the Iraqi arsenal were made in France (see
Table 4).[35] It is not impossible that U.S. soldiers will again face
European weapons on the battlefield, weapons that may even
incorporate innovations first developed in the United States. If the

European nations and the United States are unable or unwilling to harmonize their defense export policies, then the United States should consider restricting future defense industrial collaboration with Europe.

Continued transatlantic collaboration in military technology will likely increase interdependence, both in terms of shared technology and with respect to production capabilities. This would deepen penetration of the U.S. market by foreign components, and as a result, increase U.S. dependence on foreign defense equipment and technology. Dramatic escalation in strategic corporate alliances and subcontracting arrangements between U.S. and European defense companies indicate this process in already underway. Recent acquisition of U.S. defense companies by European firms, large defense cooperation staffs at the European embassies in Washington, and marketing offices of European defense firms inside the Capital Beltway also indicate increasing European penetration of the U.S. defense market.

European governments are unlikely to permit U.S. defense companies to establish a greater presence in Europe, as producers or sellers, unless there is reciprocal access for European firms. Because the U.S. Government buys more defense equipment than all of the major defense producing states of Europe combined, it is unlikely that opening up transatlantic defense collaboration and trade would benefit U.S. firms in the aggregate, particularly in a declining global defense market. Over the past several years the defense industries of Europe have consolidated, creating national champions. These defense conglomerates—such as British Aerospace (BAe) in the U.K. and Deutsche Aerospace (DASA) in Germany—are comparable to the large U.S. defense contractors in terms of financial resources, technology, production, and sales.

Finally, transatlantic exchange of defense technology and the industrial linkages on which it depends raise additional proliferation concerns. Ultimately, the United States exerts very little influence over the choice weapon systems and defense technology used by even its closest allies. Increasing internationalization of the defense industrial base means that national controls over the distribution of defense systems and technologies become weaker. At some point in the weapons development process, technology itself becomes fungible, that is, innovations of one company working closely with another contribute to the establishment of a common technology base. It then becomes possible for either party to build on a particular development, modify it for different applications (both military and civil), sell its products to third parties, or transfer it as technology to others.

Issue 3: Defense Industrial Collaboration with Japan

In 1989, the 101st Congress approved the transfer of U.S. fighter technology to Japan, as part of the FSX codevelopment agreement. Numerous committees of Congress held hearings on the advisability of permitting General Dynamics to work closely with Mitsubishi Heavy Industries (MHI) to develop a Japanese indigenous fighter. A principal concern was that the FSX project might ultimately help Japan become more competitive in civil aviation markets. But the debate largely failed to address the more immediate questions of whether or not transferring this capability to Japan would enhance or detract from U.S., Japanese, and international security.

In three respects, Japan is a special case. First, the U.S. transfers more major weapons systems to Japan than it does to any other nation. Over the past decade, Japan has embarked on a rapid defense build-up and has developed an extensive defense industrial sector, drawing heavily on licensed production from the United States. Because Japan is a major export market for U.S. defense technology, the FSX codevelopment project represented a deepening of already firmly established defense industrial ties. It also meant business opportunities for General Dynamics and its U.S. subcontractors.

Second, concerns that Japan might proliferate U.S.-licensed, codeveloped, or derivative defense technologies are somewhat mitigated by Japan's policy against export of defense equipment. Although this policy may change, it is anchored in the larger U.S.-Japan security relationship, and to the extent this alliance remains stable, Japanese restraint in defense exports will probably be preserved. If, however, trade relations between the two economic superpowers continue to sour, a new security environment could emerge in which Japan depended less on the U.S. security umbrella. Change could also result from different perceptions by the two countries of their roles and interests in the evolving post-Cold War security structure. Japan might decide to do what many U.S. policymakers have urged for decades: take on more of the burden of its own defense. In that case, the United States (and the world) would find a Japan with a strong base of defense technology, and an industrial sector fully capable of ramping up production swiftly in the event it was called on to do so.

Third, the flow in defense technology between the United States and Japan has been a one-way street to Japan, with few exceptions.[36] Supporters of the FSX project argued that Japan would make advanced radar and composite materials technology available to the United States under the terms of the agreement. While it is still early in the development process, such reverse technology transfer has not occurred, and some argue that the Japanese developments in question were overrated in the first place. In general, government and corporate leaders in Japan appear eager to receive U.S. defense technology, and at the same time, reluctant to share theirs with the United States.

U.S. policy on cooperation in defense technologies between the United States and Japan must factor in the unique circumstances enumerated above and should not ignore lessons learned from the FSX experience. Mired in political controversy from the outset, the FSX project has encountered unforeseen technical problems, and appears to be far more expensive than its Japanese supporters expected. Some now doubt the project will reach full-scale production. Many Japanese officials remain bitter about what they perceive to have been less than good faith on the part of the U.S. administration and Congress. They believed they had negotiated a firm agreement with the Reagan administration, only to have it reopened in an atmosphere of distrust and mutual recrimination.

If maintained, the present U.S. policy to permit frequent transfers of defense technology to Japan will continue to build up the defense industrial base of that nation. This, of course, raises the question of the rearming of Japan. Japan has increased its defense expenditures in real terms by about 6 percent per year for the past decade, and is by for the largest military presence in the Western Pacific. Few believe Japan intends to build its arsenals to levels associated with World War II. Nevertheless, a key component of its defense industrial strategy is to produce a large number of major weapons at very low production rates, developing the technological know-how and industrial infrastructure that would have to precede a decision to rearm.

Japan is able to reap the benefits of much U.S. defense R&D, essentially buying it through licensed production, returning little or nothing to the U.S. defense technology base (see Table 5). Japanese officials believe that technology is a precious commodity, and unlike many U.S. defense industrialists, they see it as far more valuable than short-term economic gains. Nevertheless, those who advocate collaboration argue that by transferring defense technology to Japan, the United States enhances that nation's ability to assume a greater share of its own defense and that U.S. defense companies receive monetary benefits as well. Policymakers will have to balance these benefits against the possibility that Japan could change its defense export policies, and that if it does, as many U.S. defense contractors believe it will, the United States will have helped to create another major supplier (and a mighty competitor) in the international arms market.

TABLE 5—SELECTED U.S.–JAPAN TECHNOLOGY TRANSFERS

F-15J Eagle fighter aircraft
FSX fighter aircraft
CH-47 D Chinook helicopter
KV-107/2A helicopter
Model 205 UH-1H helicopter
Model 209 AH-1S helicopter
US-60J helicopter
EP 3C Orion electronic intelligence aircraft
M-110A2 203mm self-propelled howitzer
Patriot missile battery
MIM-104 Patriot mobile surface-to-air missile
MIM-23 Hawk mobile surface-to-air missile
AIM-7F Sparrow air-to-air missile
AIM-9L Sidewinder air-to-air missile
BGM-71C I-TOW anti-tank missile

Source: Office of Technology Assessment, from data in Stockholm International Peace Research Institute, SIPRI Yearbooks, 1970 through 1990, *World Armaments and Disarmament.*

GLOBAL TRADE IN ADVANCED CONVENTIONAL WEAPONS

The final two issues address the question: What are the key considerations of a policy to restrict or permit arms trade in major conventional weapons? The Iraqi invasion of Kuwait and subsequent events have focused world attention on international transfer (both sales and grants) of advanced weaponry. On one hand, the Bush Administration has proposed major arms transfers, especially to the Middle East; and the Department of State and Defense Security Assistance Agency (DSAA) have argued to Congress that increased foreign sales are necessary to maintain domestic production of important U.S. weapons systems.[37] On the other hand, the Administration has initiated talks among the 5 permanent members of the United Nations Security Council to restrain arms sales to the Middle East.[38] These differing perspectives will form the basis of future political debates within the United States, and indeed in the other major arms suppliers.

Issue 4: The Future of Global Defense Trade
Two major objections are offered to any U.S. policy to place additional restraints on international defense trade. First, some defense industrialists contend that international sales are important to sustain selected sectors of the U.S. defense industries at present levels of production and capacity. Most industry analysts agree that U.S. Government procurement will continue to fall,[39] and that foreign markets, especially in the Middle East and the Western Pacific, offer opportunities for growth. Proponents urge government to support or, at a minimum, permit expanded foreign sales to cushion the effect of declining domestic procurement.

The second argument against placing significant restraints on international defense trade is that unilateral action, while helpful, will be insufficient, because the Soviet Union, Europe, and other producers of advanced arms would make the sale. Defense lobbyists argue that U.S. industry lost an enormous opportunity when Congress blocked the sale of F-15 fighter-bombers to Saudi Arabia in the middle 1980s. As an alternative, the Saudi government bought between $25 and 30 billion worth of defense equipment from British companies in the Al Yamamah agreements of 1986 and 1988. In a worst case scenario, unilateral U.S. action to eliminate foreign military sales might strengthen the competition at the expense of U.S. defense companies, perhaps accelerating a loss of U.S. leadership in a range of defense technologies.

U.S., European, Soviet and Chinese policymakers have, however, indicated a willingness to consider restraint in arms sales to the Middle East, based on the role of foreign arms in the Persian Gulf War and on the massive military response that became necessary to defeat them. In defense trade, governments can exert strong regulatory controls, because government is often the only buyer, helps to finance R&D and production costs through progress payments, and has the ability to regulate the output and distribution of the product. If the goal is to reduce the proliferation of potent weapons, it can be approached as a matter of public policy through concerted multilateral action by the United States and other nations with similar interests.

The U.S. Congress could enact stricter unilateral controls through modification of the congressional approval process for foreign military sales and reform of the arms transfer process (Issue 5, below). But this kind of action does not address the fundamental problem—that buyer nations can draw on diverse sources for defense equipment and technology, and that the number of such sources is increasing. The process of creating new centers of defense industry (through increased technology transfer and coproduction arrangements) will deepen this trend if it continues in the future.

At this writing, the Bush Administration is pursuing a policy of negotiating "collective self-restraint" with the other major suppliers of weapons to the Middle East. But it is also proceeding with major weapons transfers to the region, including FA/18 fighter aircraft to Kuwait, Apache attack helicopters to the United Arab Emirates and Bahrain, and F-15 fighters to Israel.[40] If this dual track approach proves unworkable, Congress could mandate a blue ribbon commission to develop a more realistic U.S. strategy for multilateral agreements on weapons trade and collaboration—considered in light of U.S. foreign policy interests and structured to enhance global political stability in a new multipolar world. Such a commission would report its findings back to Congress and to the President for additional consideration.

The Persian Gulf situation offers useful lessons. First, the $2.7 billion in advanced weapons purchased by Kuwait were of little use in defending that nation, and some ultimately fell into enemy hands. Second, the United Nations Security Council moved quickly and effectively to censure and enact sanctions against Iraq as a renegade nation unwilling to live by accepted standards of international conduct. And finally, the end of the Persian Gulf War may improve the opportunity for multinational regulation of defense trade and collaboration conducted within the region.

In the absence of an institutional mechanism to advocate restraint, however, it is extremely difficult and perhaps impossible for the Executive to resist the use of arms transfers to further its foreign policy agenda. The U.S. Government maintains an extensive bureaucracy in the Politico-Military Bureau at the State Department, its embassies, the Defense Security Assistance Agency, the Defense Technology Security Agency, and elsewhere whose purpose is to conduct international trade in arms such that (1) the foreign policy agenda of the President is promoted and (2) regulation and appropriate security is exercised over the export of defense systems and technology.

Although extensive guidance for arms transfers is provided through the Arms Export Control Act and related legislation, Congress has not altered the fundamental principle that it is the policy of the United States to sell, grant, and otherwise transfer large quantities of advanced weapons to other nations. Perhaps more emphasis should be placed on curtailing international arms transfers through multilateral agreements as part of a larger strategy to pursue objectives that contribute to greater world military and political stability.

Issue 5: Reform of the Arms Transfer Process

There are a number of steps that could be taken to make the arms transfer process more transparent and accountable for oversight and regulatory purposes.

For example, Congress could change the way in which military assistance, including coproduction and codevelopment, is considered in the authorization and appropriations process. At present, security assistance programs are viewed as an aspect of foreign assistance as part of the international affairs budget. There is, accordingly, a general understanding that assistance will be extended to allies and others in support of U.S. foreign policy goals. However, because security assistance programs cause proliferation, both of potent weapons and of defense industry, they exert effects on international relations that extend far beyond the immediate support of U.S. allies and friends. Formally separating security assistance from foreign aid programs in the legislative process would help Congress distinguish the costs and benefits of each to the United States.

Another means of achieving better visibility for congressional oversight would be to require the Bureau of Politico-Military Affairs to report regularly on the proliferation of conventional defense technology and industry, including a regional assessment of the relative capabilities of different national defense industries. Congress could also require a "proliferation impact statement" to accompany all proposed arms transfers above a specified dollar threshold. In addition, Congress could require DSAA to include an evaluation and quantitative analysis of collaborative versus off-the-shelf foreign military sales in the annual Congressional Presentation Document. For major collaborative programs, the Arms Control and Disarmament Agency could also be required to evaluate the extent to which collaboration enhances the defense industrial capabilities of the recipient nation relative to its neighbors or some other standard.

If Congress wishes to assure that proliferation aspects of large arms transfers are given greater consideration, it could establish a high-level, nonproliferation advocate, perhaps in the Bureau of Politico-Military Affairs or in connection with the National Security Council. The purpose of such an advocate would be to review all pending arms sales to determine—perhaps on a case-by-case basis—the degree to which the sale would contribute to proliferation, whether it would increase the likelihood of political instability, or otherwise damage U.S. interests according to legislatively specified criteria. If the advocate found the sale not to be in the national interest, he could be charged to make that case to the President as a part of the public record.

Congress could make security assistance programs more accountable by reforming the congressional approval process for arms transfers. By separate legislation, Congress could require that all arms sales above a specified dollar threshold be approved by a vote of both houses, thus reversing the present process where a sale can be disallowed by the same procedure. A potential problem is that Congress might then have to bring each of 120 to 130 major sales per year to a floor vote, a cumbersome and impractical process. A variation on this procedure would be to batch the different arms sales according to status of the recipient, sophistication of weapons, regional considerations, volume of sales, or some combination of criteria. In this way the legislative burden of the approval process could be reduced.

In recent years, the number of direct commercial sales (DCS) as opposed to foreign military sales (FMS) has increased significantly.[41] Congress may wish to take steps to expose DCS transfers to the same level of scrutiny as FMS transfers. Congress may wish to prohibit DCS transfers on the grounds that such sales promote direct international linkages between U.S. companies and foreign firms and their governments, and are not subject to the full regulatory spectrum Congress has mandated for domestic business. If Congress wishes to slow the pace of internationalization of the defense technology and industrial base, providing disincentives for DCS transactions would be a clear point of departure.

Congress could also change the information collecting and processing structure that results in a pattern of specific requests by other countries for arms. Currently, approximately 950 DSAA field staff members work closely with host country military and diplomatic personnel to design security assistance packages that are likely to meet both the needs of the host country and the political requirements at the State Department and within DSAA. In addition, DSAA maintains separate organizations in 56 foreign countries.[42] Because DSAA field staff are promoted according to how effective they are in arranging and managing security assistance programs in specific countries, they have a career interest in promoting sales and transfers of U.S. weapons.

Congress could change this incentive structure by making the determination of security assistance needs a stand-alone function, to be performed by staff who are not involved in the implementation of the program. It might even be desirable to separate out needs determination bureaucratically. This could be done by making Arms Control and Disarmament Agency, or some other arms control entity, responsible for evaluating security assistance needs of recipient countries, both in terms of equipment and industrial capability. This evaluating group might have its own field staff as well to enhance control over weapons transfer requests earlier in the process.

Each year approximately 80 percent of DSAA's operating budget is financed through a 3-percent fee that DSAA charges over and above the cost of the weapons that it procures and then transfers to foreign governments. This self-financing fee has amounted to an average of approximately $330 million per year over the past 5 years.[43] Because the operating budget of the agency is tied to the volume of weapons transferred, there is a powerful incentive for DSAA personnel to make as many sales as is possible, consistent with the law and with the policy direction and review it receives from the State Department, White House, and Congress. Congress could reduce or eliminate DSAA's self-financing mechanism, thus removing the incentive to maximize sales. At the same time, it would force the DSAA operating budget to come out of general appropriations, increasing congressional visibility and control over DSAA's activities.

CONCLUSIONS

There is apparent agreement that action by any country alone to stem the proliferation of modern weapons and technology is likely to fail. There are too many sources of supply, and for most weapons systems, alternative sources are available. This is partly a consequence of past U.S. policy on collaborating with our allies and friends in the production of weapons systems. It is also due, in part, to the liberal defense export promotion policies of our European allies. As a result, we are seeing today the emergence of an increasingly international and interdependent defense industrial structure in the West.

That structure is anchored in a complex set of strategic corporate linkages between U.S. companies and their counterparts in the advanced defense industrial states of Europe and Asia. It is now being gradually extended to numerous developing defense industrial nations, including Brazil, Taiwan, South Korea, India, Turkey, Indonesia, Singapore, Australia, and others. The result is loss of control over the dispersion of defense technology through the continuous development of new centers of increasingly capable defense industry around the globe.

NOTES

1. The Department of State and the Defense Security Assistance Agency contend that the United States should use foreign sales to support continued domestic production of U.S. weapons systems:

> Unless we adjust to the challenge of an increasingly diverse international defense supply environment, the United States will be unable to address satisfactorily the legitimate defense needs of our friends and allies, and thereby our own, at an acceptable cost in the coming years. Indeed, the long term survival of a number of important domestic arms programs are tied to foreign sales: M1A1 Abrams battle tank, Blackhawk helicopter, HAWK surface-to-air missile, Boeing 707 aircraft, to name a few.

U.S. Department of State and U.S. Defense Security Assistance Agency, *Congressional Presentation for Security Assistance Programs*, FY 1992, p. 6.

2. International collaboration can take many forms including, but not limited to, transfer of technical assistance, codevelopment, co- and licensed production, and licensed assembly. It may also involve a variety of business relationships such as revenue sharing, teaming (prime-sub), consortia, joint venture, and corporate alliances, among others.

3. The United States still maintains a lead in next generation defense technology and systems such as the B-2 stealth bomber and the Advanced Tactical Fighter, but it does not export these weapons or share the enabling technologies.

4. U. S. Arms Control and Disarmament Agency, *World Military Expenditures and Arms Transfers*, 1989 (Washington, D.C.: Government Printing Office, 1990), pp. 88, 111.

5. U. S. Arms Control and Disarmament Agency, *World Military Expenditures and Arms Transfers*, 1989 (Washington, D.C.: Government Printing Office, 1990), and Stockholm International Peace Research Institute, SIPRI Yearbooks 1986, *World Armaments and Disarmament* (Oxford: Oxford University Press, 1986), p. 336.

6. For an analysis of the U.S. contribution to the development of the European and East Asian defense industries, see U.S. Congress, Office of Technology Assessment, *Arming Our Allies: Cooperation and Competition in Defense Technology* OTA-ISC-449 (Washington, D.C.: Government Printing Office, May 1990).

7. In a direct offset arrangement, the seller agrees to let the buyer manufacture parts and components of a weapons system as a condition of the sale. The seller often provides training and technical assistance and transfers technology sufficient for the buyer to undertake indigenous production of the parts or components in question. According to one definition, offsets include "a range of industrial and commercial compensation practices required as a condition of purchase of military exports." See *Offsets in Military Exports* (Washington, D.C.: Executive Office of the President, Office of Management and Budget, December 1988), p. 3.

8. *The Washington Post*, March 29, 1991, p. F1; *Wall Street Journal*, March 29, 1991, p. A3; *Defense News*, April 1, 1991, p. 4.

9. U.S. Congress, *Global Arms Trade* OTA-ISC-460 (Washington, D.C.: Government Printing Office, June 1991), p. 8. Major systems transferred have included the U.S. M1 Abrams tank (to Egypt), the U.S. F-16 fighter and Multiple Launch Rocket System (to Turkey), the German Type 209 submarine (to Brazil and South Korea), the French Alpha Jet (to Egypt), the Soviet MiG-27 fighter (to India), the British Jaguar fighter (to India), the U.K. Swingfire Anti-Tank Missile (to Egypt), the French Super Puma helicopter (to Indonesia), the French Milan Anti-Tank Missile (to India), the German BK 117 helicopter (to Indonesia), among others.

10. U. S. Arms Control and Disarmament Agency, *World Military Expenditures and Arms Transfers*, 1989 (Washington, D.C.: Government Printing Office, 1990).

11. *Defense News*, February 18, 1991, pp. 4, 44.

12. The Defense Security Assistance Agency (DSAA) is the defense agency responsible for implementation of foreign military sales. DSAA may transfer equipment already in stock or it may order additional material and defense related services from U.S. companies to complete the security assistance package. Increasingly, DSAA may also handle licensed production and codevelopment transfers under the FMS program, for example, the FSX fighter program with Japan.

13. *Defense News*, December 17, 1990, p. 16.

14. For the purpose of measuring arms transfer activity, the distinction between an arms sale and an arms delivery is important. In the terms foreign military sale (FMS) and direct commercial sale (DCS), the word "sale" means that an agreement to sell has been reached and approved. Some of these "sales" are never consummated, i.e., for one reason or another, they may not result in the transfer of equipment or technology to a foreign country. For this reason, the data in this report refer to equipment or technology that has actually been delivered. Such deliveries often do not occur until 2 or more years after the "sale" is made.

15. U. S. Department of Defense, Defense Security Assistance Agency, *Fiscal Year Series*, Washington, D.C., September 30, 1989, p. 2.

16. U. S. Arms Control and Disarmament Agency, *World Military Expenditures and Arms Transfers*, 1989 (Washington, D.C.: Government Printing Office, 1990), p. 11.

17. Concern over sales to the Middle East, however, extends well back into the 1970s. For example, see Andrew Pierre, "Beyond the Plane Package: Arms and Politics in the Middle East," *International Security* 3 (January 1978).

18. U.S. Department of Defense, Defense Security Assistance Agency, *Foreign Military Sales, Foreign Military Construction Sales and Military Assistance Facts*, Sept. 30, 1989, p. 3; U.S. Department of Defense, Defense Security Assistance Agency, *Fiscal Year Series*, Sept. 30, 1989, p. 101; and U. S. Arms Control and

Disarmament Agency, *World Military Expenditures and Arms Transfers*, 1989 (Washington, D.C.: Government Printing Office, 1990), p. 93.

19. Examples include U.S.-made TOW antitank and Hawk antiaircraft missiles.

20. Thomas E. Mann, *A Question of Balance: The President, the Congress and Foreign Policy* (Washington, D.C.: The Brookings Institution, 1990), pp. 4-7.

21. Craig M. Brandt (ed.), *Military Assistance and Foreign Policy* (Wright Patterson Air Force Base, Ohio: Air Force Institute of Technology, 1989), p. 152.

22. Andrew J. Pierre, *The Global Politics of Arms Sales* (Princeton: Princeton University Press, 1982), pp. 52-66; Paul Y. Hammond et al., *The Reluctant Supplier: U.S. Decisionmaking for Arms Sales* (Cambridge, Mass.: Oelgeschlager, Gunn & Hain, 1983), pp. 266-67, and Christian Catrina, *Arms Transfers and Dependence* (New York: United Nations Commission on Disarmament, 1988), pp. 80-82.

23. Presidential Directive on Arms Transfer Policy, May 13, 1977.

24. Presidential Directive on Arms Transfer Policy, July 8, 1981.

25. *New York Times*, May 30, 1991, p. A1.

26. Cable from Acting Secretary Eagleburger for Ambassador/Charge on "Guidance Concerning Embassy Role in Support of U.S. Defense Exporters."

27. On the "defense GATT," see "The Future of Defense and Industrial Collaboration in NATO," a speech presented by Amb. William Taft to the German Strategy Forum and the Institute for Foreign Policy Analysis in Bonn, Germany, Mar. 15, 1990.

28. This would require the repeal of section 32 of the of the Arms Export Control Act of 1968. *The New York Times*, March 18, 1991, pp. A1 and D6.

29. In addition, the Administration has orchestrated forgiveness for $7 billion in past security assistance debts for Egypt and has agreed in principle to permit Turkey to sell 40 F-16 fighters to Egypt if the two countries can reach agreement on the terms of the sale.

30. The President said, "It's time to put an end to micro-management of foreign and security assistance programs, micro-management that humiliates our friends and allies and hamstrings our diplomacy." Text of the President's address, published in *New York Times*, March 7, 1991, p. A8.

31. See Virginia Lopez, *The U.S. Aerospace Industry and the Trend Toward Internationalization* (Washington, D.C.: The Aerospace Industries Association, Inc., March 1988), p. 6.

32. U.S. Congress, Office of Technology Assessment, *Global Arms Trade*, OTA-ISC-460 (Washington, D.C.: Government Printing Office, June 1991), p. 5. The OTA figures are derived from data in Stockholm International Peace Research Institute, SIPRI Yearbooks, 1970 through 1990, *World Armaments and Disarmament*.

33. For example, in the proposed Korean Fighter Plane (KFP) project, an F-16 fighter coproduction agreement, South Korean industry engineers will receive training at research centers in the United States, and General Dynamics engineers will work in Korea to transfer the underlying technologies to Korean companies involved in the project.

34. U.S. Congress, Office of Technology Assessment, *Global Arms Trade.*

35. From 1980 through 1987, the French sold $6.7 billion (current dollars) worth of advanced weapons to Iraq, including 143 Mirage F-1C fighters and 734 AM-39 Exocet missiles. U.S. Arms Control and Disarmament Agency, *World Military Expenditures and Arms Transfers*, 1988 (Washington, D.C.: Government Printing Office, 1989) p. 22.

36. To date, very little Japanese-made defense technology has been transferred to the United States. However, a significant but unknown quantity of Japanese high-technology products (with both civil and military applications) has been incorporated into U.S. defense systems. In general, the degree of DOD dependence on foreign sources of supply is unknown. See U.S. Congress General Accounting Office, *Industrial Base: Significance of DOD's Foreign Dependence*, GAO/NSIAD-91-93 (Gaithersburg, Md.: U.S. General Accounting Office, January 1991).

37. These include the M1A1 Abrams tank, the Blackhawk helicopter, the HAWK surface-to-air missile, the F-16 fighter, the Apache attack helicopter, and the Boeing 707 aircraft, among others. Several of these were deployed effectively in the Persian Gulf War and are scheduled to go out of production as early as 1993. See U.S. Department of State and U.S. Defense Security Assistance Agency, *Congressional Presentation for Security Assistance Programs*, FY 1992, p. 6.

38. *New York Times*, July 10, 1991, p. A9.

39. Salomon Brothers, "Defense Industry Update--The 1992 Department of Defense Budget: Seventh Consecutive Year of Real Decline Is Certain; Backlogs Will Fall," March 18, 1991.

40. *U.S. News and World Report*, July 22, 1991, pp. 34-35.

41. U. S. Department of Defense, Defense Security Assistance Agency, "Fiscal Year Series," September 30, 1989, p. 2.

42. U.S. Department of State and U.S. Defense Security Assistance Agency, *Congressional Presentation for Security Assistance Programs*, FY 1991, p. 49.

43. This figure is derived from data provided by the Defense Security Assistance Agency.

3
The United States: Partnerships with Europe

Joel L. Johnson

This chapter is written solely as a personal statement. It should not in any way be interpreted as reflecting official views of the Aerospace Industries Association of America, where the author is currently employed. The author wishes to acknowledge with appreciation several individuals who took the time to review this paper in draft form, including Henri Conze of France, Malcolm Haworth and Keith Hayward of the United Kingdom, and Frank Cevasco, Michael McMillan, Gerald Sullivan, David Vadas, and the other authors of this book. Their comments certainly helped improve the manuscript.

For nearly half a century following World War II, American and West European military establishments spent most of their energy and resources preparing for a massive war with the Soviet Union, in the hopes that credible preparation would prevent such a cataclysmic event from actually occurring. As allied forces prepared for war, particularly with respect to the Central European theater, it became fairly obvious that the logistics of conducting such warfare would be enormously simplified if forces fighting side by side could use the same type of fuel, ammunition, and even parts. As weapons systems grew more costly and complex, it also became apparent that greater economies of scale could be obtained from longer production runs, which argued for common weapons systems among allies.

The notion of reducing logistics problems and unit costs by cooperating in the development and production of common military hardware is blindingly obvious to the outsider. Yet with a few notable exceptions, over the past four and a half decades the actual accomplishments related to weapons cooperation between the U.S. and its European partners have been extremely limited.

This chapter will argue that governments are torn between the attractiveness of national weapons programs (providing political independence and expenditure of taxpayers funds and jobs at home) and where necessary bilateral programs (which are relatively simple), versus focusing on increased multilateral arms development, production, and even acquisition (which may provide more weapons at cheaper prices, but are more complex to administer and may result in increased expenditures off shore). The greater the external threat, and the tighter the domestic budgets, the more governments may turn to multilateral solutions; the weaker the external threat, and the more ample the domestic defense budgets, the greater the tendency to look to national solutions and to insure that expenditures are politically, as well as economically, rewarding.

Similarly defense companies prefer to produce products on their own and sell them "off the shelf" to foreign customers. They become involved in international cooperative activity only if they see real advantages related to increasing market access, reducing risk, obtaining capital at better rates, and gaining technology without having to pay development costs.

To date, the large U.S. defense market and companies, contrasted to the small individual European defense markets and companies, has made it difficult for American government institutions and private firms to work up much enthusiasm for cooperative programs. On the other hand, the small individual European defense markets, combined with a common external military threat (Soviets) and economic threat (U.S., Japan), has encouraged greater intra-European cooperation in both the civilian and military arenas.

This chapter will briefly review the efforts at weapons cooperation between the U.S. and European allies, the factors inhibiting success of such efforts, and suggest a few approaches which might improve chances of obtaining the basic objectives of more efficient weapons production and standardization. Note that this chapter is not intended to provide a comprehensive history of arms cooperation between the U.S. and Europe. Rather historical examples are raised primarily to highlight specific policy themes which must be recognized in addressing the arms cooperation issue.

Restoration of European Defense Industries

Following World War II, only the UK was still left with a defense industry that was relatively intact and operating. The French had the professional talent and most of the industrial infrastructure, and simply needed time and resources to revive. The Germans, Italians, and smaller industrialized European countries had professional talent, but much of the industrial infrastructure was destroyed. Thus U.S. policy with respect to European countries varied somewhat from one country to the other.

At the outset, as the Soviet threat emerged, U.S. cooperation in weapons systems with allies and former enemies was quite simple--the government made U.S. weapons available to them out of inventory, or from current production. In some cases the weapons were provided on a grant basis through the Military Assistance Program, in others the recipients paid. The driving force for such weapons transfers was also quite straight forward—we wanted those countries to have the weapons necessary to help provide a credible deterrent to any expansionist Soviet intentions in Western Europe.

The U.S. was also interested in encouraging the restoration of European industries, including defense industries. Obviously so were the Europeans. Hence it was not surprising that by the late fifties a shift began from transfers of military equipment to European countries, to licensed production of American defense products in those countries. Early examples included production of the F-86 and F-104 fighter jets, the M113 Armored Personnel Carrier, and various utility helicopters.[1]

Such licensed production transactions served the purpose of helping European countries provide for their own defense and of restoring their defense industries. This period, however, was also to have other long lasting implications for the United States. The Defense Department administered the program through an office reporting to the Under Secretary for International Security Affairs, known first as the Office of Programming and Control, and later the Office of Military Assistance. In 1971 this office became the current

Defense Security Assistance Agency.[2] Its mandate was to provide hardware for allied countries, and later to assist in arrangements for licensed production. To that agency, the client was the recipient government and military establishment, not the U.S. company which produced the military hardware. Put another way, its mission was to help the foreign country obtain and/or produce weapons for its own defense, not to sell American products.

Similarly, the U.S. defense industry personnel involved in selling or supporting U.S. weapons systems in Europe, or in licensing production programs, saw their role as assisting the Europeans to assimilate U.S. weapons and technology. The U.S. provided the teachers, the Europeans the pupils. This mind-set became rather fixed in the U.S. corporate outlook towards Europe.

Finally, these programs were bilateral in nature, and helped individual European countries restore their respective militaries and defense industries. They did not encourage collective European activity per se, and in fact by supplying different weapons systems and helping individual national arms industries, may well have had the opposite effect.

Advent of Offsets

A new phenomena in U.S.-European defense trade relations arose in the late 1960s when European governments began to demand offsets from the U.S. as a condition for purchasing American weapons systems, or even when they produced a U.S. system under license in their own countries. This practice, now widespread around the world, requires that the vendor of the defense hardware agree to purchase goods from the customer country. Increasingly such goods must themselves be in the defense or other high tech sectors. Often the vendor country must agree to transfer technology to the customer country in order for the customer to undertake the offset activity.

The U.S. government became involved in helping to perform some of the early offset programs, such as those involving the F-5 program in Switzerland, and the European countries (Belgium, Denmark, the Netherlands, and Norway) which coproduced the F-16. It soon found, however, that trying to fulfill offset obligations involved DOD in a variety of economic and political problems, both with the customer country and at home. Consequently, in the 1978 "Duncan Memorandum" DOD declared that in the future offsets would generally be an issue between the U.S. company selling a product, and the foreign purchasing government.[3] That position was reaffirmed by President Bush in a policy statement on offsets issued on April 16, 1990.[4]

Offsets are also a nuisance to American business. Given a choice, companies would clearly prefer to sell "off the shelf" with no offsets or licensed production. Companies participate in such programs because they have become a necessary condition of doing business with most countries. Furthermore, given the enormous U.S. domestic commercial and defense markets, American firms have a comparative advantage in performing offsets as compared to companies based in smaller European or other country markets.[5]

In limited cases offsets can have one positive impact, which is to force American companies to look at European or other countries as the possible source of components for defense products, and in the case of horizontally integrated companies, for their civilian products as well. In some instances companies have found sources of components which, even without an offset incentive, are competitive in quality and price, and hence the relationship has withstood the passing of the offset requirement. In this case, offsets, rather than being market distorting, actually serve to increase information and hence make the international market more transparent; such examples, however, are probably the exception, rather than the rule.

Multiplication of Weapons System Types

As European national defense industries reestablished themselves in the 1950s and 1960s, they once again began to design and produce weapons for their own needs and for export. It soon became apparent that such independent production was leading to an increasing proliferation of weapons systems among the Western European countries. When added to the range of U.S. armaments, this meant that the NATO allies who were supposed to be able to fight side-by-side, were fielding a hodgepodge of weapons which were incompatible—ranging from different fuels to different ammunition and even to different screw threads.

Thus began the great paradox which has bedeviled the NATO alliance to this day. On the one hand, NATO could only match the strength of the Warsaw Pact if Western Europe could pull its own weight. This meant not only reviving the European economies, but its arms industries as well. But the very revival of those national defense industries, each with a client military and elected political system, meant that the alliance seemed doomed to face a multiplicity of weapons systems, each designed to meet the national interests of the purchasing country. Each country produced its weapons in relatively low quantities and over extended time periods which meant that unit costs of individual weapons were high.

Thus not only were NATO weapons incompatible with each other, but by producing a variety of weapons at uneconomic rates, each country was getting less for its defense expenditures than if it were to purchase common weapons that were produced in longer and larger production runs. In armaments, the NATO whole was seemingly less than the sum of its parts. In the words of Tom Callaghan, one of the long time commentators on this issue, NATO was "structurally disarming" itself.[6]

This dilemma was clearly apparent to those NATO planners who focused on meeting the Soviet threat. As early as 1959 NATO established a Basic Military Requirements procedure (NBMR), which was supposed to identify common weapons needs which would be collectively funded by NATO countries.[7] The system never took hold, however, and in 1966 the system was dropped, without a single item having been cooperatively developed. From that date to the present NATO has consistently attempted to find ways to bring about greater commonality in identifying common weapons requirements, and developing and producing them cooperatively. Over three decades, the success rates have been comparable.

The Bilateral Approach

Two other themes emerged or were reinforced in the 1960s which have also continued to the present. In 1963 the U.S., largely out of frustration with the slow progress in NATO on cooperative weapons activities, signed bilateral cooperative research and development agreements with France, Germany, Italy, and the United Kingdom.[8]

The idea of working bilaterally (or at times plurilaterally) with one or more European countries has continued to the present. In the seventies a series of bilateral procurement Memorandum of Understandings (MOUs) were signed between the United States and nearly all NATO countries to facilitate the purchases of weapons systems by one country from the other. And a large variety of MOUs for specific weapons systems, mostly bilateral, have proliferated over the past two decades.

Also in the mid 1960s, partly in response to political frustration with the high cost to the U.S. of maintaining a large standing military in NATO Europe, the U.S. government began a campaign to encourage arms sales to Europe and the Third World to help offset those expenses. The notion was that European countries were economically restored, and could now afford to purchase more U.S. systems off the shelf as one way to help alleviate the economic burden on the U.S.[9]

The Two-Way Street

The effort was successful, but triggered strong complaints from the Europeans that such arms trade was a one-way street—they bought from us, but we would not buy from them. The notion that arms trade between the U.S. and each European country should be a two-way street, and presumably relatively balanced, was in large part responsible for the negotiation of the bilateral procurement MOUs mentioned above.

It should be noted that the "two-way street" argument can be one of process, or one of results. It can simply be argued that countries should have equal access to each others defense market. In other words, both lanes of the road—to and from Europe—should have the same pavement and lane width. This is an argument of process. But more often it is also argued that the result of building such a symmetrical road should be a relatively balanced trade in armaments between the two countries. In other words, the level of traffic on both lanes should be the same. This is an argument about results.

The problem here is that it is most unlikely that the former would produce the latter between individual European countries and the U.S. The U.S. currently purchases around $80 billion in military equipment a year, while Europe acquires around $40 billion. The U.S. spends approximately $34 billion on research and development for weapons systems; Europe as a whole spends less than one-third that amount. Any single European country obviously spends a fraction of the total European numbers. For example, the UK spends about $14 billion on procurement, around $4.5 billion on research and development.[10]

If the bilateral armaments street were paved identically (including transparent and fair procurement systems and an open technology transfer regime), it is almost inconceivable the traffic levels would be the same. The United States, with its much larger research budgets and greater procurement of individual weapons systems, would almost certainly dominate defense trade with Europe. In fact, it would be astonishing if, after nearly five decades of spending a multiple on research, development, and production on weapons systems compared to any European country, combined with much longer and larger production runs than is possible for any European country, the U.S. did not have a comparative advantage in weapons systems.[11]

From an economics standpoint, there would be nothing wrong or surprising with such a result. Comparative advantage and an open trading system assumes there will be asymmetries in particular product trade between nations. The U.S. imports more high fashion garments from France than it exports, it exports more supercomputers than it imports. The problem is that when it comes to armaments, such bilateral lopsided trade is generally not politically acceptable. Two arguments are made in favor of why defense trade cannot be left to market forces.

National Security
    The least important is the one that is most often enunciated—that of national security. This argument is in turn composed of two sub-claims. First is the traditional notion that foreign dependence for weapons systems can limit political flexibility in peacetime and the ability to fight in war time. For World War II-type weapons systems this might have been true, when Liberty ships could be cranked out one a day and B-24s at one every four hours. But today's complex weapons systems—fighter aircraft, tanks, radars—are dependent on

such a wide production base—domestic as well as foreign, that speeding up the line would likely take longer than a war would last, with or without foreign components. And as to political flexibility, it is not clear that Sweden, which produces its own airplane (with an American engine, it might be noted) has more political wiggle room than Canada, Australia, and Switzerland, which don't.[12]

The second subdebate concerns technology. Defense research and development, it is argued, are important to design new weapons systems, and to have an idea of what an adversary might also have discovered, so as to prepare countermeasures. Furthermore, defense technology can have important spinoffs into the commercial world. Thus if a country relies on foreign suppliers for defense technology, it loses its research and development capacity, which in turn both makes it more vulnerable from a defense aspect to foreign developments, and it may sacrifice commercial advantage as well.

There is of course some truth to those arguments, although perhaps not as much as in earlier post war years. No European country can come close to matching U.S. or Soviet levels of spending on research and development, and hence their national efforts can at best rival U.S. work in limited niche areas. Defense related research no longer drives commercial research in most fields. Indeed, some have argued that concentrating on research and development of commercial products has helped a country such as Japan dominate many civilian areas of technology.

Jobs

The second issue related to the trade balance in armaments is, put simply, jobs, or more precisely, jobs funded by taxpayers funds. It is not unusual to hear U.S. defense industrialists comment privately, and at times publicly, that Europe doesn't have a defense procurement policy, it has a defense jobs policy. Of course, when lobbying a major weapons system in Congress, these same industrialists are quick to point out how many suppliers and related workers will stand to benefit in each state and Congressional district.

The clear fact is that in industrial democracies, politicians believe it is necessary to justify weapons systems to their voters not just in terms of getting the best defense product for their money, but also in terms of jobs and other benefits as well. In fact, it is quite evident that politicians are willing to sacrifice both quality of a system and its price if there is a real or perceived increase in employment.

In Europe this has not only meant protecting defense procurement, but public expenditures on other capital goods as well. It is noteworthy that it took only ten years from the founding of the European Community in 1958 to the removal of all internal tariffs on private sector trade in 1968 (although it is true that a number of nontariff barriers such as national standards are only now being dismantled as part of the Europe 1992 exercise. However, "buy national" barriers with respect to public procurement in the so-called excluded sectors—transport, communications, water, and power generation—will only be removed in 1992, 34 years after the entry into force of the Treaty of Rome.

It will be even more difficult to remove buy national barriers in the defense arena, where arguments of national security carry greater weight. When European countries have purchased defense products from each other or worked together in joint projects, they have long adhered to the principle of "juste retour," which is the basic concept that there should be a rough equality between the amount of funds a country spends on defense procurement and the amount of defense work which is created in the country. Such a balance may be struck within a single large cooperative weapons program, or expanded to include an overall balance of defense trade between countries, over more than one weapons system and over more than one year. It is true that some of the more industrially advanced European countries have not in practice always found ways to implement the concept of "juste retour" for their less industrialized European counterparts. But certainly the stated goal is that work share should roughly equal purchase share.

As already noted, European and other countries demand offsets when they purchase a weapons system from a foreign supplier. Again, such offsets are basically designed to assure the purchasing country a level of domestic production and employment, whether directly related to the weapons system or not, in exchange for its taxpayers funds.   The United States is not immune to this phenomenon, even with respect to domestic purchases. Our states are not sovereign, and hence cannot withhold funds from the defense budget when a weapons project of particular importance is not funded. However, state delegations can make cancelling a favored project very difficult, and as noted, prime contractors make a point of spreading subcontracts widely about the country, a sort of domestic offset policy, to assure that taxpayers dollars flow back to as many districts and states as possible. Congressionally mandated small business and minority business setasides are an additional form of domestic offset, which while undoubtedly increasing the costs of weapons systems, make them more politically attractive.

When it comes to purchases of weapons systems from offshore, which the U.S. has done on only rare occasions, it has generally demanded a "warm production line" in the U.S. Examples include the Harrier jump jet, the T-45 trainer, 9 mm handgun, multiple subscriber system, and bridge erector boat. While the official rational given for such demands is related to security, not jobs, to the Europeans from whom we have purchased these systems our practice is hard to differentiate from an offset demand.

European Integration
The Europeans have long wrestled with the problem that companies which are limited to serving their small domestic markets—for both civilian and military products—may have difficulty in competing in a global market, particularly with respect to companies based in the U.S. and Japan, which has the benefit of large internal markets. In order for European companies to gain the necessary economies of scale, in 1985 the European Commission drafted a White Paper which outlined 300 measures necessary to create a single internal market with freedom of movement for goods, services, people, and capital by the end of 1992. The European Community adopted the Single European Act in December of 1985, which allowed the EC's Council of Minister to make most decisions by qualified majority, eliminating the possibility of one country vetoing even minor changes. While some EC goals will not be met by the 1992 deadline, it is likely most will.

On the defense side, the Europeans have also tried to come to grips with the problem of the dominant size of the U.S. defense establishment relative to any single European country. Traditionally, their defense companies have tried to offset the small size of their protected domestic market by seeking export markets, primarily in the developing countries. In some countries, 60-70% of total defense production has been exported, much of it to Third World countries. But this reliance on Third World markets has become questionable as weapons needed to confront the Soviet threat became too complex and too expensive for such many such buyers. Examples include air superiority fighters, main battle tanks, large surface naval vessels, and complex electronic systems and related counter measures.

The Europeans have long been aware of the need to collaborate in order to match the American defense industry. In 1969 the European NATO ministers (absent France and Portugal) formed Eurogroup, with the basic intent of encouraging greater collaboration among the European countries in identifying weapons needs, developing and producing such weapons, or even purchasing them from other sources.[13] In 1976 the Independent European Program Group (IEPG) was established, with France now a member. It had much the same mandate as the Eurogroup, but with perhaps a bit more independence from NATO itself.[14]

The IEPG was not notably effective during its first decade of existence. In 1984, however, the British Defense Secretary, Michael Heseltine, with the support of the Dutch Minister of Defense, Jan van Houwelingen (who chaired the IEPG at the time) pressed to revitalize the organization. Its governance was elevated from armaments directors to defense ministers. By 1987 the IEPG issued a report entitled "Towards a Stronger Europe",[15] which in turn led to an Action Plan that was approved in November 1988 at a Ministerial meeting. The plan urges:

- the creation of an open, transnational European defense market.

- a stronger European defense R&D effort

- development of viable defense industries in less developed member nations.

It is surely not coincidental that the resurgence of interest in the IEPG came during the same time frame as the period leading up to the passage of the Single European Act by the European Community. As in the civilian arena, the defense ministers recognized that the only way European defense industries could hold their own against the United States was through consolidation and larger, European wide markets. Ironically, the American economic threat appeared to play a more important role in the drive towards more rational defense equipment design and procurement in Europe than the threat posed by the common military enemy, the Soviet Union—and this of course was prior to the sudden decline in East-West tensions. And as with the Europe 1992 exercise, Europeans were quick to argue with the U.S. that the IEPG effort was not so much aimed at keeping the U.S. out of their markets, as it was to enable European defense industries to be truly competitive with their American counterparts.

The IEPG has been making progress on two of its major objectives.[16] By the end of 1990 all countries except Luxembourg (which was excused) and Portugal were in some fashion publishing their procurement requirements so that other IEPG countries could bid on them. It should also be noted that the IEPG program included not only the concept of helping defense industries in less developed member countries, but also of "juste retoure," to assure that an open competitive procurement process would be modified to guarantee a rough distribution of contracts proportionate to funds spent. Thus any European open procurement defense program will be modified to produce "equitable" as opposed to efficient results, at least for a "transitional period". Traffic flow on European two-way streets is to be equal roughly in all lanes.

In theory, given the bilateral procurement MOUs the U.S. has with most IEPG members, U.S. companies should be able to bid on these published national defense requirements. It is the stated policy of the IEPG that this is the case. It remains to be seen whether in practice this will happen, however, particularly given the "just retour" policy of the member countries.

The program known as the European Cooperation for the Long-Term in Defense (EUCLID), which is to facilitate cooperative R&D efforts on particular projects, also now appears about to get underway. It is similar to a number of European programs in the civilian sector such as BRITE, RACE, and ESPRITE, all of which are intended to combine national resources to help Europe stay competitive in high technology industries with respect to the U.S. and Japan.

EUCLID had been delayed in part because countries were unable to agree on how to handle ownership of intellectual property emerging from such research. With Ministers having passed this hurdle in November of 1990, there are hopes that contracts on joint research projects can be let by mid-1991. There are those in Europe that hope EUCLID can eventually move from being a facilitator of voluntary cooperation among countries on specific projects, to a truly central pool of European money which can be spent on projects agreed to collectively—sort of a European DARPA.

During this rejuvenation period, the IEPG has almost certainly served as a catalyst for action by the private sector, just as the EC-92 program has triggered major restructuring in manufacturing and service sectors in the community even before new EC regulations are in place. Similarly, in the past two years there has been a major consolidation of defense companies within European countries.

Most notable has been the establishment by Daimler-Benz of its Deutsche Aerospace (DASA) Division, which absorbed the previously independent aerospace companies of MBB, Dornier, Telefunken Systemtechnik and MTU, and the acquisition by British Aerospace of Royal Ordnance. The UK's General Electric Company (GEC) and West Germany's Siemens collectively acquired Britain's Plessey, and divided most of the pieces among the two. GEC later took over Ferranti International's radar division. France's Thompson-CSF and Aerospatiale have combined their avionics activities into a single joint venture.[17]

It should be noted that if one of the European objectives was to create defense companies of a size to compete head on with American rivals, that objective is being met. For example, DASA, with aerospace sales of $6 billion in 1988, and British Aerospace, with sales of $7 billion in the same period, compare favorably with such American giants as General Dynamics (1988 sales of $5 billion) and McDonnell Douglas ($13 billion).

European companies have also begun to create cross national joint ventures, companies, and cross holding of stock in each others companies. For example, France's Thomson-CSF and British Aerospace intend to merge their missile and guidance system divisions into a new company called Eurodynamics. Similarly, DASA's MBB and Aerospatiale are forming Eurocopter to jointly design and produce military helicopters.

European companies have, of course, worked together in government sponsored project-specific consortium for some time. Examples include the British-French Jaguar fighter aircraft, and French-German Alphajet trainer, the British, German, and Italian Tornado fighter/attack aircraft, and the British, German, Italian and Spanish next generation European Fighter Aircraft (EFA). In all these cases governments identified a common requirement, projected individual country purchases, and divided up the work share in rough proportion. While there may be competition at the subcontracting and component level, work at the prime contracting level has been a political, rather than a market decision.

The U.S. and NATO Weapons Integration

As already noted, the NATO alliance has tried some of the same approaches recently embraced by the IEPG. Beginning thirty years ago with the unsuccessful NBMR, NATO later established the Conference of National Armament Directors (CNAD), which is the primary policy-making body in NATO for procurement. It is intended to encourage greater standardization and interoperability of weapons systems, and to stimulate joint programs for research, development, and production of weapons systems. In 1987 the CNAD approved a trial program known as the Conventional Armaments Planning System (CAPS), which would provide NATO members a forum to outline their anticipated research, development, and procurement plans and to compare them with other members. The program was adopted by NATO ministers in 1989 as a permanent part of the NATO planning machinery. It is hoped that CAPS may lead to common programs among members.[18]

Congress has on occasion given a positive push to such NATO weapons collaboration. In 1975 it passed the Culver-Nunn amendment which encouraged the U.S. Department of Defense to engage in cooperative activities with NATO countries. In 1979 it began the Foreign Weapons Evaluation program, which included funding, to stimulate the Services to examine whether existing foreign weapons systems might meet U.S. mission requirements.[19] In 1985 the Nunn-Warner and Quyale amendments were passed. The former provided funds for codevelopment programs with NATO allies, and the latter removed a number of legislative obstacles to cooperation with and procurement from our allies.

Yet the same Congresses consistently passed Buy America legislation which sends an opposite signal to industry, the U.S. services, and our allies. The basic Buy America law of 1933 requires federal procurement officers to add 6% to the price of foreign bidders on defense contracts in comparing their bids to American firms. DOD has by policy increased the preferential margin to 50%. This preference, however, has been waived for essentially all NATO countries under the provisions of our bilateral reciprocal procurement MOUs. The Congress has also added product specific Buy America provisions which cannot be waived, ranging from specialty metals (since repealed), stainless steel flatware, anchor chain, textiles, and naval vessels. As recently as September of 1990 the House passed an extension of the Defense Production Act which encourages the President to purchase all military hardware and components from U.S. sources within five years (the provision was dropped in conference).

The executive branch in general, and the Department of Defense (DOD) in particular, also send mixed signals to European allies and U.S. industry as to its enthusiasm for cooperative undertakings. On the one hand there has been a long series of supportive policies and statements from Presidents, Secretaries of Defense, and U.S. Ambassadors to NATO on cooperative programs. As recently as March 15, 1990, the U.S. Ambassador to NATO William Taft, IV, made a speech endorsing defense industrial cooperation, early agreement among NATO partners on future military requirements, a definition of our industrial base to include NATO countries, and a mechanism to expand intra-NATO trade in defense products (a "NATO GATT").[20]

But the executive branch and the services have also thrown numerous obstacles into the path of cooperative programs. The services have always preferred equipment which is tailor made for their own requirements—requirements which often are more specialized for a specific mission and more generalized to cope with a variety of external conditions than our NATO allies need or can afford. Cooperative programs have often been seen as requiring compromises to service requirements, and as adding time, cost, and complexity to the management of a program.

It is not surprising therefore that the services have historically not been enthusiastic about cooperative programs, except in rare instances when they didn't see any other way to obtain a desired piece of equipment (such as the Harrier jump jet). The Nunn program, for which the Congress earmarked specific funding levels, attracted the services as long as the costs associated with the program were covered by Nunn funds, rather than the services' own resources. But the U.S. dropped out of several of these programs when, after two years, service money had to replace the Nunn funds, and when the services perceived that the Office of the Secretary of Defense had lost some of its earlier enthusiasm for such programs.

The Technology Transfer Problem

The offices charged with watching over the transfer of U.S. technology, both in the services and in DOD (the Defense Technology Security Administration, or DTSA), have also been less supportive of collaboration than the sponsors of these programs. There is considerable apprehension that if U.S. companies are allowed to bring their best technology to a cooperative program, the technology itself might be compromised, or knowledge of our capabilities might become known to potential adversaries. As a consequence, restrictions on technology transfer for cooperative programs can make U.S. technology unattractive to potential partners, who are often capable of providing their own technology at the level we are allowed to transfer. However, if only second best technology is available for a cooperative program, then both the U.S. service and alliance partners will quickly lose interest in the product. Thus all too often U.S. technology transfer policy results in our closest allies producing less capable equipment at higher unit costs than would be possible if U.S. technology were made available.

Similarly, the U.S., both through legislative statute and administrative oversight, has insisted on stringent controls over the export of products containing U.S. technology, even when produced in other countries. Even when the U.S. government agrees in advance to designating a set of countries to which sales might be made, it still withholds the right to unilaterally change the eligibility of a given country. As already noted, most European defense products must be exported if production runs are to be at all efficient. Hence Europeans are understandably reluctant to compromise their ability to export a defense product because it contains some U.S. technology.

The technology issue has been further complicated in the past two years as some in Congress and in the executive branch, particularly in the Commerce Department, have regarded cooperative defense programs as a conduit whereby U.S. technology may be transferred to countries which are our military allies, but commercial competitors. The recent efforts by Congress and the Department of Commerce to become more involved in establishing offset policy and to review product and procurement MOUs, plus the Congressional hostility to the FSX codevelopment program with Japan, are dramatic evidence of these concerns.

The Empty Street

The net result of these mixed signals is, not surprisingly, rather limited cooperation between the U.S. and Europe in weapons design, production, and trade. There have been stellar examples of such programs. Often noted are the F-16 fighter program; the Multiple Launch Rocket System (MLRS), with the U.S., UK, France, Germany and Italy; the Sea Sparrow, which included Belgium, Canada, Denmark, Germany, Greece, the Netherlands, Norway, Portugal, Turkey and the U.S.; the AV8-B attack aircraft, with the U.S. and UK; and the X-31, involving Germany and the U.S. But these have been the exceptions, rather than the rule.

Currently the U.S. procures roughly $3 billion a year from off shore out of a defense procurement budget of approximately $80 billion. This 4% of the market compares to European imports of roughly $5 billion from the U.S., out of a procurement budget of around $40 billion, or about 12% of its expenditures. As recently as the mid 1980s, Europeans complained that the ratio of European imports of defense equipment from the U.S. was about eight times that of U.S. imports from Europe. Today that ratio is about 1.4 to 1. However, the ratio has changed more because European imports from the U.S. have dropped sharply than because of increased U.S. imports from Europe, which are rising at a steady but slow rate. The two-way street is becoming more evenly traveled, but traffic is decreasing.

By way of comparison, it is noteworthy that in the United States about 29% of our automotive market is served by foreign producers (both imports and U.S. based foreign companies). In civil aviation, the U.S. imports about 38% of its demand, Europe around 77%. These figures would indicate that were open trade in defense products possible, it is likely there would be a considerably higher percentage of procurement accounted for by imports or foreign owned domestic production on both sides of the Atlantic.[21]

The Government's Perspective: Where You Stand Depends on Where You Sit
So why have nearly three decades of initiatives to bring about greater arms cooperation between Europe and the U.S. produced such meager results? The reasons lie with both governments and industry. From the government standpoint, cooperation seems to have foundered on the inability of governments to find an appropriate balance between three sets of contradictory objectives:

Independence versus Interdependence: Individuals, bureaucracies, and nations all prefer to maintain their freedom of action. In the defense arena, this has meant that services want to obtain equipment designed for their particular mission requirements. Politicians and military planners want as autonomous an industrial base and research and development capacity as possible. International relations practitioners want wide latitude to conduct foreign policy, including the ability to impose trade sanctions. Cooperative arms programs, while hopefully increasing the total military power available to the NATO alliance, will generally reduce the individual freedom of action of each participant. For the U.S., with its huge domestic defense market, cooperation has historically not been an economic necessity to produce our own systems, but rather something we wanted others to do in order to increase their military effectiveness. We wanted it both ways—to maintain our own independence of action with respect to the design and production of weapons systems, while encouraging European interdependence (which is to say dependence) with the U.S.

Efficiency versus Equity: Put crudely, most economically efficient systems force individuals and organizations to compete against each other, with the least efficient losing jobs and business. Governments traditionally set the rules within which such competition occurs, and often feel impelled to intervene in the results of such competition in order to bring about "equitable" results. In democratic systems, this often means results in which the desires of politically active groups must be offset against the common welfare. In the case of defense cooperation, this means the proponents of "two way streets" and "open defense markets" must deal with the political requirements of "offsets," "juste retour," and "pork barrel" politics.

Multilateral versus Bilateral: The more participants there are in a program, the more compromises are necessary in arriving at a common policy, and the less satisfied each party will likely be with the decision. Hence it is easier to conduct bilateral programs than multilateral ones. The U.S. deals with European countries, not Europe, in most instances, as witness the individual bilateral reciprocal procurement MOUs. Since there is as yet no *European* defense procurement agency or industry, U.S. government and industry must deal with European countries and companies on an individual basis. But bilateral programs, while increasing standardization and (hopefully) efficiency between two countries, by no means resolve the problem of the U.S.-European alliance as a whole.

Multilateral programs, while being more complex, also allow a wider dispersal of costs and risk. The more partners, the longer the production runs, and hopefully the lower the unit costs. Furthermore, the greater the number of participants, the wider the spread of standardization around a single system. Finally, broadly based multilateral programs may be less vulnerable to the departure of any one partner from the program.

For individuals in European and U.S. governments, the more a government official has been preoccupied with fighting the Russians, the more oriented he is likely to be towards interdependence, efficiency, and multilateral solutions. Hence most initiatives for cooperative programs have come from NATO officials and representatives to the organization, Ministries of Defense, senior legislators on armed services committees, and scholars. Conversely, the more one is focused on getting reelected, maintaining the strength of a uniformed service, or keeping foreign policy options open on a global basis, the more skepticism an individual may have towards arms cooperation, and the more sympathetic he may be with arguments centering on independence, equity and bilateral relations.

The Industry View: What Does the Customer Want?
The other player in the cooperation arena is industry. While the defense industry faces a peculiar customer base—essentially a limited number of governments—it acts in many respects as any other industry. In particular, it will participate in international cooperative activity for four basic reasons:

Gain Market Access: It is always useful to be close to your customer. Having a foreign partner, or an investment in the customer country, can help accomplish that objective. As the customers for defense products are governments, a foreign partner, production in the customer country, or purchases from that country may be a political or legal necessity. U.S. companies thus may have little choice but to seek licensed production or that with foreign business offset agreements. A European company bidding on a large contract with the U.S. must have a domestic partner and/or a U.S. subsidiary to have a reasonable chance of winning a competition; hence the recent direct investment by European defense companies.

Once again, the asymmetry between the U.S. market (about 50% of the Western defense market), and the European national markets, comes into play. It is quite obvious to European defense companies that buying into the U.S. market is a sensible investment. It is by no means as obvious to U.S. companies that entering into a relationship with a single company in one European country provides enough market access to make such a deal attractive. Ironically, one major advantage for a U.S. company of establishing a relationship with a European company might well be in Third World markets, where Europeans may have better access, strong political and financial support for exports from their own governments, and less of the political and legal restrictions which impede U.S. companies from selling directly to Third World countries.

Share the Risks: For U.S. aerospace companies, it is conventional wisdom that launching a new civil aircraft or engine involves "betting the company." In recent years companies have spread the risk by taking on foreign partners. In the defense industry, the risk has historically been less as the government has generally covered most development costs. As DOD in recent years shifted towards requiring more risk capital by the defense companies, the firms responded by forming teaming arrangements with American partners. Over time, U.S. firms may seek foreign partners or will if the defense project has potential in both U.S. and foreign markets.

Raise Capital: Related to the above, launching increasingly complex and expensive civil projects requires large amounts of capital. International partnerships can help raise such funds in different capital markets. In the international arms cooperation arena, it is governments that generally fund such projects, and the increasing cost which drives them to work collectively, particularly within the European market.

Obtain Technology: Companies in the defense industry have long taken advantage of technology from off shore through buying components or obtaining production licenses. As technology development becomes increasingly complex and expensive, companies will find it attractive to search out partners for product development which have complimentary technologies—both basic and production—so as to minimize the up-front costs. This can only happen across borders, of course, if government controls on technology transfer do not preclude such arrangements.

For companies, as for governments, international cooperation is often harder than going it alone. This is particularly true in the defense industry. Most companies have excess capacity, and it makes little economic sense to establish a new production line outside of the home country. This observation is not necessarily true in the case where a European product is being considered by the U.S., as a single buy from DOD may be a multiple of the domestic European country market, and hence domestic production facilities might well not be adequate to produce for a large U.S. purchase. Security regulations make cooperation with foreign nationals complex. Thus barring incentives of the types noted above, defense companies will prefer to avoid cooperative undertakings.

In general the primary customers for defense companies are the uniformed services, and to a lesser degree the parliamentary bodies (particularly in the case of the U.S.) which must approve military budgets. These customers generally regard cooperative programs as an annoyance, and enter into them only under duress or with a strong enticement (such as free Nunn money in the case of the U.S.). In Europe, small national markets and increasingly expensive weapon systems are slowly forcing customers to overcome their antipathy to cooperative programs, as the only alternative to such programs is buying offshore or doing without. In turn, companies have responded by forming system specific, and more recently, product specific alliances.

So What Happens Now?

As defense budgets in Western Europe and the U.S. decline, the procurement of weapons systems on a national basis will mean each country will have to reduce the variety of systems it can produce, and to pay higher unit costs for those weapons which are purchased. Thus the economic arguments of cooperation and the larger production runs and lower unit costs associated with such cooperation become even stronger. Europeans may be driven to accelerate the efforts of the IEPG, and NATO may see arms cooperation as one of the areas for increasing activity in an institution looking for new directions.

At the same time, the receding Soviet threat which has precipitated those budget declines in turn will reduce the political and military pressure on Western democracies to make the perceived sacrifices needed to increase cooperation. European governments may well become preoccupied with absorbing Eastern Europe, while the U.S. becomes increasingly concerned with regional instability outside the European theater. The Europeans may well cancel a number of new systems, build and upgrade enough current systems to keep domestic defense industries alive, while the U.S. increasingly turns to development and procurement of equipment suited for force projection outside of Europe, such as airlift and sealift, lighter and more lethal weapons which can be readily transported, and equipment for light infantry combat.

As is usually the case with such dichotomies, the likelihood is that some of both will happen. Military services will increasingly find that diminished budgets and the tyranny of the linkage between unit costs and length of production runs will mean that they have to buy equipment from offshore (including the possibility of licensed production onshore) or engage in cooperative programs if they are to continue to purchase a variety of systems at anything resembling acceptable costs. At the same time, new systems in Europe and the U.S. are likely to be deferred or cancelled, and ways found to make do with current equipment or modifications of that equipment. European involvement in the war with Iraq is likely to remind the allies that they must be able to respond to events outside of the European Continent if they are to be credible as global players.

Proponents of cooperative programs should recognize political reality. Neither the U.S. nor Europe is likely to agree to any scheme wherein they go out of the business of designing and producing major defense equipment such as capitol ships, fighter aircraft, or tanks. Here the best that can be hoped for is that European integration moves forward through cooperative programs so that the Europeans at least reduce the number of models of such equipment they produce.

While these systems may not compete against each other in home markets, they will do so in third country markets, which should help press the producers of both U.S. and European systems to design and manufacture quality products.

This function of Third World markets, by the way, is reduced when Congress refuses to allow sales of military hardware to certain countries without a similar boycott by European countries, or when European companies can use business methods, subsidized credits, or political pressure not available to their American competitors. In such cases, particularly in the Middle East, the Europeans have been able to attain markets even when their quality and price were not equal to that offered by American companies. This in turn encourages Euro-nationalists to produce parallel systems. The U.S. government and industry get the worst of all possible worlds in such a situation. The government loses influence over the customer country, U.S. industry loses sales which, and the Europeans get longer production runs.

With respect to such major weapons systems, the best role NATO might perform is to encourage greater standardization wherever possible, ranging from ammunition and fuel to other consumables (filters, treads, etc.) to subsystems and support equipment. Joint basic research projects, such as the X-31 enhanced fighter maneuverability program being undertaken by Rockwell and MBB might also be stimulated by NATO, future DARPA-EUCLID cooperation, or individual countries, thereby increasing common knowledge on which U.S. or European programs might be based.

With respect to medium sized systems, such as many missile programs, wheeled vehicles, communications gear, and infantry weapons, as well as for large subsystems on major weapons programs, a gradual increase in competition across the Atlantic would seem advisable. Here again, the emergence of a truly integrated European defense market may be a prior requirement for cross Atlantic cooperation to emerge. Only when the European market as a whole is of sufficient size to allow the Europeans some confidence in their ability to take on American companies will such two-way competition be practical. Without such market symmetry, European companies will continue to find it important to team with American companies or to purchase American subsidiaries in order to penetrate a market which is a multiple of any European country, while U.S. companies will primarily seek out export marketing opportunities (with associated offsets or licensing) for individual European and Third World national markets.

Even with such medium sized systems or major subsystems, neither Europe nor the U.S. is likely to be willing to see domestic capacity lost all together. Thus partnerships, licensing arrangements, or dual sourcing will almost certainly have to be employed in the immediate future to assure design and production capability on both sides of the Atlantic.

As to minor or highly specialized weapons systems, and components of all weapons systems, competition across the Atlantic should be allowed to the maximum extent possible. The total U.S. plus European market should be large enough to assure the survival of several firms for any given product, particularly if major weapons systems are designed to use standardized or compatible components to the maximum extent feasible.

On the European side, therefore, it is probably necessary for European integration to move forward rapidly if trans-Atlantic cooperation is to increase. On the U.S. side, perhaps the single major contribution the U.S. government could make would to be decrease controls on technology transfer. If U.S. companies cannot bring their best technology to the table, neither the Europeans nor the U.S. military services will have much interest in collaborative programs. If we insist on unilaterally dictating to which countries end items with even modest amounts of U.S. technology can be sold, Europeans will avoid using American technology will endeavor to create their own.

Overall, the best policy for governments to take is one that creates a framework which allows for maximum competition and cooperation among firms on both sides of the Atlantic. Given that customers are governments, such a framework will always have to take into account more political and security than commercial factors, and hence will never wholly emulate other product markets. The challenge is to take the most advantage of larger markets and the economies of scale a common defense market could provide, and to stimulate as much competitive behavior as is realistic among defense producers.

NOTES

1. Thomas A. Callaghan, Jr., *U.S./European Economic Cooperation in Military and Civil Technology*, prepared for the Department of State by Ex-Im Tech, Inc., August 1974, p. 41.

2. Defense Society Board, *Industry-to-Industry International Armaments Cooperation: Phase I-Nato Europe,* report to the Office of the Under Secretary of Defense for Research & Engineering, June 1983, p. 84.

3. *International Coproduction/Industrial Participation Agreements*, report of the Department of Defense Task Group, August 15, 1983 (known as the Denoon Report, after its principal author, David B. H. Denoon), pp. 5-6.

4. See Policy Statement and Fact Sheet released by the Office of the Press Secretary, The White House, April 16, 1990.

5. For an example of industry attitudes towards offsets, see "Views of the Aerospace Industries Association on a U.S. Government Policy on Offsets Related to Military Sales"; submitted to the Office of Industrial Resource Administration, Bureau of Export Administration, U.S. Department of Commerce, January 30, 1990, in response to a request in the *Federal Register* of January 8 for public comment on offsets.

6. Thomas A. Callaghan, Jr., *Pooling Allied and American Resources to Produce a Credible, Collective Conventional Deterrent,* prepared for the Department of Defense, August, 1988, p. 19.

7. Callaghan, *U.S./European Economic Cooperation in Military and Civil Technology*, p. 40.

8. Ibid., p. 40.

9. Ibid., p. 41.

10. Data from Research Center, Aerospace Industries Association, and the "Statement on the Defence Estimates, 1990," a report to the Parliament by the Secretary of Defence, April, 1990.

11. Andrew Moravcsik, "1992 and the Future of the European Armaments Industry," Economic and National Security Program, John M. Olin Institute for Strategic Studies, Harvard University, September, 1989, p. 6.

12. A number of recent studies on the industrial base have addressed this range of problems. See for example *Bolstering Defense Industrial Competitiveness*, report to the Secretary of Defense by the Under Secretary of Defense, Acquisition (known as the Costello Report), July 1988; *Industrial Base: Defense-Critical Industries*, a briefing report to the Honorable John Heinz by the U.S. General Accounting Office, August 1988; and *Lifeline in Danger: An Assessment of the United States Defense Industrial Base*, The Air Force Association, September 1988.

13. Callaghan, *U.S./European Economic Cooperation in Military and Civil Technology*, p. 65.

14. For a simple guide to the various institutions and programs related to Europe 1992 and European integration of the defense sector, see Aerospace Industries Association, *European Integration: Background and Definitions*, 1990.

15. *Towards a Stronger Europe*, vol. 1, report by an independent study team established by Defence Ministers of Nations of the Independent European Programme Group, December 1986.

16. See the "Copenhagen Communique" and accompanying "Policy Document on the European Defence Equipment Market" issued on November 16, 1990, by the IEPG Defence Ministers for more detail on procurement and EUCLID.

17. Data from Aerospace Industries Association Research Center.

18. Aerospace Industries Association, *European Integration: Background and Definitions*.

19. Francis M. Cevasco, "The United States and Europe: State of the Future Relationship," *Revista Espanola de Defense*, 1990.

20. The Honorable William H. Taft, IV, "The Future of Defense and Industrial Collaboration in NATO," presented to the German Strategy Forum and the Institute for Foreign Policy Analysis, Bonn, FRG, March 15, 1990.

21. Data from Aerospace Industries Association Research Center.

4
Arms Cooperation in the Pacific Basin

Jack Nunn

Dr. Nunn is a senior analyst with the Office of Technology Assessment, U.S. Congress, Washington, D.C. This chapter, however, reflects only his own views and not those of the U.S. Government or any Agency thereof.

The Pacific Basin poses the greatest arms cooperation challenges to United States policymakers in the last decade of the twentieth century.[1] However, the region also offers some of the greatest arms cooperation opportunities. The dichotomy lies in the changing nature of the region. It is after all, the Western Pacific, and not Western Europe, that has been the focus of the most contentious arguments over U.S. international arms cooperation. For it is in this economically dynamic region that the security and commercial aspects of arms cooperation have so openly clashed in the past, and are most likely to clash in the future. While it is clear that the United States can gain from regional arms cooperation, it is also clear that we have not yet found the proper mechanism to deal with nations and firms whose concerns are far more commercial than military. With the end of the Cold War, the economic and competitive aspects of arms collaboration agreements will become even more central to the political debate on both sides of the Pacific.

The arguments for United States participation in international arms cooperation have been presented in detail elsewhere in this book. These arguments generally include: improving and cementing overall security ties with allies and friends; promoting common weapons (rationalization, standardization and inter-operability: RSI); and most importantly in the early days of the Cold War, developing the arms industries and military capability of America's allies for common defense against the Soviet Union and associated military threats. In addition to these national justifications, the past decade has witnessed a growing need for U.S. defense industrial firms to participate in various forms of arms cooperation in order to sell military systems abroad.

However, the world's changing political, economic and military landscape raises questions about future security ties and the size and character of the global defense industrial base. Although most of the prior justifications remain valid, future international arms cooperation decisions will rest on more complex calculations. Cooperation is no longer automatically assumed to be in the best interests of the United States. It is now seen to carry increasing economic and military security risks that must be matched against expected security returns.

In the Pacific Basin, cooperation is considered desirable, not only to improve local security, cement security ties, and clinch critical arms sales, but increasingly because of the potential for technological reciprocity from a foreign partner. The United States, for example, already draws on Japanese industry for critical subcomponents in some of its most important military systems.[2] These "dual-use" technology inputs into U.S. defense systems result in both cost savings and qualitative improvements in weapons' performance on the battlefield. There is potential for much more "reverse" technology transfer to the United States, but gaining access to that technology for use in U.S. military systems will be difficult.

Regardless of the desirability of arms cooperation in this new environment, cooperation is viewed as risky because of the technological and commercial competition America faces from its allies—particularly in this region.[3] Defense cooperation carries the possibility of transfer of technology from the United States that might have significant adverse commercial implications for U.S. business. Negative commercial possibilities are viewed with the most alarm in the case of Japan, but are also increasingly worrisome with regard to South Korea and Taiwan.[4] In addition to commercial concerns, fears over the development of new defense competitors for the global weapons market are very real. The People's Republic of China, Taiwan, South Korea and Singapore have all emerged in the past decade as arms exporters.

Despite the acknowledged risks, arms cooperation is considered necessary not only because the United States potentially stands to gain access to future militarily useful technology, but also because the United States is, and remains, a Pacific power. The United States government will continue to find arms cooperation a valuable national tool in maintaining overall security arrangements with Pacific nations and American firms will find cooperation both useful and necessary in doing business in what might be a very lucrative future arms market. However, the conditions of the Pacific Basin pose special challenges. The region has always lacked the common view of a military threat that cemented the NATO alliance and provided some rationale for weapons development planning. Further, the commercial threat from arms cooperation differs from the European experience in that many of the technologies of interest can be used in the private sector, and the governments of the Pacific Rim are more supportive of unbridled commercial competition than are European governments. Playing off the risks, desirability and necessity of regional arms cooperation creates a difficult challenge to those seeking to develop policies to manage that cooperation.

This chapter examines the motivations for regional arms cooperation, explores the development of regional arms cooperation objectives and policies for achieving those objectives, and considers the implications of the policies for United States national security.

REGIONAL IMPORTANCE

For over forty years, arguments for maintaining United States forces in Western Europe were buttressed by the observation that the United States had in this century fought two wars to protect its vital interests. In that context it should also be noted that the United States, in the past half century, has fought three major conflicts in the Pacific. The region is important to U.S. security, but the basis of that importance is changing. Increasingly, our national security will be affected not by the population, geography and raw materials of the region, but by its economic power and potential technological and industrial developments, and finally by the underlying military security threats in the region.

Economic Power and Potential

Japan is an economic and industrial superpower. South Korea, Taiwan, and several of the ASEAN countries in Southeast Asia are also important exporters of manufactured goods. Other countries remain key exporters of raw materials. The region's size and growing technological sophistication clearly increase its importance to the United States. The Western edge of the Pacific Basin contains a third of the world's population and has become one of the world's most economically and technologically dynamic areas. While individual country economic trends are far from stable, the regional trend has remained clearly upward. Excluding the United States and Canada, the countries of the region contributed over a quarter of the world's GDP in the late 1980s.[5] This percentage is expected to continue to rise into the next century.

Technology and Industrial Development

The economic explosion of the Pacific Basin's Western edge is principally due to the growing industrial and technological prowess of the area. The region is a prodigious producer of consumer products (for example, over 50% of the world's 1987 TV set production and more than 25% of its automobile production),[6] and is becoming a major exporter of high-technology products. In 1986, the United States high-technology trade balance showed a $22 billion deficit with Japan, and a $7 billion deficit with the East Asian newly industrialized countries.[7] In 1988, Pacific Rim nations constituted more than 50% of the world's exports of micro-electronics, about 30% of computer exports, and about a quarter of its machine tool and robotics exports.[8] While some portion of both the regional trade deficit with the United States and the world exports can be attributed to off-shore production of U.S. firms (for example, integrated circuits and other electronic devices from such U.S. firms as Texas Instruments, IBM, National Semiconductor, and Motorola), national firms in Japan, Taiwan, and Korea are increasingly either leaders, or tough competitors, in key electronics sectors. However, regardless of whether the producers are owned by the United States or foreign countries, the critical factors are regional production, technological development of new products, and ultimately the increasing interdependence of the United States' manufacturing sector with those of Pacific Rim countries.

Military Security Threats
U.S. security is affected by the military threats in the region. The region is now at peace and the current trend is toward increased stability. Few direct military threats exist. There are internal security problems in the Philippines, and to a limited extent in some other countries (Indonesia and Malaysia), but these internal problems argue less for arms than for economic development. Vietnam still presents concerns to Thailand, but this is a much diminished threat. The startling security changes that have occurred in Eastern Europe and the former Soviet Union are having an impact on the region. The Republics and their former eastern block allies present no military threat in Southeast Asia and far less threat in the north than the PRC perceived in the late 1960s and early 1970s. Further, it appears possible that Russia may make a deal with Japan on the "Northern

Territories."[9] The two Koreas are talking, and the PRC and Taiwan are increasing their "unofficial" contacts. The PRC is also seen as a diminished threat to much of the region. Thus, in the short term there are few military threats.

However, the long-term threat assessment is less sanguine. There are several future military threat possibilities. The petroleum resources of the South China Sea and the territorial disputes over the Spratly Islands are potential sources of conflict. A dispute at sea might spread into renewed border fighting between Vietnam and the PRC. In the absence of sustained economic growth, the population explosion in the Philippines can only increase the instability of that nation. Religious and/or ethnic turmoil in Malaysia might affect Singapore. The uncertain path of North Korea after the death of Kim Il Sung is another potential threat to stability, as is the leadership transition in Indonesia after Suharto. A further concern for South Korea is the possibility that the North might be developing a nuclear capability.[10] Finally, the path of change in the former Soviet Union remains unknown, with some potential for renewed threats to the nations of the region.

Thus, despite current stability and positive near-term trends, many Pacific States can be expected to continue to modernize their military forces as a hedge against the uncertain future. The power and potential of the Pacific Rim region, as well as the long-term threat potential, argue for a continuation of United States interest in regional security and arms cooperation on the part of the U.S. The following section explores current and future policies to manage that cooperation.

DEVELOPING PACIFIC BASIN ARMS COOPERATION POLICY

U.S. government arms cooperation policy has nominally supported the limited development of indigenous arms production by allies and friendly nations in the region. However, this support has differed from that in the NATO arena in several important ways.

Regional Characteristics
Lacking an overall treaty umbrella, U.S. Pacific policies have been bilateral and far more country-specific than in Europe. Further, the relative lack of technological sophistication (with the exception of Japan) that existed until a decade ago, and still exists in many of the countries, combined with the fragmented regional defense industry, made it even more difficult to develop a "two-way street" in defense trade in the Pacific. A third difference is the relative importance of the United States as a military supplier in this area. Our Pacific allies have been predominantly armed with American weapons, and have sought to continue this relationship through licensed production of American military equipment. In this environment, the U.S. has used the transfer of weapons technology as a tool both to enhance its own political influence and to allow the cooperating country to provide for its own security. However, policies directed at more industrial countries (Japan, Australia), have differed from those directed at countries with immediate security needs (South Korea and Taiwan).

National Approaches
The most important regional ties and subsequent arms cooperation relationship have been with Japan, where the United States has assisted the government in developing a significant arms industry. This arms industry relationship began in 1947 with the United States using Japanese labor to overhaul and repair American weapons in the Pacific region, and received a major boost during the Korean War.[11] For many years, U.S. policy toward Japan included the "unilateral transfer of technology through licensed production of advanced systems."[12]
The initial objective of U.S. policy was to shore up the Japanese as a bulwark against communism, but subsequently a principal objective became, in the words of one American government

participant, "to offer advanced technology as an inducement to larger defense expenditures and commitments by the Japanese."[13]   U.S. policy further changed in the 1980s as the United States sought to develop a Pacific version of the "two-way street" that allowed the U.S. acquisition of advanced Japanese technology for U.S. military systems. A Memorandum of Understanding (MOU) signed in 1983 sought to facilitate the transfer of military technologies and related dual-use technologies from Japan to the United States. Given the relative paucity of Japanese military R&D, the Japanese technologies of interest were indeed principally the dual-use technologies developed in the civil sector, but with military application.[14] The much debated U.S./Japanese agreement on the FSX fighter in 1988 included a further effort at providing U.S. access to Japanese technology as well as continuing Japanese access to U.S. military technology.

For its part, Japan has certainly used the U.S. arms relationship to develop an arms industry capable of providing its forces with a wide array of weapons systems. However, observers have noted that it has done so in ways that have "offered the greatest technological benefits to domestic industry,"[15] rather than maximizing military benefits. Japan's approach enhanced the domestic technology base in ways that have positive effects on non-defense production.[16]

While U.S. arms cooperation with Japan was driven by the Soviet threat, cooperation with South Korea and Taiwan developed from more immediate concerns. United States support of South Korean defense industry is much more recent. South Korea initiated a policy of military self-reliance in the 1970s, in part due to the perceived weakening of the U.S. security commitment.[17]   This program has been built around licensed assembly agreements between U.S. and Korean firms, but Korea has also sought to diversify import sources for military items.[18] The Korean government has actively intervened through "tax incentives and other favorable treatment for industry [that] have encouraged the development of defense production across major sectors."[19] South Korea also sought to use the Korean Fighter Program (KFP) to gain technology and know-how from the United States in order to boost the country into the top tier of the world's aerospace industry.[20] That might be an overly optimistic objective given the country's size, but it demonstrates the economic as well as the national security component of Korean developments. The U.S. government has responded with reluctant support when facing potential diversification away from U.S. sources. Currently, South Korea has an extensive, but under-utilized, defense base. There has been much discussion between the U.S. and Korea over "Third Country" sales and use of Korea as a part of the United States mobilization base—both of which Korean industry desires, but the U.S. either officially, or unofficially, opposes.[21]

The U.S. security commitment to the Republic of China (Taiwan) goes back to 1950. U.S. military deliveries consisted entirely of grant assistance until 1967. Direct sales exceeded grants by 1974, and grants ended entirely by 1979.[22] According to one study, "Taiwan's licensed production efforts parallel the decline in grant assistance and were augmented by the implications of U.S. rapprochement with the PRC."[23] Thus, in common with South Korea, concern about the long-term viability of United States commitment has been a driving force behind local arms development. Defense industrial cooperation between the United States and Taiwan is currently governed by the Taiwan Relations Act. Although there are limits on the technology that can be transferred, the U.S. has allowed a number of private U.S. firms to provide technical engineering support for development of new weapons, such as the Indigenous Defense Fighter (IDF) being developed in cooperation with General Dynamics.[24]

Other countries of the region have developed important, but much more limited defense industrial capabilities—many with assistance from the United States. Australia, a longtime American ally, has focused its efforts on developing a capability to maintain and repair major systems purchased abroad (principally from the United States) and to engage in licensed coproduction. While U.S. policy has generally supported this approach, there have been disagreements over the transfer of specific technologies.

U.S. policy toward the ASEAN countries has allowed some weapons production, but has sought to limit the technology transferred to systems that appear appropriate to the threat and the technological capabilities of those countries. Singapore has a small, highly diverse and very capable arms industry, which includes a number of programs with U.S. firms. Indonesia, in keeping with the spirit of industrial independence developed during its fight for freedom from the Netherlands, wants defense industrial independence, but still has a limited arms production capability. However, there are several cooperative arrangements with U.S. and European firms, principally in aerospace. Indeed, Indonesia reportedly has sought to use offset programs to make the country "self-sufficient in weapons systems, independent in naval shipbuilding, and to create a regionally dominant civil and military aircraft industry through joint ventures."[25] Thailand, Malaysia, and the Philippines also aspire to some defense industrial capability, but actual arms capabilities remain quite limited.

The People's Republic of China (PRC) represents a very special arms cooperation case for the U.S. The largest regional producer of military systems and a major exporter of military hardware, the PRC developed its arms industry with major assistance from the Soviet Union. This cooperation was curtailed in the early 1960s, and the Chinese subsequently sought, and achieved, self-sufficiency in military systems, largely based on 1950s Soviet designs.[26] Since the rapprochement between the United States and the PRC in the 1970s, the United States has attempted to use arms cooperation as an aid in developing better relations. Projects ranged from conventional ammunition facilities to the upgrade of some of the PRC's fighter avionic systems.[27] European firms also undertook industrial cooperation programs in the 1980s. However, the events in Tiananmen Square in June 1989 put a hold on all U.S. defense cooperation.[28]

In response, the PRC reportedly turned back to the Soviet Union for new military technology, but it appears to favor acquisition of Western technology for both its defense and non-defense sectors, and will continue to be interested in cooperation with the United States in the future. However, barring some dramatic world event that increases the PRC's immediate importance to the U.S., improvements in arms cooperation between the two countries will probably await changes in leadership in the PRC. In the meantime, it might buy extensive technology from Russia and other republics.

These national approaches indicate that while the United States government has nominally supported regional arms cooperation, it has been restrained in that support. This restraint resulted from concern over: the possible transfer of inappropriate technology (either technology the recipient could not adequately use, or technology that might provide the recipient with capabilities the U.S. desired to control); the possibility of developing new international arms competitors; and the non-defense commercial implications of the transfer of some technologies. Commercial concerns have grown rapidly (as evidenced by the arguments over the FSX agreement). The Iraq War increased concern over the potential for inappropriate transfers of arms production technology. Under these conditions, U.S. arms cooperation policy will be under close review in the future. In the relatively stable military threat environment currently forecast, any changes are likely to be evolutionary rather than revolutionary.

Other Factors Affecting Arms Cooperation

Whatever the trends in overall regional arms expenditures, and U.S. concerns over the implications of regional defense industrial developments, actual arms cooperation agreements are likely to increase. This is partly due to the fact that current levels of cooperation are very low. Further, unlike Europe, where many local defense firms already exist, none of the Pacific Rim countries have a sufficiently independent defense industrial capability, or a sufficiently large defense market base (the PRC and a future Japan are possible exceptions), to attempt to "go it alone." Arms cooperation will remain important to Pacific Rim nations as a means to: (1) gain technology for military or civilian use, and/or (2) gain access to a market (through possible joint ventures or offset agreements that include some export production). As noted earlier, such arms cooperation will also be the "price of admission" for American and European firms to the local market.[29] With no major threat in Europe and general over-capacity in arms production, Pacific Rim countries will have increased leverage to press their offset demands on U.S. and European defense firms attempting to make sales to stay alive. A further incentive for the U.S. and its European arms competitors is the increasing possibility of gaining militarily relevant technology from the Japanese. In this environment, the aerospace industry presents excellent business opportunities for United States firms. Not only is the U.S. the world's leader in military aviation, but it is also involved with the current leading regional high-performance aircraft programs—FSX in Japan, KFP in South Korea, and the IDF in Taiwan.[30]

There is much more international competition in training aircraft and helicopters. Nations in the region are expected to undertake major modernization programs in training aircraft and helicopters in the future, and European firms from the United Kingdom and Italy have strong positions.[31]

There will also be increased competition from regional allies. It has been argued that South Korea may "become one of the best examples of an indigenous defense production and consequent export capability that may create foreign policy dilemmas for the United States."[32] The desire by Korea to sell weapons to third parties, and indeed to undercut U.S. prices, has been the source of friction between the two countries for several years. Not only have U.S. firms been concerned about the business losses, but the U.S. government has been concerned that these sales might provide arms to potential adversaries.

Developing Regional Arms Cooperation Objectives

Given all these factors, how should regional arms cooperation objectives change to accommodate the new environment? Current Department of Defense arms cooperation objectives include:

- Providing DOD access to, and use and protection of, the best technology developed by our allies, and comparable allied access to, and use and protection of, the best U.S. technology, thereby avoiding unnecessary duplication of development.

- Deployment and support of common, or at least, interoperable equipment with our allies.

- Providing incentives for allies to make a greater investment in modern conventional military equipment.

- Developing economies of scale through coordinated research, development, production and logistics programs.[33]

These objectives are far too narrow to guide future policy. Furthermore, portions appear to be of questionable relevance and/or have limited potential for U.S. acceptance in dealing with Pacific nations. Using a broader definition of security that includes: (1) economic as well as military factors, (2) a forecast of relative stability, and (3) much reduced regional threats, a more appropriate list of U.S. regional arms cooperation objectives includes:

- Maintain security ties to regional powers.

- Maintain general stability through appropriate arms development.

- Provide U.S. access to allied technology and allies access to U.S. technology.

- Deploy common military systems for mutual defense.

- Develop economies of scale in research, development, production and logistics.

With a smaller direct military threat, industrial cooperation might be more appropriate than troop deployments for maintaining regional security ties. At the same time, the general objective of providing incentives for greater allied investments in conventional military equipment might be dropped. A larger global defense industrial base does not appear to be a near-term requirement. If arms cooperation is managed properly it might promote general regional stability. A factor here is the control of the types of military technologies available in the region. Control will require more than a unilateral U.S. effort. While cooperation from Europe and the former Soviet republics will be required, developing regional economic and political groupings would also be useful, and will be discussed later.

Providing U.S. access to allied technology and allied access to U.S. technology will be an increasingly important objective, but one that will remain terribly difficult. This objective raises issues of how much foreign dependence the United States will accept in development and production of materiel, and how much risk (commercial and military) the U.S. is willing to accept in the transfer of its military technology. What security future do U.S. planners foresee and what future do our allies anticipate? Kazuo Nukazawa, long the principal economist for Keidanren (the association of major Japanese manufacturing firms) is reported to have assessed the future U.S./Japanese relationship as follows:

As I see it, the United States will still be a bigger power than Japan in every sense twenty years from now and we will still be ultimately dependent upon you for our survival. But because we will be so advanced technologically you will also be dependent upon us for some critical elements of your military power—microcircuity or whatever the newest thing will be by then. And that's precisely what the relationship between our two countries ought to be: mutual dependence for mutual survival.[34]

While such a symbiotic relationship has advantages, it carries disadvantages as well. Probably the most important (certainly the most discussed) is the risk that a country's dependence is misplaced and its partner fails to support its national security objectives in crisis—one of the chief concerns that have driven much of the arms production development of our allies.[35]

Deployment of common weapons systems remains a worthwhile objective and works in synergy with the development of economies of scale in research, development, production and logistics—all important in a world with fewer arms.

These somewhat broader objectives provide opportunities for both continuity and necessary change in future regional cooperation.

Future U.S. Regional Arms Cooperation Policies

Future arms cooperation policies in the Pacific will of necessity continue to be more tailored to country circumstances than has been the case in Europe. This is a function of the diversity of the region. However, the general grouping noted in the earlier discussion of past policy will continue.

Japan, critically important for world stability, will continue to stand in a category by itself because of the potential for technology exchange. However, given Japan's long history as an importer of military technology rather than an exporter, the key policy challenge for the United States will be to develop conditions that promote meaningful technology exchange, especially with regard to so-called dual-use, or civil-military technology.

South Korea, Taiwan and Australia all fall into a second category. The potential for technological reciprocity is more limited with these countries, but still exists. But, the need for commonality of equipment and the potential for economies of scale in research, development and production are both important objectives. Further, their importance as long-time allies and friends means that the U.S. needs to maintain its military ties during a period of reduced military threat.

The ASEAN countries are unlikely to provide technological reciprocity. The objectives stressed with these nations will be on maintaining security ties and general stability through appropriate arms development.

Finally, arms cooperation policies toward the People's Republic of China will be influenced by the internal policies of that government, especially in the area of human rights.

Although regional policies will remain tailored to individual countries, there is potential for more multilateral cooperation. The U.S. should support such cooperation. The potential for this change exists in developing the economic and political groupings of the region. These are embryonic now. The Association of Southeast Asian Nations (ASEAN) has developed very slowly since its establishment as an economic, social, cultural, and technical grouping in 1967. It has long resisted a military component, but the withdrawl of the United States from Vietnam prompted increased military consultation, and individual members have subsequently worked together on arms projects.[36] Cooperation is increasing and becoming formalized in an association provisionally named "the ASEAN Confederation of Defence Manufacturer's Association." The proposed organization would "loosely unite the ASEAN countries through their respective national defense manufacturer associations, which are private organization although leading members include government-controlled companies."[37] Singapore is particularly keen to improve the economic relationship.[38] If this happens, it could have a major impact on regional arms cooperation too. The Asia-Pacific Economic Cooperation (APEC), which held its second ministerial meeting in July 1990, groups the six ASEAN states with Australia, Canada, Japan, New Zealand, South Korea, and the United

States. The PRC, Taiwan and Hong Kong are potential future members.[39] It remains to be seen how APEC will develop. However, the association could be an important future factor in regional arms cooperation. More informal, but potentially more important are the private groupings developing through business investments. In this area Japan's actions will be critical. Japanese companies are the leading investors in the Asian region and there is some desire for rationalization of production among Japanese industrial leaders. The extent to which this rationalization is accomplished will have an effect on individual country's and the region's arms production capabilities.

A policy promoting a regional multilateral approach might help maintain general regional stability by limiting arms developments. It would also support the objective of economies of scale in all aspects of arms development and production.

An associated policy would be to establish joint (including a significant U.S. commitment) defense research facilities in the region. A joint U.S./Japan research facility might improve the exchange of technology between the two countries. It might also act as a catalyst for additional cooperation at all levels.

Implications for U.S. Security

These policy initiatives—tailored cooperation, supporting multilateral approaches, retaining limits on arms technology, and establishing regional research facilities—would fully support the arms cooperation objectives outlined earlier.

If the region continues to grow in importance, continued arms cooperation can play an important role in maintaining a U.S. defense presence in the region. Cooperation can also enhance security by providing access to new technologies that might otherwise be unavailable. And, if cooperation develops a more multilateral flavor, it might also help to limit the perceived need for rapid modernization of regional armed forces.

SUMMARY

The growing importance of the Pacific region mandates some continued arms cooperation. The United States has much to gain from such cooperation; however, it is clear we have not yet found the proper mechanism to deal with nations and firms whose orientation is far more commercial than national security. Arms cooperation provides an opportunity to continue a security association in a period in which the "threat" that previously drove military cooperation no longer is sufficient to promote allied actions. It also provides access to advanced technology.

U.S. policy toward Pacific Rim allies with high technology capabilities must stress reciprocity in technology transfer. This is particularly difficult in Asia. Japanese resistance to sale or trade of technology is real, but can be overcome. Japanese firms will share technology in a strict business relationship. Current government relationships provide insufficient reasons for reciprocity.

U.S. policies toward allies lacking high technology must still seek reciprocity in terms of an identifiable return. The Pentagon's Pacific Rim Task Force recommended cooperative maintenance and logistics improvements. These would appear useful goals. However, it is difficult to properly value such an exchange.

In both these cases, however, it must also be noted that cooperation with allies and friendly nations is going to become more difficult because of the lessening of direct ties to the U.S., and the desire of these countries to buy military materiel from diverse sources. Doing business will become harder for U.S. firms precisely at a time when export sales are of growing importance to them. U.S. defense firms will be under great pressure, and the U.S. government arms cooperation policy must recognize this fact.

Lastly, arms cooperation in the Pacific region will demand the attention and cooperation of many more elements of government than just those in the Department of Defense. Countries of the region have become masterful at playing off various parts of the U.S.

government. There is a need for close governmental cooperation if the nation is going to answer adequately the question posed by the Defense Science Board: "What defense industrial cooperation policies will maintain adequate military security without harming U.S. industrial and technological competitiveness?"[40]

NOTES

1. The following countries are included in this discussion of the Pacific Basin: the United States and Canada (the North American Defense Industrial Base), Japan, the People's Republic of China, South Korea, the Republic of China, the ASEAN countries (Indonesia, Thailand, Singapore, Philippines, Malaysia, and Brunei), and Australia.

2. Martin Libicki, Jack Nunn and Bill Taylor, *U.S. Industrial Base Dependence/Vulnerability Phase II--Analysis*, Mobilization Concepts Development Center (Washington, D.C.: National Defense University, November 1987), p. 44. Examples of identified dependencies on Japan for U.S. precision guided munitions (PGM) included: silicon field effect transistors, galliym arsenide field effect transistors, and precision optics. PGM are some of the most important weapons in the U.S. inventory and were used with great effect in the Iraq war.

3. Defense Science Board, *Defense Industrial Cooperation with Pacific Rim Nations*, Office of the Under Secretary of Defense for Acquisition, Washington, DC, October 1989 (Hereafter referred to as *DSB Pacific Rim Study*), p. iii, notes the nature of both the risk, and the security and economic relationships between the United States and its Pacific allies and friends. The report argues that: "Economic concerns are beginning to dominate our thinking as military tensions subside. We are engaged in intense economic competition largely centered on technology, and are concerned about our ability to compete. The formation of new economic blocs is occurring, with the Pacific Rim the most powerful by the end of the century."

4. Michael W. Chinworth, "Industry and Government in Japanese Procurement: The Case of the Patriot Missile System," *Comparative Strategy* 9 (1989), p. 218. Chinworth points out that the Patriot program provided Japanese industry experience in systems integration and automated production methods and in technologies that could ultimately be used in Japan's civilian space programs.

5. *Asian Yearbook 1989* (Hong Kong: Far Eastern Economic Review, 1988). *World Development Report 1988* (Washington, D.C.: World Bank, 1988).

6. *The Economist World Atlas and Almanac* (New York: Prentice Hall Press, 1989), pp. 92-93.

7. The Aerospace Education Foundation, *Lifeline in Danger* (Arlington, Va.: AEF, 1988), p.3.

8. Central Intelligence Agency, *Handbook of Economic Statistics 1989*, CPAS89-10002, Washington, D.C., September 1989, p. 156.

9. Charles Smith, "Bargaining Counters," *Far Eastern Economic Review*, 30 (August 1990).

10. L. Dunn, D. Dwyer, and D. Louscher, *Diffusion of Military Technology and Its Implications for U.S. Defense Policy*, Technical Report for The Director, OSD Net Assessment, prepared by Science Applications International Corporation, 1990, p. A-263.

11. Reinhard Drifte, *Arms Production in Japan: The Military Applications of Civilian Technology*, Westview Special Studies on East Asia (Boulder, Colo.: Westview Press, 1985), p. 9.

12. Defense Science Board, *Defense Industrial Cooperation with Pacific Rim Nations*, p. viii.

13. Dr. Malcolm Currie, speaking at the Eighth Annual Executive Conference on International Security Affairs, May 15-17, 1984, reported in *Proceedings of the Pacific Basin Defense Corporation*, American Defense Preparedness Association, p. 9.

14. Jack Nunn, Martin Libicki and Herbert Glazer, "United States Access to Japanese Technology," unpublished working paper, Mobilization Concepts Development Center, National Defense University, 1988. Interviews by the authors with many of the participants confirmed that the focus was principally dual-use technologies.

15. Chinworth, "Industry and Government in Japanese Procurement," p. 197.

16. The *DSB Pacific Rim Study* was one of the first comprehensive efforts to address these issues.

17. Andrew Ross, *Security and Self-Reliance: Military Dependence and Conventional Arms Production in Developing Countries*, UMI Dissertation Information Services, part 2, pp. 495-496.

18. Dan C. Boger and Man Won Jee, "Korea Contribution to U.S. Defense Mobilization Base," paper presented at the 1987 Industrial College of the Armed Forces Mobilization Conference, National Defense University. The authors note that South Korea also sought equipment from West Germany, Italy, and Sweden. South Korea sought to reduce its arms dependency on the United States.

19. David J. Louscher and Michael D. Salomone, *Technology Transfer and U.S. Security Assistance: The Impact of Licensed Production* (Boulder, Colo.: Westview Press, 1987), p. 158.

20. Alex Gliksman and Jack Nunn, "Military Aerospace in the Pacific Rim," *National Defense*, April 1990.

21. Boger and Jee, "Korea Contribution to U.S. Defense Mobilization Base."

22. Louscher and Salomone, *Technology Transfer and U.S. Security Assistance*, p. 141.

23. Ibid.

24. Glicksman and Nunn, "Military Aerospace in the Pacific Rim."

25. Lindsey Shanson, "Building on Offsets," *Jane's Defence Weekly*, December 15, 1990.

26. China's arms exports reportedly totalled $3 to $3.5 billion between 1958 and 1979, and $7.2 billion between 1980 and 1986--much of the latter to Iraq and Iran. *DMS Market Report: Latin America & Australasia*, China (PRC), Jane's Information Group, 1989, p. 7.

27. Ibid. The avionics deal and all other on-going projects fell through as a result of Tiananmen.

28. L. Dunn and D. Dwyer and D. Louscher, *Diffusion of Military Technology and Its Implications for U.S. Defense Policy*, p. A-215.

29. Virginia Lopez and Loren Yager, *The U.S. Aerospace Industry and the Trend Toward Internationalization* (Washington, D.C.: Aerospace Industries Association of America, 1988), pp. 59-65.

30. DSB, *Pacific Rim Report*, p. 51.

31. Roy Braybrook, "Rash of New Trainer Projects," *Pacific Defense Reporter*, November 1989, pp. 59-62. *Diffusion of Military Technology and its Implications for U.S. Defense Policy* reports a deal between South Korea and the U.K. for Hawk trainers that involves significant transfer of manufacturing technology.

32. David J. Louscher and Michael D. Salomone, *Technology Transfer and U.S. Security Assistance: The Impact of Licensed Production*, p. 164.

33. *Memorandum for Secretaries of Military Departments for the Deputy Under Secretary of Defense Acquisition, Subject: Policy for Negotiation of International Agreements for Cooperative Projects and Follow-On Activities*, Reported in *DSB Pacific Rim Study*.

34. Robert C. Christopher, *The Japanese Mind* (New York: Fawcett Columbine, 1984), p. 309.

35. Although the Japanese have provided steady support for the U.S. in the past (for example, providing logistical support during the Vietnam War despite the fact that the Japanese public opposed the war), the changed relationship could modify this support. The observations by Shintaro Ishihara, in *The Japan That Can Say "No": The New U.S.-Japan Relations Card*, that Japan could tip the strategic balance by providing microchips to the Soviet Union rather than the United States, while incorrect now, might well be true in the world envisioned by Nukawaza. While the U.S. may neither be able to avoid such a mutually supporting world nor have the desire to do so, we must certainly be aware of the implications of such relationships.

36. Jack Nunn, "ASEAN Defense Industry: its Impact on Economic Development," in Dora Alves, ed., *Pacific Security Toward the Year 2000: The 1987 Pacific Symposium* (Washington, D.C.: National Defense University, 1988), pp. 235-250.

37. *Jane's Defence Weekly*, September 15, 1990, p. 488.

38. Michael Vatikiotis, "Triangular Vision," *Far Eastern Economic Review*, July 26, 1990.

39. "Faltering First Steps," *Far Eastern Economic Review*, August 9, 1990.

40. DSB *Pacific Rim Study*.

5
Transnational Industrial Cooperation in Defense Programs

Robert H. Trice

Dr. Trice is with the McDonnell Douglas Corporation. He wishes to thank Charles A. Lanczkowski and Shannon Christensen for their valuable assistance in the preparation of this chapter.

Belated recognition of the positive impact of military-related exports on the U.S. economy has heightened interest in better understanding this sector and its underlying mechanisms and processes.[1] Issues associated with the current and future prospects for transnational defense industrial cooperation have recently caught the fancy of a growing number of political scientists and economists as topics worthy of serious investigation. Even Congress and government bureaucracies that traditionally have all but ignored the implications of the defense sector on the U.S. balance of trade, such as the Department of Commerce, are now clamoring for major roles in regulating specific business arrangements associated with cooperative arms projects.[2]

A working premise of this paper is that, all other things being equal, defense companies and national governments would prefer to develop and produce advanced weapons on their own for their national military establishments. The continuing increase in the number of collaborative projects reflects the fact that political and economic realities often prevent them from doing so. Thirty-plus years of experience has shown that transnational cooperation makes sense when it leads the participants to expanded markets, reduces relative costs, enhances weapon systems commonality,[3] provides shared access to new technologies and increases prospects for follow-on weapons developments and sales.

The logic for increased cooperation will only be strengthened as the size of national armed forces and defense budgets continue to decline, excess defense industrial capacity grows, technological prowess becomes more diffuse, capital requirements for new weapons become unmanageable for any single firm, and the creation of significant barriers to unidirectional defense trade grow. As we prepare for a new era in arms collaboration, we should review the principles of success and lessons learned from past and current programs. Many recent studies have focused on the important role played by governments in determining the fate of defense collaboration efforts.[4] Less attention has been paid to the essential role of defense companies in implementing multinational programs and turning long term visions into complex military systems that are ultimately produced for and procured by multiple governments.

This paper examines from an American industrial perspective the varying forms that defense cooperation can assume, outlines several of the complex contractual and managerial arrangements established to implement actual programs, and suggests some requisites for future success.

Defense industrial cooperation is not new. After World War II, the U.S. first helped rebuild foreign military establishments by offering modest coproduction and licensing arrangements.[5] As European and Japanese economies strengthened and their defense industries re-emerged in the 1960s and 1970s, their governments sought more formal mechanisms for "offsetting" the enormous cash outlays required to purchase new advanced weapon systems from the United States.[6] These offset arrangements, described in more detail below, created mandatory requirements for transnational defense industrial cooperation, and formed the basis for the elaborate programmatic structures that have evolved over the last 15 years or so. As competition increased among U.S. suppliers, and between U.S. and European firms, purchasers were able to set new standards of expectations regarding offsets. The final outcome of industrial negotiations from the last major sale became the benchmark for the initiation of discussions on the next. A flurry of intense military aircraft competitions beginning in the mid-1970s and running through the 1980s,[7] involving U.S. and European producers and abetted by a laissez-faire U.S. Government attitude,[8] have created a situation in which the dollar value and quality of the industrial offerings now rival the technical qualities and price of the system as criteria for weapons selection. Even nations that do not pay for the weapons they acquire from the U.S., but rather use "forgiven credits" provided by the United States, routinely demand and receive offsets. The U.S. Government's 1989 decision to restrict the value of the offsets that could be offered by General Dynamics and McDonnell Douglas to the Republic of Korea at 30 percent of the contract value for the 120 aircraft Korean Fighter Program represents the first time in at least a dozen years that the government has restricted a military-related offset negotiation.

OFFSETS AND LICENSING

An offset is an agreement under which a seller agrees to engage in business activities that provide economic benefits to the buyer of a military system. It is a term used to describe a range of commercial practices, usually required as a condition of purchase, through which some portion of the purchase value is "offset" by the supplier in the purchasing country.[9] There are various types of offset programs:

· A "direct offset" is any reciprocal business activity that relates specifically to the products or services sold to a foreign country. The most common form of direct offset is co-production.

- "Co-production" is a form of direct offset whereby a foreign government, or selected foreign contractor, is permitted to acquire the technical information needed to manufacture all or part of the U.S.-origin defense article being purchased. This can involve limited parts production, final assembly of the product or more complex arrangements where components produced internationally are utilized in U.S. or other foreign production.

- "Indirect offset" refers to any directed business activity on the part of the manufacturer that benefits the purchaser but is not directly related to the product or services sold. For example, in aircraft sales, sellers have purchased consumer items from the customer country for export and resale, invested in hotels or other businesses, and established unrelated manufacturing facilities in customer countries.

All direct offsets involve some degree of transnational industrial cooperation. So do "licensed production" agreements under which a foreign government or company purchases from the original manufacturer the right and capability to build a given product. Coproduction and licensed production arrangements related to the sale of major weapon systems have been the standard mechanisms through which defense industrial cooperation has occurred to date.

"Codevelopment" projects, in which companies and governments agree to jointly develop and produce a military system, represent a quantum leap over traditional methods of transnational industrial cooperation and significantly increase the complexity, as well as the financial and technical risks of new weapons programs. However, the worldwide diffusion of technology, the need to share capital requirements in return for R&D and production work share, and the dwindling ability of most nations to provide a sufficient internal market to guarantee an affordable unit price for advanced systems, will only increase the drive toward codevelopment projects.

U.S. and European firms have more codevelopment experience than is generally recognized by those who have only recently discovered transnational defense cooperation as a policy issue.[10] The British Aerospace-Dassault Jaguar; the Panavia (UK-FRG-Italy) Tornado; McDonnell Douglas-BAe Harrier; and the McDonnell Douglas-BAe Goshawk trainer are positive examples of transnational codevelopment. The outcome of new and more intricate collaborative efforts such as the General Dynamics-Mitsubishi FSX and the BAe-DASA-Aeritalia-Casa European Fighter Aircraft (EFA) programs should provide instructive lessons for structuring future projects.

The importance of how the governmental defense establishments in North America, Western Europe and Japan evaluate the ultimate costs and benefits of current efforts such as EFA and FSX cannot be overemphasized. The logic for transnational cooperation and the experience base in industry necessary for success are only likely to increase over time. But negative outcomes on high visibility ongoing programs could drive the only entities capable of funding future efforts to the conclusion that codevelopment is not worth the political, economic or military risks.

Equally relevant will be the fate of major U.S.-only collaborative programs such as the Navy's A-12 Avenger and the Air Force's Advanced Tactical Fighter. The January 1991 cancellation of the four-year A-12 codevelopment effort exemplifies the worst case outcome for industry of tackling a beyond-the-state-of-the-art program through the mechanism of a fixed price development contract. The combined technical and financial strengths of General Dynamics and McDonnell Douglas, America's two largest defense contractors, were not sufficient to overcome the obstacles inherent in such an ambitious undertaking. The lessons learned from the demise of the A-12 and their applicability for international cooperative programs are not yet fully understood. Clearly, however, teaming is not a financial panacea for defense companies undertaking high risk ventures. Nor does it appear that industrial base arguments in support of troubled cooperative programs are likely to carry the day with governmental customers faced with overwhelming demands for dwindling resources and domestic defense industries already in general decline.

CURRENT COOPERATIVE PROGRAMS

A review of General Dynamics' and McDonnell Douglas' current international programs provides a basis for determining the prerequisites for successful international cooperative ventures.

Both McDonnell Douglas (MDC) and General Dynamics (GD) have enjoyed considerable success in the international arena over the years. Charts 1 and 2 depict the range of business arrangements these companies have entered into around the world in conjunction with the sale of military aircraft.[11] As is readily apparent, few of these sales have been "off-the shelf." International cooperative agreements have played an integral role in the production of the F-4 Phantom, F-15 Eagle, the F/A-18 Hornet, the AV-8B Harrier II, the T-45 Goshawk, and the F-16 Fighting Falcon. More than 85 percent of all foreign purchasers of these systems are involved in some form of industrial participation as co-producers, suppliers or indirect offset partners. The success of these American products can be attributed not only to their design, performance and continual enhancements, but also to the innovative business arrangements that have been developed to meet customers requirements in a highly competitive marketplace.

How then does a transnational defense industrial cooperative program actually work? In order to answer this question I will review three cases: the Spanish purchase of 72 F/A-18 Hornets in 1983, the continuing development of the AV-8 Harrier by British Aerospace and McDonnell Douglas, and the European Participating Governments' purchase of 348 F-16 Falcons in 1975.

CHART 1—McDONNELL DOUGLAS BUSINESS ARRANGEMENTS

Aircraft Program	Customer Country	Direct Offset					Indirect Offset	Licensed Production	Cooperative Production Program	Cooperative Development
		Final Assembly	Component Manufacture	Sub Component Manufacture	Aircraft Engine Assembly	Aircraft Engine Component Manufacture				
F-15	Saudi Arabia									
	Israel		●	●		●	●			
	Japan	●	●	●	●	●		●		
F/A-18	Canada			●	●	●	●			
	Australia	●	●	●	●		●			
	Spain		●	●			●			
	Kuwait									
	Korea	●	●	●	●	●	●	●		
AV-8B	United Kingdom						●		●	●
	Spain						●			
AV-8B II PLUS	Italy/Spain/U.S.A.								●	●
T-45	United Kingdom								●	●

CHART 2—GENERAL DYNAMICS BUSINESS ARRANGEMENTS

Country	Direct Offset									Indirect Offset	Suppliers	Licensed Production	Cooperative Development
	Aircraft Assembly	Engine Assembly	Aircraft Components	Engine Modules	Aircraft Subcomponents	Avionics	Mechanical Subsystems	Alternate Mission Equipmnt	Support Equipment				
Belgium	●	●	●	●	●	●	●			●			
Denmark	●			●	●	●	●	●	●	●			
Netherlands			●	●	●	●	●			●			
Norway			●	●	●	●	●	●		●			
Israel						●	●	●		●			
Egypt			●								●		
Korea					●					●		●	
Pakistan											●		
Venezuela													
Turkey	●	●	●					●		●			
Greece			●							●			
Singapore					●					●			
Thailand					●								
Indonesia								●		●			
Bahrain										●			
Japan												●	●

SPANISH F/A-18 PROGRAM

Spain signed a contract with McDonnell Douglas to purchase 72 F/A-18 Hornets in 1983, a sale valued at $1.54 billion in 1981 dollars. In return, McDonnell Douglas proposed a package of industrial benefits designed to help Spain accommodate this expenditure. Included was an offset commitment equal to 100 percent of the contract value of the sale.

The offset program was divided into four parts. Direct offsets involved development of Spanish capabilities to maintain their fleet of Hornets, manufacture of some Hornet parts, and the transfer of technologies to Spain to aid in achievement of the first two goals. The second part provided other aerospace related opportunities to Spain, while the third addressed non-aerospace, but defense related activities. Finally, indirect offset projects were developed to boost Spanish exports and encourage new foreign investment in Spain. In direct support of the Hornet, Spain received new technology in composite bonding and aluminum honeycomb core carving, numerically controlled machining, ion vapor deposition (a patented MDC process), and hot titanium forming. All of these projects were carefully reviewed by the U.S. Government to ensure that sensitive technologies were protected.

Additionally, Spain received offset commitments from Hornet engine manufacturer General Electric, and Hughes, the radar supplier. Many other suppliers and subcontractors participated in the direct offset program, allowing Spanish co-production of many and various parts of the aircraft.

In order to develop the export of Spanish goods and stimulate foreign investment in Spanish companies, McDonnell Douglas included the services of its International Business Center (IBC) as part of its indirect offset offer. The IBC was created in St. Louis in 1980 and serves as McDonnell Aircraft Company's in-house offset implementation group. It is staffed with experienced professionals and concentrates in several areas: aerospace and electronics, export development, foreign investment work, commercial technology development and other diversified activities.

The total offset credit of the arrangement between Spain and McDonnell Douglas will eventually reach 100 percent of the original contract value. This does not, however, mean that MDC and its

CHART 3—SPANISH F/A-18 PROGRAM BUSINESS RELATIONSHIPS

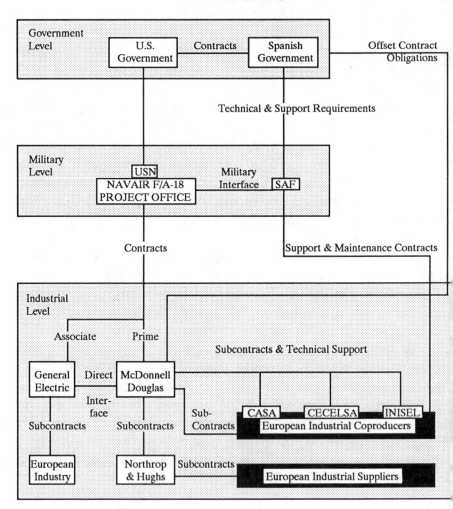

partners will necessarily spend a billion dollars to offset a billion dollars of aircraft sales. In some instances, offset credits can be accumulated on a leveraged basis. Most suppliers attempt to negotiate with the purchasing government multiple dollars of offset credit for projects that are of particular value to the purchaser, who ultimately "keeps score" of the dollars credited against the commitment. For example, MDC operates an internship program for Spanish engineers which returns multiple offset credit for each dollar actually spent on the program.

Chart 3 illustrates the contractual and offset relationships associated with the Spanish F/A-18 program. While MDC's contract for delivery and performance of the aircraft is with the U.S. Navy/U.S. Government (which in turn delivers the aircraft to the Spanish Government under Foreign Military Sales procedures), its offset commitments are directly with the Spanish Government. As the prime contractor, MDC is responsible for seeing that its major subcontractors--Northrop, Hughes, General Electric--place work with Spanish industry and meet their share of the total commitment.

Each quarter McDonnell Douglas and representatives of the Spanish Ministry of Defense meet to review the credit requests submitted by the MDC team and to ensure that key cumulative milestones are achieved. Over each of the seven years of implementation, MDC has exceeded its offset requirements. The MDC team believes that the successful results of the Spanish offset program will be a discriminating factor in future international competitions, as well as providing long-term, economically viable relationships with Spanish industry.

THE HARRIER PROGRAM

In 1975 McDonnell Douglas and the United States Marine Corps (USMC) began to develop an upgraded version of the BAe Hawker Siddeley AV-8A.[12] This improved aircraft was designated the

AV-8B Harrier II. A cooperative production program was then initiated between McDonnell Douglas and British Aerospace which would meet the aircraft requirements of both nations. MDC became the prime contractor for 323 Harrier II's to be supplied to the USMC, and BAe became prime contractor for the 96 advanced Harrier II's supplied to the Royal Air Force (RAF). MDC builds the Harrier II under license from BAe. To date, over 400 advanced Harrier IIs have been produced under this cooperative agreement.

In the case of the Harrier, a major American aerospace company was the recipient of advanced vertical take-off and landing technology generated overseas. The development of the Harrier II has permitted both MDC and BAe, as well as British engine producer Rolls Royce, to continually enhance their engineering and production capabilities. The result has been an improved aircraft for both the U.S. and British militaries as well as a vibrant production program for American and British industry.

The latest chapter in the Harrier story involves the creation of a complex, second-order international industrial relationship evolving from the original MDC-BAe arrangement. In the fall of 1990, the governments of the United States, Spain, and Italy signed a Memorandum of Understanding (MOU) which will launch a $165 million co-development effort to integrate the Hughes APG-65 radar into the Harrier II. This new version of the aircraft will be called the Harrier II Plus. Chart 4 shows the structure of the Harrier II Plus program. The three governments will establish a joint program office in Washington to administer the effort. McDonnell Aircraft Company will be the prime contractor for the airframe and will be responsible for creating acceptable work packages for Spanish and Italian industry as the program transitions to the production phase. The Joint Program Office will contract directly with Spanish and Italian "primes" on simulation, maintenance training, weapons integration and support equipment. This makes it unlike the traditional Foreign Military Sale (FMS) with a single prime contractor and associated offset agreements.

CHART 4—HARRIER II PLUS CODEVELOPMENT PROGRAM

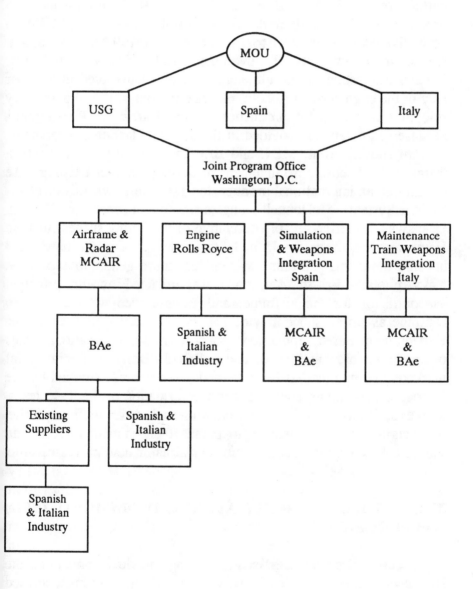

What is interesting is that the U.K., which initiated the original Harrier program more than 15 years ago, is not a development partner on the Harrier II Plus. The U.K.-U.S. arrangement to produce the Harrier II in the mid-1970s has now evolved into a derivative cooperative industrial program in the 1990s encompassing two entirely new sets of government and industry participants. Equally interesting is that although BAe is not involved in a major way in the engineering effort to integrate the radar, it will play a key role in the subsequent production of the Harrier II Plus aircraft because of guarantees provided in the original Harrier arrangement.

On another front, MDC and BAe have recently entered into a teaming and licensing arrangement to develop another existing BAe design into an international product--the T-45 Goshawk Advanced Jet Trainer System. McDonnell Douglas secured an order for 300 T-45 Goshawks, a carrier-suitable derivative of the highly successful BAe Hawk aircraft, from the United States Navy. The Goshawk will become the primary training system for future generations of U.S. Navy pilots. British Aerospace was retained as the principal subcontractor for the airframe, and Rolls Royce was selected to continue as prime subcontractor for the engine. Again, as in the Harrier cooperative production program, future international sales opportunities are anticipated, and a BAe-McDonnell Aircraft joint marketing committee has been formed. The success enjoyed by the Harrier program was a vital link in the formation of the T-45 team. Two experienced companies familiar with each other, their respective products and markets, teamed to pursue their mutual interests and succeeded in winning a competition for a major new program.

THE EUROPEAN PARTICIPATING GOVERNMENTS (EPG) F-16 PROGRAM

Specific circumstances existed during the development of the EPG program that provided for its success. Several nations identified a clear requirement for a new fighter aircraft. At the same time, there was also a push for standardization within NATO that provided an incentive for a common aircraft among these air forces. In addition, the United States expressed an interest in a low-cost fighter as a complement to the F-15 and intended to purchase it in significant numbers. Thus, a definite requirement for a minimum number of aircraft was established among several nations that was sufficient to support a major co-production program.

Shortly after the U.S. Government selected the F-16 as the USAF's lightweight fighter aircraft in 1975, the European Participating Governments (EPG)—Belgium, Denmark, the Netherlands, and Norway—reached a consensus to purchase the new American fighter. The four EPG countries signed a Memorandum of Understanding (MOU) with the U.S. Government in June 1975 that outlined the conditions of sale as well as an extensive F-16 co-production program to be implemented in the four EPG countries and in the United States. In addition to the benefits of enhanced national security and NATO interoperability, the EPG countries have seen a return of approximately $7 billion (then-year dollars) to their respective economies since the program began. This agreement was a conceptual and political breakthrough in international cooperation in the defense arena and established perhaps the largest guaranteed business base to date for a modern aircraft program.

The principal conditions of this landmark cooperative venture, as outlined in the MOU, are as follows:

- The USAF would purchase a total of 650 F-16s, and the European governments would buy a total of 348 (these numbers exclude follow-on buys).

- The European countries would have access to F-16 advanced technology, with some exceptions.

· Three assembly lines would be in operation—General
  Dynamics Fort Worth in the USA, Fokker in the
  Netherlands, and SABCA and SONACA in Belgium. All
  three lines would use parts and subassemblies produced in
  the United States and Europe.

· European industry would participate in the manufacture of
  the aircraft in the following percentage of value:
  - 10 percent of all F-16s bought by the USAF
  - 40 percent of all F-16s for the European Air Forces
  - 15 percent of all F-16s sold to non-consortium countries

· The consortium established a mechanism to fix the exchange
  rates of the participants' currencies at the rates prevailing in
  October 1974. European and U.S. contractors would not
  realize gains or bear losses due to currency exchange
  fluctuations. The European governments provided all the
  currencies required for their 348-aircraft program.
  European companies were paid in their national currency.
  The United States provided American currency for the
  650-aircraft USAF program.

The contractual arrangements for the 998-aircraft program placed
significant responsibility upon General Dynamics and its Brussels
program office. Basically, the EPG countries contracted with the
United States Government to buy an initial quantity of 348 aircraft.
The U.S.Government added this total to its own requirement for 650
aircraft, and placed a prime contract with General Dynamics for a
grand total of 998 fighters. The ultimate responsibility for the
delivery of aircraft fell to General Dynamics. General Dynamics
shared the production responsibilities by placing production contracts
with firms in Europe and the United States. European governments
did not place a single contract with participating companies, and the
United States Government contracted only with General Dynamics.

One of the major challenges of the EPG co-production program was to coordinate the production parts and subassemblies from both sides of the Atlantic and supply them to three separate production lines with strict adherence to quality and delivery schedules. The

CHART 5—EPG PROGRAM BUSINESS RELATIONSHIPS

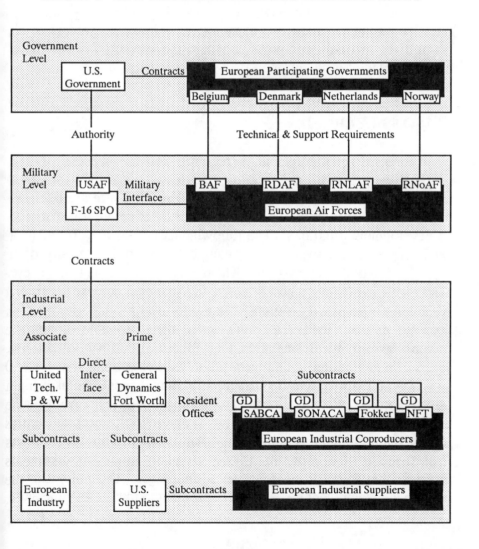

approach of General Dynamics Fort Worth Division was to establish contracts with U.S. suppliers, which in turn issued contracts to component suppliers and manufacturers in Europe. Chart 5 depicts the business relationships established for the EPG program. The size of the 998-aircraft program was sufficient to warrant the risks the contractors accepted to meet quality, cost, and delivery schedule requirements. The continuation of the F-16 program has permitted the EPG countries to purchase additional F-16s and retain production lines, employment, and R&D capabilities. Almost 50 percent of all major F-16 airframe components except the forward fuselage have been manufactured in Europe.

LESSONS LEARNED

There are certain elements required for the success of any cooperative program, and heeding the lessons learned from past experiences such as those that have been described here are likely to be critical in determining the success or failure of future transnational co-development programs. The following assertions are offered as a candidate checklist by which to gauge the potential viability of a proposed international program. The message is a simple one: There is no magic to creating a cost effective transnational defense program. Although no proposed program is likely to meet all the criteria, if it does not measure up against some set of the reasonable economic, military and political standards that follow, it probably will not succeed in generating a long term production program.

1. At the outset, ensure that the program is identified as a high priority project among all the participating countries. Above all, there must be a consensus that the program will meet a clearly recognizable military requirement. An imbalance in the relative importance of the program among member nations is likely to threaten the stability of long term funding. Technological or industrial development goals may be sufficient to initiate an endeavor,

but they are unlikely to sustain it into the production phase unless the system is attractive to the multiple military customers.

2. Limit the number of participants. While it is impossible to set an ideal number of participants, be aware of the likelihood of increasing organizational complexity and costs associated with rising membership. The fact that there were five governments in the EPG project was mitigated by the fact that there was only one prime contractor responsible for managing the entire program.

3. Look for programs that are likely to generate and sustain support from among various internal political constituencies in their respective countries. The political clout of a strong supporter or group can be a significant factor in determining a program's future, but it is not a hedge against the vagaries of political life. Broad bipartisan support is the best guarantee for program longevity.

4. Obtain a commitment from the participating countries for a minimum purchase sufficient to achieve "critical mass," defined as a number that permits the non-recurring development costs to be allocated while maintaining a total per unit cost that is politically and economically affordable. Defense products resulting from cooperative programs, in particular, are going to be viable only to the extent to which they are produced in economic quantities.

5. Provide sufficient industrial incentives to overcome political obstacles. Cooperation by itself is not enough reason to either enter into or continue involvement in a program. Each industrial participant needs to expect to gain substantial future sales and earnings from its involvement.

6. Be aware of potential corporate conflicts of interest among program participants, and sort-out how to handle possible future problems at the outset. International cooperation has become so extensive that the potential for conflicts exists even for companies within the same country. As the number and complexity of defense consortia grow, so do the chances that teammates on one project may be rivals on another. Lack of trust is likely to destroy any prospects for success.

7. Understand the potential impact of the technology transfer issues on the ultimate marketability of the product. Participants with unduly restrictive export policies can negatively impact sales potential even in cooperative ventures, and it does no one any good to develop a system that cannot be sold in sufficient quantities to warrant the investment in time and money.

The incentives for future defense cooperation continue to grow. And those limited number of projects that meet the tests of equitable technology and work share for the industrial partners, and strong and continued military and political support on the part of the governments, are likely to produce new systems in quantities that can meet future military requirements. American firms are anxious to build on past successes and enter into new relationships that support the mutual interests of the transnational partners. The central issues that need to be addressed in the immediate future are whether sufficient demand for advanced systems will exist to launch many of these long term projects, and whether the highly classified technologies imbedded in new systems will preclude meaningful co-development with potential foreign partners. Even more creativity and reciprocity is likely to be required to meet these challenges in the future than has been demonstrated in the past efforts of American defense companies and their international partners. Above all, governmental defense establishments in the major nations will have to decide that the benefits of transnational cooperation outweigh the potential programmatic and technological risks. Without their active and continuing support, even the most imaginative and cost effective initiatives from industry are unlikely to result in successful international defense programs.

NOTES

1. Among the obvious exceptions is the work of Raymond Vernon and his associates over the past two decades. See, for example, Raymond Vernon, ed., *The Technological Factor in International Trade* (New York: Bureau of Economic

Research, 1970), and Jacques S. Gansler, *The Defense Industry* (Cambridge, Mass.: MIT Press, 1980).

2. See, for example, the 1987 report of the National Academy of Sciences panel, *Balancing the National Interest: U.S. National Security Export Controls and Global Economic Competition* (Washington, D.C.: National Academy Press, 1987); the 1989 Office of Technology Assessment report, *Holding the Edge: Maintaining the Defense Technology Base*, OTA-ISC-420 (Washington, D.C.: Government Printing Office, April 1989); and former Commerce official Clyde Prestowitz's book, *Trading Places* (New York: Basic Books, Inc. 1988).

3. Ethan B. Kapstein, *Corporate Alliances and Military Alliances: The Political Economy of NATO Arms Collaboration* (Cambridge, Mass.: Olin Institute for Strategic Studies, November 1989).

4. For example see Theodore H. Moran, "The Globalization of America's Defense Industries. What is the threat? How can it be managed?" Unpublished paper, September 1989; and Andrew Moravcsik, *1992 and the Future of the European Armaments Industry* (Cambridge, Mass.: Olin Institute for Strategic Studies, September 1989).

5. Keith Hartley, *NATO Arms Co-Operation: A Study in Economics and Politics* (London: Allen & Unwin, 1983).

6. For an excellent overview of this entire subject, see Grant T. Hammond, *Countertrade, Offsets and Barter in International Political Economy* (New York: St. Martin's Press, 1990).

7. In particular: The European Participating Government's F-16 program, Canada (F/A-18), Australia (F/A-18), Turkey (F-16), Greece (F-16), Saudi Arabia (Tornado), Korea (on-going), Switzerland (on-going), Japan (General Dynamic's FSX).

8. The annual reports produced by the Office of Management and Budget provide a convenient summary of U.S. Government policy, dating back to then Under Secretary of Defense Duncan's 1978 "hands-off" memorandum concerning defense offsets. See, for example, Office of Management and Budget, *Impact of Offsets in Defense-Related Exports: A Summary of the First Three Annual Reports*, (Washington, D.C.: OMB, December 1987).

9. Considerable portions of this and subsequent sections are based on an earlier paper; see Robert H. Trice, *International Cooperation in Military Aircraft Programs*, Olin Institute for Strategic Studies, November 1989.

10. See Casey Wardynski, *European Multinational Development of Combat Aircraft and the Prospects for a Competitive European Arms Market*, Olin Institute for Strategic Studies, April 1990.

11. These charts are accurate as of mid-1990. However, they should be considered illustrative rather than definitive because these industrial relationships are constantly evolving.

12. For more details see Bill Yenne's book, *McDonnell Douglas: A Tale of Two Giants* (Greenwich, Conn.: Bison Books, 1985), pp. 241-3.

6
Managing International Cooperative Projects: Rx for Success

C. Michael Farr

Lieutenant Colonel Mike Farr is an Associate Professor at the Air Force Institute of Technology in Dayton, Ohio. He is a graduate of the U.S. Air Force Academy and holds a Ph.D. in Operations Management from the University of North Carolina at Chapel Hill. He has been associated with the defense acquisition community since 1980.

Speaking to *Defense News* in October 1988, Deputy Undersecretary of Defense Robert McCormack stated that:

. . . the need for international cooperation is driven by economics as well as the strengthening of the relationship with the allies. It is sort of a two-track road there. And the more people look at the economics of it, the more apparent it is that we need cooperation.[1]

Since then, the world has changed dramatically with the advent of glasnost, the reunification of Germany, progress toward an integrated European market (EC 92), and cuts in defense spending. One thing that has not changed, however, is the continuing debate over the contentious issues that divide those who support armaments cooperation from those who do not.

International programs present unique opportunities for the U.S. in light of today's skyrocketing weapons costs and increasingly capable allies. From a corporate perspective, this view was best illustrated by a Boeing executive who described going it alone on major aerospace projects as literally a "bet the company" proposition.[2] On the other hand, international ventures also present risks related to the potential loss of domestically developed technology, further aggravation of trade imbalances, increased foreign competition, and the decline of an already fragile U.S. industrial base.

As the heated controversy over the Japanese "FSX" fighter program[3] aptly demonstrated, the debate over international programs is very much alive, and is often centered around interrelated political, military, economic, and technological issues.[4] While government policy will continue to evolve, and the relative merits of any specific cooperative opportunity may always be debated, it is nonetheless a reality that U.S. involvement in these types of projects has grown over 3,000 percent since World War II, and the majority of that growth has occurred since 1976.[5] Further, with the expected downsizing of defense markets and the increasingly transnational nature of technology, many experts are predicting that the logic for continued arms collaboration is more compelling than ever before.[6]

These realities provide the motivation for this chapter. Put simply, there is an urgent need to improve the management of international armaments projects. Previous research has demonstrated mixed success in managing international military projects. Many international programs have failed for a variety of reasons while others have succeeded despite similar obstacles, suggesting that improved management is both necessary and possible.

THE STUDY

This chapter summarizes the results of two major studies on the management of international cooperative projects.[7] Focusing on successful project management, three research objectives were examined using a comprehensive literature review, a review of project records, and through approximately 140 personal interviews. The following fourteen international military projects were analyzed through extensive case analysis. Six of the projects were rated as fully successful while eight were rated as less than successful. The project distribution included three from the Air Force, five each from the Army and Navy, and one project that requested anonymity.

FIGURE 1

FULLY SUCCESSFUL PROJECTS	LESS THAN FULLY SUCCESSFUL PROJECTS
F-16: Fighter Aircraft	ROLAND: Missile Defense Against Low Level Air Attack
NATO AWACS: Airborne Warning and Control System	M1E1: Competition to Sell Main Battle Tank to the Swiss
MLRS: Multiple Launch Rocket System (Launcher & 12 Rockets Per System)	ISRAELI HYDROFOIL: Hydrofoil Patrol Boat
NATO SEASPARROW: Defense Against Anti-Ship Missiles	NATO SEA GNAT: Decoy Against Radio/Heat Seek Anti-Ship Missiles
MLRS/TGW: Terminal Guided Weapon (Smart Warhead) for MLRS	APGM 155: 155 Millimeter Smart Munition
NATO AAWS: Anti-Air Warfare System (Anti-Ship Missile for Frigates)	RAM: Rolling Airframe Missile (Low-Flying Anti-Ship Missile Defense)
	MSOW: Stand-off Missile
	PROJECT X: Requested Anonymity

MEASURING SUCCESS

Formal Criteria

To provide any meaningful analysis of management principles, a first order of business is to set forth criteria for judging project management and execution. Both studies used six formal criteria for judging the projects. The first three criteria, well known to those familiar with project management, included cost, schedule, and technical performance. The fourth criterion, familiar to those with experience in armaments cooperation, was fulfillment of offset[8] commitments.

These first four criteria were evaluated in two ways. First, each interview respondent provided a measure of *perceived* success by rating a program against these criteria using a numerical rating scale of 1 to 5. This scale placed each program on a continuum ranging from unsuccessful to fully successful. Second, objective measures of the actual performance (e.g. extent of cost overrun, months of project delay, mission capable rate of the weapon system, percentage of any offset commitments that were actually achieved, etc.) were recorded to the extent possible. The fifth criterion noted whether any of the partner countries withdrew from the project because of dissatisfaction with some aspect of its management. Similarly, the sixth criterion noted whether the project was terminated prematurely because of problems among the participants.

Informal Criteria

The mere existence of problems or adversity does not necessarily signal an unsuccessful program. In fact, it would be difficult to name any armaments program, domestic or international, that has not faced serious obstacles. The 1990 interviews with our European allies[9] further supported this position when they essentially concluded that few programs are "completely successful or completely unsuccessful." Therefore, two additional "informal" measures of success were used to judge the projects in the more recently completed study.

The first was armed services' satisfaction with the results, which may in fact be the eventual measure of success for any program. If a real need is being met, if the user is happy with the product, and if a reasonable value for the money is perceived, then a project will probably be considered successful even though it may have suffered considerable problems along the way. For projects still in development, an indicator of this type of support would be the user community defending the project if its need (i.e. continuation of the project) is questioned during budget reductions.

The second informal measure was described as partner consensus, which relates to the somewhat vague but important concept of whether the governments involved *believe* the project is a success. For example, while the cost and technology of the Tornado fighter aircraft may not compare favorably with front line U.S. fighters, European governments in that program consider it a success. Reasons include the fact that it was completed as a European-managed project and that sales have been made outside the countries that built it. This criterion postulates that, like beauty, success often lies in the eyes of the beholder.

Internal versus External Determinants of Success
The studies reported here focused on internal management and organizational structures that may have important influences on project success. The aim was to help future managers improve their chances for a successful project. The research found that certain management practices do indeed make a difference in the success of a project. However, while the research found that poor internal management will result in an unsuccessful project, it also found that good internal management does *not* conversely guarantee a successful result.

For example, one of the projects examined in the study was highly touted as a premier example of a successful project by the U.S. Army. When the program was examined, the organization and internal management of the project were (as advertised) excellent. Yet, within 6 months after the study, the project was terminated. The reasons for failure of the project were related to external factors over which the project manager had little or no control.

Therefore, the research concluded that projects can fail in one of two basic ways: poor internal project management or through the overriding influence of external factors. Examples of such external factors include politically motivated decisions (by the Administration, Congress, or DOD) to withdraw from a project; unplanned budget reductions imposed by Congress or DOD; and a variety of problems within the military hierarchy (e.g. pursuing multiple programs for the same requirement with limited funds, and information "disconnects" such as terminating an international project because a high level decision maker did not realize that international commitments were at stake).

Figures 2 and 3 summarize the measures of success used in this study and the basic ways that a project can fail.

FIGURE 2

CRITERIA FOR MEASURING SUCCESS

Formal Measures

1. Cost Performance

2. Schedule Performance

3. Technical Performance

4. Achievement of Offset Goals

5. Withdrawal of Dissatisfied Partners

6. Termination of Program (for negative reasons)

Informal Measures

1. Client/User Satisfaction

2. Partner Consensus

FIGURE 3

TWO BASIC TYPES OF PROJECT FAILURE

1. Inadequate Internal Project Management, e.g.
   - Low Project Management Authority
   - Failure to Harmonize Requirements/Goals
   - Excessive Focus on National Interests versus Project Success

2. External Factors, e.g.
   - Politically Motivated Decisions
   - Externally Imposed, Unplanned Funding Cuts
   - DOD Hierarchy (Multiple Programs, Same Requirements)

Conclusion: Good Internal Management Does Not Guarantee Success!!!

RESEARCH FINDINGS

The findings of this study are reported as they relate to the three research objectives mentioned earlier. Also, while many of the interviews in the U.S. and overseas were with members of defense industry, the studies focused on the role of government program management offices.[10]

Research Objective #1: Program Initiation

The first objective sought to determine whether certain actions early in a project might affect project success in a significant way. International managers were asked whether there were factors that either created barriers or facilitated a successful start. Four of the most important experiences are recounted on the following page.

(1) The requirements and goals at the outset of several programs were characterized as "loose" and "not really harmonized". At the highest levels, participating countries thought they had a good match, i.e. common requirements based on agreed perceptions of the threat. Later in these programs, and on closer examination, countries found differing perceptions of the threat which in turn prompted differing operational doctrines and technical approaches to counter the threat. Examples of the resulting disagreements included disputes over the intended targets, range of the weapons, size and weight of the weapons, methods of delivery, and whether the missions were offensive or defensive in nature. Choices of this sort drive a program toward specific technical solutions that can have profound effects on the cost of the system and the schedule for fielding it. Some readers may be tempted to conclude that these disagreements sound rather innocuous, however, requirements disputes of this type were cited as the primary reason for the failure of several programs.

(2) Also, serious problems resulted whenever program management offices were not jointly manned and managed. Programs that failed to locate international managers in a single office experienced the following problems: poor communications, inability to develop a team spirit, lower commitment to the project, slow decision making, diverging goals, cultural barriers, and adversarial attitudes (the proverbial "us and them" mentality).

(3) The process of negotiating the Memorandum of Understanding (MOU), which serves as the cornerstone of any international project, was mentioned as critical in several respects. First, problems were experienced when the program manager (PM) was not involved in the MOU process. The presence of the PM during negotiations is likely to sharpen the focus on whether the agreements being made are realistic, and decreases the likelihood of politically motivated promises that cannot be fulfilled once the management task actually begins. The PM also ensures that adequate attention will be paid to the technical and managerial aspects of the project, in contrast with the more political, financial, and legal perspectives that may dominate the thinking of other team members.

Also, concern was voiced by both American and European participants in arms collaboration projects that U.S. managers are often not trained or experienced at MOU negotiation, and are at a disadvantage when faced with the professional cadres typically found in other countries. Compounding this problem is the duration of the process, sometimes taking one or two years for completion. U.S. negotiating teams are much more likely to suffer personnel rotations, leaving the team with not only an inexperienced negotiator but also one that lacks continuity and corporate memory on the project in question.

Finally, several programs experienced problems because the MOU was left vague on important issues. For example, one MOU indicated that "workshare would be 'equitable' with cost share", but did not describe what "equitable" meant or how this goal would be achieved. There is a strong temptation at the outset of an international project to put tough issues aside for resolution at a later time, or to adopt general approaches that leave interpretation to each participant. These practices may create the illusion that goals and requirements have been harmonized when in reality they have not.

(4) Managers universally stated the need for strong, symmetrical project commitment, a real need for the product, and clear support from the armed service that will receive the weapon (recall that one of the informal measures of success was user satisfaction). All eight of the less successful projects experienced varying degrees of difficulty with this concept. Some PMs encountered outright opposition to or a distinct lack of interest in their project. Others experienced divided user support, e.g. one Army program faced "politics between the gun guys and the missile guys."

Project managers quickly feel the impact of ambivalent or unclear commitment when important program needs (funding, personnel, decision making, etc.) begin to receive inadequate attention. Strong commitment and clear user support are vital whenever the success of a project is challenged by difficult problems.

Research Objective #2: Management Principles
The second research objective examined management characteristics and organizational structures in a search for factors that may systematically influence the success of international projects. Eight such management principles were found to have significant

influences on project success. In general, these principles deal with organizational and management structure, mechanisms for resolving conflict, and coping with externally imposed influences on the program. The following sections summarize the most important findings with one exception. The overriding importance of harmonizing goals is omitted, as it is discussed among other findings.

THE ROLE OF PROJECT STEERING COMMITTEES

All six successful projects were governed by effective steering committees while only two of the eight unsuccessful projects had effective committees. A steering committee is a high-level, executive group that functions much like a corporate board of directors. An effective committee provides vital benefits such as (1) a clear source of policy guidance, (2) an accessible forum for resolution of conflicts and difficult issues that cannot be settled at the working level, (3) a buffer from political and administrative interference, and (4) a mentor or advocate that represents the program within the national hierarchies whenever important issues arise or important decisions are needed.

There are several important operating guidelines for effective steering committees: (1) The committee must be vested with real decision authority (and be willing to exercise it) and be able to provide timely decisions whenever difficult issues arise, (2) The committee must meet often enough (a minimum of 2-3 times per year and emergency sessions, if needed) to remain effective in their knowledge of the program and in their ability to function as a group, (3) All participating nations must be represented so that all decisions reflect the agreement and consensus of the entire group, and (4) The steering committee should remain in its "top level, strategic" role and not be tempted to meddle in the daily management of the program.

PROGRAM MANAGER AUTHORITY

All six successful programs employed internationally staffed teams located in a single office and led by a single manager with overall program authority. The benefits of such an arrangement were described earlier and will not be repeated here. Five of the less successful programs experienced difficulties with their management structure. Three programs failed to locate team members in a single office. In one case (the Roland Missile), what began as a transfer of European technology to the U.S. for licensed production slowly diverged into full scale modification of the European design, with over 49,000 engineering change proposals. The presumed savings in development time and costs disintegrated, and unit costs escalated to three times the original estimate.

Further, a recent trend in organizational structures has raised some concerns for successful and unsuccessful programs alike. Many programs are now establishing both an International Program Office (IPO) and national program offices. The IPO is supposed to manage the contractual work performed by industry while the national offices are supposed to handle the interface with the national hierarchies, including funding issues. In practice, the national program managers have sometimes given directions to the contractors without going through the IPO. If these organizational structures are to work successfully, mechanisms must be found to prevent multiple sources of contractual direction to the contractors.

EQUITABLE PARTNERSHIPS: KEEPING BENEFITS IN PROPORTION TO CONTRIBUTIONS

The more successful programs in this study had partnerships characterized by cooperation rather than dominance. Team members on these programs exhibited a win-win attitude that was described by several respondents in various ways, "Everyone should be equally happy or unhappy with the results" and "No partner should prosper at the expense of another." A major goal of such arrangements is to keep the benefits accruing to each partner roughly symmetrical with their contributions to the project.

Predominant areas of concern are cost share, work share, technology transfer, access to third country sales, and equitability. The MOU must address these issues so that each partner has accurate expectations about what they will put into the project and what they will get back. The trick is to prevent the perception by any partner that their contributions have been exploited. Most experienced international managers agree that this task is easier among partners with similar industrial, economic, and technological capabilities. However, other partnerships can and do work successfully as long as the "quid pro quo" arrangements remain in some agreed balance.

Most unsuccessful programs experienced problems with this management concept. On one program, the U.S. unilaterally withdrew the right of the partners to cooperatively produce the system even though the partners had shared in funding the development program and we had agreed in the MOU to permit cooperative production. European participants further indicated that the true status of the development program, which ran five years behind schedule and four times the original cost estimate, was concealed by the U.S. program manager. Two of the five partners withdrew from the project, placing financial strain on the remaining countries.

On the Roland Missile program, the U.S. decision to "Americanize" the European design led to dramatically increased costs, political controversy, and finally to U.S. withdrawal from the project. The Europeans lost licensing fees on units not produced, and also felt the U.S. pull-out hampered export sales opportunities by damaging world opinion of the system. The Europeans were also suspicious that the U.S. intended to exploit their technology by marketing a similar system under a new name.

THE VALUE OF PREVIOUS EXPERIENCE

This study examined the effects of experience on project success. Three specific dimensions of experience were investigated: the extent to which key managers had previous management and/or technical experience, how much experience industry had with the relevant technologies, and whether the partners had previous international experience.

Consistent with previous results, the findings revealed that management experience and sound business skills are absolutely vital for a project manager. For a PM, technical experience is desirable but can be acquired from other sources if necessary. The presence or absence of appropriate management skills and experience was a clear and consistent discriminator between successful and less than successful projects. Further, managers unanimously reported that experience must be complemented with education and training programs.

One unsuccessful program appointed a PM with no management experience, no management training, and no international experience on a part-time basis. His lack of general business skills greatly hampered the program, which deteriorated into a "technical playhouse" with serious cost and schedule overruns.

Low management experience at the outset of a joint U.S.-Israel hydrofoil patrol boat program was cited as *the* key reason for the cost and schedule problems that plagued the remainder of the project. A contract was structured that would have been appropriate only if design, development, and test of a prototype had already occurred. As it was, the delivered systems were also essentially the development prototypes. To attempt to meet contract terms, the contractor was forced to design and build at the same time. Further, Israeli industry had less experience with important manufacturing technologies than was initially assumed. This inexperience complicated the technology transfer, causing it to take longer and cost more than originally planned.

THE ALLIES' PERSPECTIVE

Although this study has focused on the American perspective on international arms collaboration, equally important are those of our alliance partners. This section presents the results of focused interviews with officials from Canada, France, Germany, The Netherlands, Spain, and the United Kingdom.

Embassy Interview Results

As to what makes cooperative projects successful, embassy respondents reiterated the importance of agreement on the threat, common requirements, jointly managed program offices, and commitment ("the will to cooperate from both sides"). They also noted the need for experienced program managers who possess management and business skills. They felt it is vital for PMs to understand political, cultural, economic, and business decision processes; and that, for a program manager, management skills are more important than technical knowledge. Though many studies support this notion, and while U.S. managers also agreed with this view; the U.S. Air Force has consciously removed people with non-technical degrees from the program management career field.

As to barriers to cooperation with the United States, two frustrations were uniquely reported by the embassies. The first was concern over what was described as the "wild card" influence of the U.S. legal community. In Europe, there are far fewer attorneys involved in the process and their opinions are generally treated as advice for the program manager who then makes a decision. In the U.S., legal opinions are frequently perceived as binding on the program manager; this apparent veto power frustrates our allied partners (as well as many U.S. program managers) during the negotiation process.

The other barrier to cooperation was described as the international capabilities of U.S. team members. It will come as no surprise that U.S. team members generally possess relatively poor language skills. While not considered a fatal problem, this fact certainly places U.S. managers at a disadvantage, sometimes clouds understanding of important issues, and hampers the development of personal relationships which are important to successful business dealings with many Europeans.

Next, Europeans were described as having a long history of reliance on exports and the economic necessity for cooperation. The U.S. has largely been more self-reliant and, in the European view, is comparatively inflexible about compromising on requirements. Therefore, it was suggested that many U.S. team members need to develop what was called "cultural awareness," which includes knowing how and when to compromise to satisfy collective needs, and how to "think like the other guy."

Finally, lack of knowledge about the acquisition and decision processes of partner countries was believed to hamper the ability of U.S. managers to negotiate and compromise effectively in the international arena. Interestingly, U.S. managers almost unanimously reported this topic as an area in which increased education and training would produce a large payoff for DOD.

European Interview Results

Interviews conducted in Europe posed questions in five major areas: critical success factors, partner selection, program initiation, judging success, and the future of international cooperation. This section highlights the findings with regard to critical success factors and the future of international cooperation. The most frequently mentioned factors that European respondents considered crucial for successful international programs are enumerated below.

(1) Making it unanimous, the European interviews indicated overwhelming concern over the need for common, harmonized requirements. While seemingly redundant with previous findings, the European observations on this subject are reported for two reasons. First, the clear consensus throughout every aspect of the research provides evidence that the relationship of harmonized requirements to project success is overriding and vital.

Second, the Europeans offered several important refinements to the notion of harmonizing requirements. They noted two barriers to the harmonization process. The worldwide missions typically undertaken by the U.S. often dictate more diverse performance requirements than are necessary for scenarios limited to only the European theater. Hence, harmonization with the U.S. is often more difficult than within European-only projects. Also, multilateral programs with a large number of partners face a greater "multiplicity of requirements" that may prove difficult to resolve.

Further, harmonization must occur on at least two levels: the high level goals of each country (e.g. technology, jobs, sharing of costs, etc.) and the operational performance requirements of the system. Harmonization at level two (operational requirements) must occur early, must involve the users, and must occur before the acquisition process "gets too far along."

Finally, a harmonized requirement is *not* a sum or aggregation of each country's requirements. Several projects made this mistake. At best, this practice raises the cost of the program. But worse, and more likely, this practice exposes the program to subsequent requirements disputes that may kill it.

(2) A preference was expressed that the U.S. participate in perhaps fewer, but more selectively chosen programs. Europeans would prefer that the U.S. carefully select projects that enjoy a high priority within the user, acquisition, and political communities; and are therefore backed by a genuine commitment. Numerous unsuccessful projects were cited in which the requirement did not exist, the requirement had a low priority in the parent service, or competing systems addressed the same or similar requirement.

While Europeans acknowledged their withdrawal from certain projects, they indicated the U.S. is much more likely to pursue multiple programs aimed at the same requirement. Predictably, it is not possible for all of these projects to lead to production. Conversely, European countries simply cannot afford multiple development programs that do not lead to production—one respondent aptly expressed the sentiments of most Europeans when he said, "don't begin if you don't intend to finish." For this reason, most Europeans unambiguously feel that cancellation of a program is tantamount to failure.

A problem with the implementation of so called "Nunn Amendment" programs has also hampered U.S. commitment to the continuation of several international projects. The intent of the Nunn Amendment has been explained as follows:

> The Nunn-Roth-Warner amendment to the Fiscal Year 1986 Defense Authorization Bill gave a political and economic push to codevelopment projects. It authorized the expenditure of up to $200 million per year in joint research and development projects with our allies and an additional $50 million per year for cooperative tests of European weapon systems to encourage the procurement of off-the-shelf foreign systems.[11]

DOD has imposed an additional stipulation that "Nunn money" fund only the first two years of an international project; then the sponsoring service must use its own funds to continue the project. The military services and our allies welcomed this initiative as a "step in the right direction".

However, pressure to obligate the expenditure of the money within the time allowed coupled with the absence of an equivalent pot of money in Europe has sometimes tempted the services to "force low priority programs into cooperation just because we have the money." Two years later, when the sponsoring service must spend its own funds to continue these relatively low priority projects, the inevitable result has been U.S. withdrawal.

(3) The European interviews also revealed the need for a clearly defined international hierarchy with a high level advocate within the U.S. Department of Defense. This concern had several dimensions. Corroborating the opinion of many in the U.S., Europeans felt that organizationally "the international process in the U.S. has been without leadership." With many burning issues vying for their attention, international programs have suffered a rather low priority under current and recent Under Secretaries of Defense for Acquisition. Europeans and U.S. representatives overseas have complained that "no one with enough horsepower" in Washington D.C. is listening to the needs of international programs.

Further, there are "many players" or organizations with various responsibilities and roles to play in the international arena. Unfortunately, this process is "not organized at the top" nor is it directed by a high level advocate with appropriate authority. The process was described as being driven more by individual personalities and attitudes than by institutionalized procedures or conscious strategies. This situation has contributed to the existence of "too many low level detractors of international programs" that can say no to a program, and are rarely challenged to justify or support their position.

The concept of advocacy has been further explored by the U.S. Mission to NATO in their analysis of lessons learned for successful international programs.[12] They noted that international advocates may come from the military services, Office of the Secretary of

Defense (OSD), Congress, or Industry. They observed that individual international programs and armaments collaboration in general cannot survive without appropriate advocacy. Their analysis revealed the following about advocacy for individual programs.

DOD programs have the best chance for success when both the Service and OSD favor the project. Service proposed programs usually gain OSD approval and advocacy. Conversely, OSD initiated programs do not always gain Service approval and, if this conflict is ignored, these projects usually result in failure.

(4) Export sales are considered an economic necessity by most of our Western European allies. Therefore, another stumbling block for armaments cooperation is the U.S. penchant for imposing restrictions on "third country" sales. French respondents acknowledged the legitimacy of U.S. concerns about national security and whether unfriendly countries may receive Western technology. However, they feel that decisions about third country sales constraints must be made earlier in the program. In some cases, last minute vetoes of proposed sales may be economically tantamount to terminating the project for European countries. Further, several longstanding allies perceived that U.S. policy does not always distinguish friend from foe, as they occasionally feel they have been treated with the same suspicion accorded our enemies.

Finally, Europeans noted the need to distinguish truly sensitive, classified technology from that which, although it may be state of the art, is already available on the world market. To do otherwise penalizes weapons programs as well as the companies that lose export opportunities. In a related fashion, the military services need a clearing house for technology release decisions. In the past, the U.S. Army has withheld technology that had already been released by the Air Force.

Technology transfer restrictions by the U.S. were considered understandable ten years ago. However, the increasing globalization of industry and technology have dramatically changed the world.[13] Albeit a formidable task, the challenge for the U.S. is to develop a strategy that balances the downside risk of technology loss with the opportunities for export sales and access to foreign state of the art technology.

(5) A complicated bureaucracy and overly complex procedures make cooperation with the U.S. more difficult than within Europe. Several respondents noted that over the years the European Economic Community has agreed on rules for bidding, awarding contracts, taxation, and other business principles. There are no equivalent agreements with the United States. An Italian respondent cited onerous government procedures such as the requirement for review of any contract over $25,000. As he said, "you can't even buy an automobile for that much."

Europeans believe there are far too many agencies with a voice in U.S. international programs, and each has a potential veto. Compared to the role of the Parliaments in Europe, the U.S. Congress is also considered too influential in arms procurement decision-making.[14] This situation makes what the Europeans describe as "political override" more likely when dealing with the United States. Finally, a particularly aggravating aspect of bureaucracy is the legal disclaimer that the U.S. includes in all of its international agreements. The Memorandum of Understanding (MOU) is viewed by many Europeans as having the force of a treaty. The U.S. reserves the right to disavow its commitments under the MOU if it is later determined that the agreement violates U.S. law.

The Future

Each European respondent was asked to comment on future prospects for armaments cooperation. The most important themes are described below.

(1) As in the U.S., European countries were anticipating the effects of reduced defense budgets. They expect no "new start" programs for approximately three to five years, and foresaw more modification and mid-life upgrade programs instead. While reduced budgets will undoubtedly spur some near term flirtation with protectionism and "national entrenchment," there was a unanimous consensus that the long term logic for cooperation will be more compelling than ever before. Many experts already considered complete self-sufficiency in defense equipment an unaffordable proposition.[15] Certainly within Europe, successful cooperative programs are expected to become ever more an economic necessity.

Several respondents commented that there will be a need for international sized rather than national sized markets.

(2) Each European country was in the process of reassessing security threats and the future role of its military forces. In general, Europeans foresaw less emphasis on East-West conflict and more concern for potential North-South conflicts such as the Middle East, Africa, and terrorist threats from countries such as Libya. Less emphasis on offensive weapons and more on defensive weapons is also expected.

Increased emphasis on non-traditional roles such as rescue, drug interdiction, anti-terrorism, dealing with illegal immigrants (a growing problem in Italy), and disaster relief were contemplated. Also, a number of new opportunities were described: the opening of Eastern Europe, a pressing need to deal with environmental concerns in Europe, reforestation, and technologies needed for verification of arms agreements.

(3) A high priority among the more industrialized countries in Europe is to compete more equally with the United States. Consequently, Europeans will increasingly investigate the possibility of "Europe-only" alliances on new projects. Certainly the impetus of the European Community 1992 initiative as well as commitments under the auspices of organizations such as the Independent European Program Group clearly illustrate this goal.

There are other important influences on the European inclination to search for Europe-only partnerships. One reason has already been mentioned. Cooperation within Europe is easier in many respects. Problems stemming from geographical separation and cultural differences are greatly reduced. Further, solutions for many of the "bureaucracy" problems have been devised *within* Europe but not with the United States. Finally, achieving "complementarity" (the ability to contribute equally to the project) is easier with European firms of more nearly equal size than with larger U.S. companies. Several European respondents referred to this concept as the "comfort factor."

(4) Having acknowledged the previous concept, it is also important to note that there will be opposing forces at work. Representatives from every European country also indicated that U.S.

involvement in armaments projects will still be desired for several reasons. One such reason is U.S. quality and technological competence in defense systems. Of overriding concern to Germany, technological competence is also of vital importance to other European countries as well. The sheer size of the U.S. defense market is also significant, and Europeans realize they cannot afford to ignore it. Finally, longstanding U.S. experience with specific technologies and with large scale integration of complex systems is a strength desired by any project team.

(5) In his 1990 book, John Naisbitt asserted, "As we turn to the next century, we will witness the linkup of North America, Europe, and Japan to form a golden triangle of free trade."[16] Echoing the sentiments of other noted experts, Peter Drucker has further stated that U.S. companies that fail to think globally in the 1990s will simply not survive. The European interviews agreed heartily with these assertions, unanimously predicting the continuing globalization of industry.

An experienced government official in Italy commented, "The market makes the reality more than the paper." His remark aptly represented European opinion that industry is already leading the way toward global interdependence through alliances, mergers, and consortia that will compete for armaments business around the world. The European respondents felt that industry is best suited to make international cooperation work successfully because governments are often unable to act quickly enough and become hamstrung by political debate.

(6) Consistent with many other sources, Europeans expect major growth in the Pacific Rim by the year 2000.[17] With the increasing importance of economic power relative to military might, many Pacific Rim countries are expected to ascend, with some of the fastest growing economies found in Singapore, Malaysia, South Korea, Thailand, and China. As mentioned earlier, the Pacific Rim will join North America and Europe as the most important markets in the world. Forward thinking companies are beginning to position themselves to take advantage of all three of these "golden markets."

CONCLUSIONS

International cooperation on armaments projects is likely to continue for a variety of reasons, yet these projects pose an exceptionally difficult management challenge. However, the two studies summarized in this chapter suggest that there are proven methods for increasing the probability of success. First, it is imperative to harmonize requirements and to develop user support at the very beginning of a project. Second, careful attention to the management structure and organization of the project plays a paramount role in assuring eventual project success. While some of the management tenets may seem simple or "just common sense," hard-won experience has demonstrated that their effective implementation is not a matter that should be left to chance. Third, though our allies obviously have their own "agendas" (as does the U.S.), we must examine their perceptions and experiences carefully if we are truly committed to successful international *cooperation*. Finally, this research has shown that good internal project management is necessary for project success; all of the successful projects also had good management structures while only one of the less successful projects had a good management structure. However, the bad news is that good internal management does not *guarantee* a successful result. It is sometimes possible for external factors to overcome the best efforts of any program manager.

NOTES

1.   Robert McCormack.   "Interview with Robert McCormack, Deputy Undersecretary for Industrial and International Programs," *Defense News* 31 (October 1988).

2.   Personal interview at Boeing Aerospace, Seattle.

3.   See Thomas P. Griffin for a concise summary of the FSX history and debate, and C. Michael Farr, "The FSX Debate: Implications for Future U.S. International Armaments Programs," *Program Manager, Journal of the Defense Systems Management College*, July-August 1989.

4. For an excellent and comprehensive review of these issues, see Thomas P. Griffin, "The Debate Over International Armament Programs: Integrating Current Knowledge and the FSX Case," Master's Thesis, Air Force Institute of Technology, Dayton, Ohio, September, 1989.

5. C. Michael Farr, "An Investigation of Issues Related to Success or Failure in the Management of International Cooperative Projects," Ph.D. diss., University of North Carolina, Chapel Hill, 1985.

6. Ambassador William H. Taft, U.S. Permanent Representative on the North Atlantic Council, "Toward Defense Industrial Cooperation in NATO," Alliance Paper No. 23, U.S. Mission to NATO, Brussels, Belgium, 1990. This view was also supported in over 30 personal interviews with European government and industry experts on international collaboration (conducted by the author in six European countries during May-September 1990).

7. Farr, "An Investigation of Issues Related to Success or Failure in the Management of International Cooperative Projects."

8. Offsets are a means of compensating country "X" for its purchase of arms from country "Y." Offsets are sometimes imposed as a condition of sale when country "X" demands that a certain percentage of the development or production work on a weapons project be placed within their economy (known as a direct offset). Indirect offsets, which provide benefits to country "X" that are not directly related to a specific weapons project, may also be used.

9. These interviews were conducted during May, June, and September of 1990 by Farr and Kwatnoski as part of the research for the Advanced International Management Workshop.

10. See the chapters by Joel Johnson and Robert Trice for additional industry perspectives.

11. William G. McCarroll, "The Future of Cooperative Programs," *The DISAM Journal of International Security Assistance Management* (Fall 1990), p. 82.

12. The U.S. Mission to NATO, Armaments Cooperation Division, reviewed a sample of international projects, conducted a survey of government and industry representatives, and reviewed historical documents looking for important influences

on the success of international projects. The findings were compiled by Major John Compton (USAF) and Captain Karl Krumbholz (USN).

13.   ICAF/Harvard Conference, May 2-3, 1990.   A common theme was the profound impact that "globalization" will have on political, military, and economic decision making in the 1990s.   One speaker specifically noted the inevitable and irreversible diffusion of technology around the world.

14.   Also see Chartrand et al., "International Defense Cooperation Agreements," *Program Manager Magazine*, September/October 1990.

15.   Though supported by others as well, Professor Raymond Vernon of Harvard University argued that the notion of self-sufficiency, though deep-rooted, is increasingly improbable.   ICAF/Harvard Conference, op. May 2-3,1990.

16.   John Naisbitt and Patricia Aburdene, *Megatrends 2000: Ten New Directions for the 1990s* (New York: William Morrow and Company, Inc., 1990), p. 23.

17.   Austin and Knight Kiplinger, *America in the Global '90s*, is one such source on expectations within the Pacific Rim (Washington, D.C.: Kiplinger Books, 1989).

7
The Role of Offsets in Arms Collaboration

Grant T. Hammond

Grant T. Hammond is Professor of International Relations at the Air War College, the senior service school of the U.S. Air Force. He has studied countertrade and offsets for some time and written *Countertrade, Offsets and Barter in International Political Economy* (New York: St. Martin's Press, 1990; London: Pinter Publishers, 1990) and an earlier article "Offsets, Arms and Innovations," *The Washington Quarterly* 10 (Winter 1987), pp. 175-183. Some of the material presented here appeared in these works as well. The views expressed here are those of the author and do not represent the policy of the U.S. Government, the U.S. Air Force or the Air War College.

When weaponry is sold overseas, it is often with the use of a business practice called "offsets." Offsets are compensatory, reciprocal trade agreements arranged as a condition of the export sale of military materiel and support services. They are, in effect, countertrade in the defense sector. Countertrade is defined as any purchase arrangement which is not conducted solely on a cash basis.[1]

The purpose of offset agreements is to compensate the buyer for acquiring a foreign good or service. As such it seeks to "offset" the attendant costs. At their best, offsets are a collaborative endeavor between purchaser and seller for mutual advantage. At their worst, they are an added cost of doing business forced on the seller in order to make the sale. More positively, offsets can be characterized as a marketing tool to compete for foreign defense sales.[2] The term and practice are so ensconced in the aerospace/defense sector that it has become a separate form of countertrade. This is particularly true for sales of fighter aircraft, on which this essay will concentrate.

There are two principal kinds of offsets. *Direct offsets* refer to benefits that are linked to the product being purchased. They require compensation in related goods and usually involve some form of coproduction, licensing, or joint venture agreement. When a government purchases advanced fighters, for example, it may seek as part of the offset package the guarantee of producing a certain percentage of the planes or their components "in country." *Indirect offsets* involve goods and services unrelated to the defense materiel being sold. An aircraft producer may commit to increasing business by stimulating tourism, increasing foreign investment, purchasing raw materials, or marketing a diverse set of products such as marble, olive oil or clothing as a part of an aircraft sale.[3]

In selling the goods to the buyer, the seller incurs an offset obligation to generate a certain value of the transaction, for the purchaser. The idea is that the agreement will help replace the foreign exchange for the transaction, or increase investments, coproduction, or technology transfer over the life of the agreement. This "offsets" some or all of the cost of making the initial purchase. Military offsets normally range from 25% to 130% of the original purchase contract and are generally negotiated through side agreements. Offsets can be implemented in a number of ways. Among these are such arrangements as:

Coproduction: This is an agreement for a foreign government or producer to acquire the technical information required to produce a certain product or component. Such arrangements are generally government-to-government agreements but can be between a government and a private manufacturer. There are numerous variations usually involving joint ventures of some kind.

Counterpurchase: This is an agreement whereby the initial exporter buys or undertakes to find a buyer for a specified amount or value of unrelated goods from the initial importer within a certain time. Where the arrangement involves goods only, it is often referred to as parallel barter. Such transactions often involve cash plus products under separate contracts for each good or service and each hard currency involved in the transaction.

Overseas Investment: Investment resulting from a countertrade or offset agreement usually involves a subsidiary or joint venture arrangement, although output from an independent manufacturer may be used in lieu of cash dividends in computing compensation. Increasingly common, it is a way for the purchasing party to increase investment, create jobs, and stimulate the domestic economy even when making foreign purchases.

Technology Transfer: This refers to the transfer of technology mandated as a part of a countertrade or offset agreement other than coproduction or licensed production. It may be in the form of R & D, technical assistance and training, or patent agreements between manufacturers. In some countries, such as South Korea, it is mandated as a part of defense offsets.

While not the entire range of implementing mechanisms for offsets, these are the major ones. A combination of direct and indirect offsets are used most transactions. The attractiveness of the offset package is often the primary reason for the purchaser's selection of one weapons system or supplier over another. Indeed, when the Greeks decided to purchase F-16s from General Dynamics and negotiated the contracts, it was the Greek Minister of Industry, not the Defense Minister, who represented the Greek government.[4]

ORIGINS

A specialized form of countertrade and a variation on barter, the term "offset" is relatively new, but the practice is not. Argentina in the 1890s and Germany in the 1930s had used barter and countertrade to cope with economic difficulties and a lack of hard currency. What had started to gain favor in times of economic hardship came to have advantages in the rebuilding of the international economy after the war and in confronting the Soviet military threat in Western Europe.

The investments in plant, equipment, personnel, facilities and technologies required to revive indigenous European industries were enormous. Among the industries developed were indigenous defense companies. But these eventually could not sustain themselves on domestic sales only. Export sales were required. Once begun, the effort to gain market share in the international arms market meant that each sale, foreign and domestic, was crucial to one's competitiveness. Few countries could afford the luxury of a solely national defense industrial base. Only the superpowers could practice autarky.

Although national purchases are critical, international sales are increasingly important. They do several things: they increase market share, keep design and production teams together and working, lower unit costs for the product, encourage upgrades and modifications, and most importantly, position the defense contractor for the next large order. Increasingly, they represent a larger portion of corporate profits for defense contractors. The small size and infrequent purchases of their national governments meant European arms manufacturers could not exist without exports.

Initially, many companies were reluctant to pursue offsets, both direct and indirect. But in an increasingly competitive international arms market, the demand for offsets became critical, and eventually, routine. Internal costs and complications increased dramatically when working on the legal and financial arrangements involved in joint venture, coproduction and licensing schemes. The political wrangling involving the governments of both the United States and its NATO allies seemed interminable at times. The time lag between initial contacts and actual production was measured in years. In the sale of General Dynamics F-16 fighters to the European Participating Governments (EPG)—Norway, Denmark, Belgium and the Netherlands—the negotiations spanned nearly eight years. To defense contractors in the U.S., the spread of offsets among First World allies was a necessary evil to get the contracts. To see the practice spread to Third World nations was something they would have preferred to avoid.

Originally, when offsets started in the defense industry, they were at the 10% to 30% level. That is, the amount of offset sought by the purchaser amounted to 10% to 30% of the value of the contract. The first of such deals in the defense sector occurred in the late 1950s. The practice increased dramatically in the 1960s for a variety of reasons. Among these were:

> ...the desire of arms buyers to create a national defense industrial base, acquire modern technology and management techniques, and solve balance of payments problems. It was also clearly in the interest of the United States because it bolstered the defenses of both ourselves and our allies, improved our allies' industrial capability and strengthened their economies.[5]

The practice spread and demands made by purchasers escalated rapidly until the offset percentage was 100% routinely. Indeed, the first offset of over 100% occurred in 1982 with a sale made by McDonnell-Douglas/Northrop for F-18s purchased by Canada. The offset demand was 130%. How high the offset percentage can go, particularly in a market that is increasingly saturated with advanced weapons systems and in which financial difficulties are still extreme, remains to be seen.

DOMESTIC EMPLOYMENT AND THE DEFENSE INDUSTRIAL BASE

Despite the underlying logic, offsets have become subject to intense controversy, particularly in the United States. One of the biggest criticisms levelled at offsets is that in licensing coproduction, transferring technology and entering into joint venture agreements overseas, we are sapping our own industrial might and preeminence in the most vital area of national security.   Many argue that the erosion of our defense industrial base that occurs in purchasing foreign sourced goods is sounding the death-knell of American status as an economic and military superpower.

There are several aspects to this critique.   Perhaps the most important issue concerns whether offsets reduce employment in the U.S.?   How much, if at all, do they reduce employment in both prime contractors or sub-tier producers?   These and other questions are addressed in a U.S. government study mandated by section 309 of the Defense Production Act of 1984, published in April of 1990.[6] Before assessing the specific impact on employment, the nature of offsets in the U.S. —numbers, impact, size, frequency, etc.—is in order.   Among other things, this study assesses the role of offsets in the U.S. economy from 1980 through 1987.   The general picture it paints is as follows.

The information is based on a survey of 52 of the top 100 defense contractors on all offset agreements of more than $500,000 based on export sales contracts signed between January 1, 1980 and December 31, 1987.   Of the 336 offset sales studied, involving 30 countries in $35 billion worth of sales, 97% were required by the purchaser.   1983 had the highest offset volume ($8.7 billion) and 1986 the lowest ($2.2 billion). The total offset obligation of all sales studied averaged 57% of the value of the sales and ranged from 5% to 175%.   Six countries (Canada Spain, the UK, Turkey, Israel and Australia) along with the European producers of the F-16 accounted for 72% of the dollar value of the offset obligations.   Spain, Sweden and the UK had offset requirements of more than 100%. 53% of the offset agreements were indirect and 47% were direct with the implementation time ranging from 6 to 21 years with an average of 11 years.[7]

In winning foreign offset sales, a U.S. producer may apply component and subcontractor work to the offset obligation by contracting for them to be supplied abroad. In doing so, American sub-tier producers lose contracts and jobs. Some argue that this is eroding the defense industrial base and hurting the American economy. Others suggest that while jobs are lost to offsets in some sectors they are added in others and there is actually a net gain in jobs produced.[8] The conclusion of the latest Office of Management and Budget (OMB) study in this regard is as follows:

> In general, this analysis shows that offsets have little effect, if any, on overall U.S. employment. Furthermore, theoretic considerations suggest that the economic inefficiencies introduced by offsets have little to do with their adverse effect on overall U.S. employment. This does not mean that specific contractors or subcontractors may not suffer declines in domestic employment from offsets, but that these declines are likely to be offset, in some instances more than offset, by employment gains in other sectors of the U.S. economy.[9]

The relatively minor impact suggests that fears of wholesale unemployment in certain sectors caused by offsets are overstated, though unemployment may well result from specific offset agreements and the use of foreign sources to satisfy offset obligations abroad.

TECHNOLOGY TRANSFER AND FUTURE CONSEQUENCE

Technology transfer and the possibility of creating new competitors is another major concern of those who criticize offset agreements. The fear was summarized by an official at Raytheon who said:

> Offsets are turning the world upside down: They are selling the products. Genial offsets are over. There will be no

more quietly arranged country-to-country memoranda of understanding as in the heyday of RSI—now it is all out war. The weapon they use is offsets. We have shot ourselves in the foot and have created a Frankenstein. We are creating our future competitors for a quick buck today.[10]

Currently, there are a host of coproduction arrangements being implemented for major weapons systems among First World countries and their allies. Japan coproduces the F-15 Eagle and the AIM-9L Sidewinder missile. The F-18 Hornet is coproduced by Australia, Canada and Spain. The Raytheon Patriot air defense system is coproduced or licensed with Japan, West Germany and the Netherlands. South Korea will soon coproduce F-18s. F-16s are now produced in Denmark, Norway, the Netherlands, Belgium, Israel, Greece, Turkey, and Indonesia, all under offset arrangements. It would appear that offsets and coproduction of aerospace/defense goods are facts of life in the international political economy.

But whether offsets are sowing "dragons teeth" that will cause irreparable harm later is difficult to determine for a variety of reasons. First, technology is not some single source of knowledge and power, a modern day version of the Holy Grail. It is a general term for highly complex bodies of knowledge, research capabilities, educational programs, industrial know-how, marketing expertise, financial methods, and opportunities and the like that are often sectorally unique. We must specify before going too far down this road. Second, there is a huge difference in the pace of development among technologies and the "half-lives" of particular breakthroughs in an increasingly dynamic environment. What is currently competitive may not be "state of the art," let alone "cutting edge." A great deal of technology may be transferred to many nations without direct military or economic threat occurring as a consequence. This is particularly true in a world driven by specialization and cooperation as well as competition and market dominance. What is terribly significant for one country is far less so for another. Finally, a significant amount of what a number of other countries seek to find out is readily available through education and scientific publishing on the one hand, and industrial espionage and reverse engineering on the other. The greatest security "problem," if it can be called that, has always been the proliferation of knowledge that might threaten those in control of the status quo. We are not likely to change that—even if we wanted to.

OFFSET DEALS

In order to get a better understanding of these abstract arguments, a few specific examples are instructive. Three different offset agreements are described below.

The F-16

One of the largest sales that enshrined the practice of offsets in the defense industry was a consortium purchase of 348 F-16s announced in a Memorandum of Understanding (MOU) in June 1975 between European purchasers and the U.S. Government. This involved the so-called European Participating Governments (EPG) program created for the adoption of the General Dynamics F-16 "Fighting Falcon" for NATO.[11] It contained a very complicated set of coproduction arrangements. But the arms selection process began long before offsets emerged as a major component of the deal. Although the selection of the F-16 for European NATO occurred in 1974-1975, the program did not really get underway until 1981. The demand for offsets, however, did not occur until 1982. This provides a good example of an "obscelescing bargain"; once the F-16 deal was struck, the EPG found they had significant unexplained market power.

The U.S. and a good many other governments, particularly NATO ones, have at least indirectly supported direct offsets, especially certain co-production arrangements.   They enhance standardization within the NATO alliance, reduce redundant R & D costs and improve national security and alliance cohesion. Thus in the government-orchestrated package, the EPG buy of the F-16 allowed NATO member countries (Norway, Denmark, Belgium and the Netherlands) to coproduce 10% of the value of the initial U.S. aircraft buy, 15% of the value of all third country buys, and 40% of the value of all EPG buys. The U.S. government portion was a buy of 650 planes for the U.S. Air Force.

The EPG have realized a return of nearly $7 billion in 1975 dollars as a result of this multilateral offset agreement. General Dynamics, Fokker in the Netherlands and SABACA and SONACA in Belgium all had production lines for the project. As Robert Trice points out in his chapter, this deal involved complex side agreements on currency rates, payments in national currencies, and a mammoth coordination of the production and delivery of parts and sub-assemblies. It is the largest multi-nation, multi-corporation offset scheme ever implemented involving not only coproduction but a wide array of indirect offsets as well. European suppliers, such as DAF, have created new businesses, in this case landing gear manufacture, and now compete for other jobs throughout the world.

Peace Shield

Despite having a mono-export structure based on oil and considerable export receipts, Saudi Arabia has turned to offsets, particularly on big ticket military purchases, as oil revenues have fallen from their previous highs. As long as the oil market remained soft and budget deficits grew, countertrade policies continued to increase, despite a traditional policy of opposing countertrade in crude oil and derivatives. Saudi Arabia has countertraded oil for jet aircraft with Boeing in the U.S., for jet engines with Rolls-Royce in the UK, and for its "Peace Shield" air defense system with a General

Electric-led consortium in the U.S., the UK and West Germany. The total dollar value of these three transactions is over $7 billion.[12]

The latter project above, the "Peace Shield," is a complex and forward-looking offset deal. It was originally a $4 billion project for a ground-to-AWACS electronic communications system.[13] A Boeing-led consortium won the reduced $1.3 billion agreement in competition with ones led by Litton and Hughes Aircraft. It requires 35% offset and began in 1985 for a ten year period. Originally, there was no mention of offsets in the bids. Now Saudi Arabia has a permanent Economic Offset Committee which is pursuing non-military countertrade as well. What is important about this agreement is the degree to which the Saudi Arabian government has tried to utilize offsets as part of a national development strategy to supply technology, materiel and expertise it did not have and that it deemed important to its future growth and needs both in regional and national terms.

Saudi Arabia sought energy-intensive and capital-intensive high technology ventures. Boeing had several advantages over its competitors, having good relations in the country as a result of the preceding AWACS sale, a friendship of sorts with the King, and a willingness to accept oil as payment for ten 747s sold to Saudi Arabia in mid-1984. Hence, it had a demonstrated commitment to countertrade with Saudi Arabia.

There are nine separate joint ventures, carefully selected to provide Saudi Arabia with capabilities it does not now have. These include a helicopter production firm, an aircraft maintenance facility, an applied technology center, a power engineering venture, a telecommunications center, a bio-technology research lab, computer systems and services capability, an advanced electronics center, and a medical products manufacturing facility. These are all high technology initiatives in important and growing areas of research, development, or manufacturing. The aircraft service center will ultimately be a regional facility. The combination will help advance the Saudi capabilities across a range of products and services that are all increasingly important to it and the Gulf Cooperation Council states. This combination of new initiatives goes a long way to providing technology, facilities and training to diversify the Saudi economy.

The FSX Deal
The most recent and controversial offset deal involving the Japanese and Americans is the debate over the FSX (Fighter Support Experimental), a new generation fighter to be jointly built by General Dynamics of the U.S., the Japanese government, and Mitsubishi Heavy Industries for the Japanese Self Defence Forces. Signed in November, 1988, the deal would provide 35% to 40% of $1.3 billion of work for developing the prototype, a new follow-on version of the F-16. The Japanese government would buy as many as 170 fighters in the mid-1990s. Just who builds them will be negotiated in 1993. The deal has been the subject of intense political controversy and a debate about the economic costs and benefits since it was first discussed some time ago.[14]

The Americans, for their part, are divided about the deal and how to proceed. One group sees the deal as sounding the death knell of one of the last areas in which the Americans still have unquestioned technological superiority compared to Japan—aircraft manufacture. This group sees the agreement as a giveaway of American technology (which they value at $7.5 billion) for the small participation in the joint development of the plane and the jobs at General Dynamics involved in its manufacture. This group maintains that if the Japanese want a new fighter, they should buy F-16s "off the shelf" for far less money and not complicate things with a joint development strategy.

Another group maintains that the technology to be transferred by the Americans is essentially a decade old. They would get nowhere near the sophisticated technology involved in the Grumman X-29, the Lockheed Stealth fighter (the F-19) or even the General Dynamics own hoped for next generation fighter, the ATF. Meanwhile,

Americans would get access to Japanese technology in miniaturized phased array radars and Fuji Industries' composite materials technology. They see the agreement of the Japanese for technology flow-back to the U.S. as critical and ushering in a new era of cooperation between the two nations. This may well include advanced industrial ceramics, a field in which the Japanese are superior. More to the point for this group is that in the joint arrangement the Japanese do not demonstrate—yet—the capacity to build state of the art jet fighters and thus compete directly with the Americans in the defense sector. But it may be only a matter of time before they do compete in the aerospace/defense sector as well as in commercial aviation.

CONCLUSION: OFFSETS AS A POLICY DILEMMA

For most of the postwar period, the U.S. government had adopted a "laizzer-faire" attitude toward offsets. But the Bush Administration has intervened to focus some attention on the use of offsets and to try to limit the practice. The U.S. government intervened directly in the Korean Fighter Program (KFP) negotiations between General Dynamics, McDonnell-Douglas and the Republic of Korea in the summer of 1989, seeking to hold the level of offsets to no more than 30% or about $1 billion on the transaction. Both Secretary of Defense Cheney and Secretary of Commerce Mossbacher discussed the issue with Korean officials. President Bush established a National Security Council Ad Hoc Working Group on Military Offsets consisting of representatives from the Departments of State, Defense, Labor, Commerce and Treasury as well as FEMA, ACDA, USTR, CEA, OMB and the NSC Staff in August of 1989. That group completed its initial investigation and recommendations in March of 1990. On April 16, 1990, the President announced that he viewed offsets as inefficient and market distorting and stated that: "No agency of the U.S. Government shall encourage, enter directly into, or commit U.S. firms to any offset arrangement..." Further, it is the President's intention to undertake discussions with foreign nations "with a view to limiting the adverse effects of offsets in defense procurement."[15]

Whether or not the U.S. is successful in limiting the use of offsets in defense sales remains to be seen. The policy is in keeping with the stated views of the IMF, the GATT and other governments, most especially, the U.K.[16] On the other hand, U.S. companies have continued to engage in offsets in pursuit of foreign arms sales, and the practice shows little sign of diminishing relative to the total amount of defense sales activity going on at the moment. Despite rather clear preferences, it is doubtful if the United States can abolish the practice on its own or seriously curtail it without having an undesirable and politically as well as economically damaging impact on U.S. export sales. An international agreement would be more effective but seems even less feasible given similar self-interests. The use of offsets is not the preferred means of doing business, but it is a virtual requirement for doing business in aerospace defense, despite the fears and efforts of many in the U.S. and elsewhere to make it otherwise.

NOTES

1. Hesham El Abd and Michael Kenny O'Sullivan, "Encountering Countertrade," *Journal of Defense and Diplomacy* 2 (June 1984), p. 23.

2. In some quarters, especially in Canada, the term "offset" has been supplanted by the phrase "industrial benefits" (IBs), a more positive euphemism for the conditions of the sale. See K. Barry Marvel, "The Evolving World of International Offset Contracting," *Military Technology* (October 1989), p. 44.

3. Among some of the better sources of information on just how offsets work and the variations on a theme are Gilbert Nockles and Alan Spence, *Offset, 1990s: Securing Competitive Advantage and Economic Development* (London: Financial Times Business Information, Ltd., 1987); and William Weida, *Paying for Weapons:*

Politics and Economics of Countertrade and Offsets (New York: Frost and Sullivan, 1986).

4. Interview with General Dynamics executives, St; Louis, Mo., May, 1986.

5. James R. Blaker, Deputy Assistant Secretary of Defense, *Policy Analysis, Statement on "The Impact of Offsets,"* before the Subcommittee on Economic Stabilization of the House Committee on Banking, Finance and Urban Affairs, 24 July, 1985.

6. Office of Management and Budget, *Offsets in Military Exports* (Washington, D.C.: Government Printing Office, April 16, 1990). Despite the date on the report, it was not submitted to Congress until July 16, 1990.

7. Ibid., pp. 34-38 plus tables 1 through 10.

8. *Impact of Offsets in Defense Related Exports*, Executive Office of the President, Office of Management and Budget, Washington, D.C., 1985. This report is mandated annually by Section 309 of the Defense Production Act Amendments of 1984, and is supposedly prepared annually in December by OMB, but usually appears in March or later.

9. OMB, *Offsets in Military Exports*, p. 44.

10. Cited in John van der Puil and Jan G. van der Puil, "Countertrade: Fad or Economic Evolution?" *Countertrade and Barter Quarterly* (Summer 1986), p. 33.

11. For a comprehensive treatment of the so-called "deal of the century," the EPG buy of the F-16, see Ingemar Dorfer, *Arms Deal: The Selling of the F-16*, (New York: Praeger, 1983).

12. For information on these deals, see, among others, Leo G. B. Welt, "The Offsetting Factor," *Defense and Foreign Affairs* (December 1985), p. 18.

13. On the Peace Shield, see Richard G. O'Lone, "Boeing, Saudi Arabia Tie Defense System to Economic Package," *Aviation Week and Space Technology* 3 (June 1985), pp. 155-158 and Nockles and Spence, *Offsets, 1990s: Securing Competitive Advantage*, pp. 70-75.

14. Of the many articles on the FSX and its attendant costs and consequences, economic, technological and military, is Richard F. Grimmett, "Japanese FSX Fighter Controversy," Washington, D.C.: The Library of Congress, Congressional Research Service, June 20, 1990.

15. Ibid.

16. See Grant T. Hammond, *Countertrade, Offsets, and Barter in International Political Economy*, (New York: St. Martin's Press, 1990), Ch. 4.

8
Technology Transfer Policy
and Export Control Practice

Stanley Sienkiewicz

Stanley Sienkiewicz is a Commerce Department Official. This chapter, however, reflects only his own views and not those of the U.S. Government or any Agency thereof.

The words "technology transfer" bring to mind at least two separate sets of policies which the United States has pursued simultaneously since World War II. On the one hand, "technology transfer" can refer to policies aimed at encouraging the transfer of technologies in pursuit of economic development or western security. On the other hand, these words can also refer to policies aimed at controlling or preventing the transfer of some technologies to friends and adversaries alike.

The United States has pursued both approaches as instruments of national security policy over the past four decades. We have encouraged the transfer of some technologies to our allies in order to strengthen collective military capabilities, and we have sought to prevent the spread of some technologies to our adversaries in order to create or preserve technological advantages of military value. These policies have been pursued in support of the same broad security objectives, have been largely complementary over the years, and have generated consequences for defense industrial collaboration as it exists today and will evolve tomorrow. This chapter is intended to trace the evolution and interaction of these policies over the past 40 years, and to the degree possible, project how they might evolve in the foreseeable future.

THE EARLY POST-WAR INTERNATIONAL CONTEXT

It is not surprising that the enduring framework of U.S. security policy was shaped in response to the major geopolitical consequences of World War II. The adversary we faced after 1945 was both large and globally expansionist, necessitating a policy of containment and an array of political-military alliances.   That meant collaborating militarily with a large number of countries. Some, like Britain, Japan or Germany, were industrialized nations needing to rebuild from the War's devastation.   Others, in the Far and Near East and in Southern Europe, were largely underdeveloped.

For some years after the War, conditions obtained which made defense collaboration relatively easy. At the end of World War II, American armed forces stood at something like 12 million, and a commensurate equipment stockpile existed. As we demobilized, the vast majority of that equipment became surplus, and thus available for transfer to friends and allies cheap or for free. We had the equipment, our allies needed it, and we all agreed that the severity of the threat justified making it available. These conditions have been replicated to a lesser degree in the wake of the Korean and Vietnam Wars, although the recipient countries changed.[1]

At the same time as this policy of arms transfers was emerging, Washington and other Allied capitals were reaching the elements of a consensus on the other aspect of technology transfer policy, that is, on the control aspect. It soon became apparent to those governments that the Communist Bloc would maintain significantly larger armed forces, and thus the Western governments realized that they would have to rely upon other factors to compensate. One of these, of course, was a substantial technological-industrial advantage. A policy to collaborate with the allies on technology denial was deemed necessary for several reasons:

First, a collaboration was necessary simply because the United States could not count upon keeping a monopoly in militarily-important technologies. With Japan and NATO as partners, however, industrialized nations could ensure something like monopoly control over a wide-range of defense-related technologies. Thus was born the Coordinating Committee, or COCOM, in 1949,[2] consisting eventually of the members of NATO (minus Iceland), plus Japan, and most recently including Australia.

Second, a larger proportion of defense technologies were derived from military research and development and/or were predominantly military in their applications than is the case today. That made it politically easier to impose restrictions on exports than for technologies invented in the private sector and holding promise of profitable civilian markets. With changes in the relationship between military and civil technology, pressures for loosening the controls have been built up.[3]

Finally, the rates of technological change in the early days of COCOM were substantially slower than is the case today, making agreement on and maintenance of control lists a relatively easier task. Appropriate export control lists in some technologies are today almost impossible to maintain.

Thus, in most respects, the technology transfer policies—both aimed at cooperation and control—erected in the early Post-World War II period, were sensible, effective, and appropriate to the circumstances extant at the time. We were in a position to help arm our Allies efficiently and effectively as well as to erect an export control regime that has in retrospect been an effective and important instrument of U.S. national security policy for over 40 years.

Even as these policies were being put into place, however, circumstances were changing in directions which would test our abilities to adapt. These changes have continued and if anything accelerated, so as to challenge the fundamental premises upon which these policies have been based.

THE COLD WAR EVOLUTION OF POLICY AND PRACTICE: 1960-1980

As the industrialized countries rebuilt their economies from the devastation of the War, those which could shifted increasingly toward producing more of their defense equipment domestically. The reasons are as obvious as they are enduring. Nations have historically sought self-sufficiency with respect to national security. From an economic perspective, nations have generally sought to keep defense spending and the associated jobs at home. Furthermore, there are widely-held views to the effect that defense industries spin off civilian industrial benefits, though this is increasingly challenged.

One result of western rearmament has been the dispersion of defense production capability and as a corollary, the emergence of concerns about rationalization, standardization, and interoperability (RSI) within the NATO force structure. Such concerns in the 1970s, coupled with Congressional concerns about duplication and waste in the procurement of defense equipment, led to some increase in emphasis and even special funding to support defense-industrial collaboration with the allies. These developments also foreshadowed impending changes in the policies on technology cooperation and technology control.

Subsequently, still another fundamental trend has emerged in international defense industry which poses even greater difficulties with respect to the intersection of these two sets of policies, to which we will return below. That trend is not merely the global spread of defense industry, but also its global "integration," that is, the emergence of industrial division of labor and collaboration on a transnational basis.

With the spread of technology and technological prowess, it became steadily more difficult for COCOM alone to maintain effective controls. Eventually, this problem was recognized and measures were developed to cope with it. Most specifically, a diplomatic effort, labeled the Third Country Initiative, was begun during the Reagan Administration. Its purpose was to develop cooperative arrangements with countries outside COCOM which were developing the capacity to provide technologies which COCOM wished to continue to embargo. This effort was reasonably effective and produced COCOM-like agreements with a handful of emerging technologically-competent countries. The objective of this effort was formally recognized in the Export Administration Act when provisions were included making such cooperation the basis for more favorable export treatment of cooperating countries.[4]

A second important trend is that the military importance of technologies originating in the civilian/commercial sector and/or having substantial civilian/commercial applications has also grown apace. That makes export controls harder to impose because the sacrifice of profit from commercial activities resulting from export denials tends to be larger. Companies and those who represent them object more often and more strenuously. The pressures for a more narrowly construed set of export controls grows, and the ability to effectively control the military uses of technologies widely available in the civilian market is obviously questionable.

One need only briefly consider the wide and growing range of military applications for computers, coupled with the extent to which innovation in that industry is today generated by private investment for commercial ends, to realize how fundamentally intertwined are the commercial and military industrial sectors. Legitimate civilian applications pose an even greater difficulty in the area of "foreign policy controls" to which we will turn below.

Finally, technological change is certainly more rapid today than ever before and that fact poses steadily increasing difficulties for efforts to control the spread of selected technologies. Technological innovations emerge, are sold abroad and only then are military applications discovered. Proscribed technologies become outdated but continue to be proscribed. New techniques arise for fulfilling military needs, circumventing export controls upon some existing technology, and so on. The risk, then, is that in the face of rapid technological change we find ourselves controlling the export of technologies we shouldn't regulate and not regulating technologies which we should try to control.

THE CONTEMPORARY EXPORT CONTROL FRAMEWORK

It is in this kind of evolving world that our export control and technology collaboration policies have had to be designed and redesigned. We and our allies have on balance managed that process reasonably well. The export control framework that has evolved in the United States, in part as a result of these international arrangements, is complex and not always efficient in its operation. Its essential elements, however, are reasonably clear:

(1) The export of arms is not treated as a matter of commerce but as a matter of foreign policy. Hence, the responsibility for overseeing arms transfers is vested in the Secretary of State. With respect to our main adversaries of the Postwar period, the Soviet Union, other Warsaw Pact countries and Peoples Republic of China, commodities and technologies defined as arms have effectively been embargoed. This policy was modified for China during the Reagan Administration thaw, and will almost certainly change eventually for the Soviet Union and Eastern Europe. The legal basis for the controls is currently embodied in the Arms Export Control Act.

(2) The export of so-called "dual-use" commodities or technologies (items with both commercial and military applications) is regulated by the Commerce Department. The goal is to balance considerations of

"commerce" and the need for regulation. The legal basis for this control regime—the Export Administration Act—sets forth three criteria for such controls: national security, foreign policy, and short supply.

National Security controls are intended to implement the COCOM regime, that is, they are aimed at the so-called COCOM-proscribed destinations and are multilateral. It is worth noting that in this arena "national security controls" is a term of art somewhat different from the common sense meaning. It refers, here, only to technologies and commodities, controlled by COCOM for purposes of export to the Soviet Union, its former Warsaw Pact Allies and the Peoples Republic of China. Regulations controlling the export of commodities and technologies useful in the development or construction of nuclear-capable missiles to non-COCOM proscribed countries, for example, are, in this parlance, not national security, but foreign policy controls.

Foreign Policy controls are, as one might expect, normally established at the request of the State Department, and are usually unilateral, although they need not be. They include the implementation of legislation limiting trade with South Africa, for example, or export controls aimed at Libya and other countries designated as terrorist-supporting by the Secretary of State. They also include control regimes aimed at inhibiting the spread of specific military capabilities such as chemical and biological weapons or nuclear-capable missiles, as well as nuclear weapons-related commodities and technologies. Such controls are not considered "national security" controls because they are not normally directed at the COCOM-proscribed destinations. In fact, some foreign policy controls, such as those based upon nuclear non-proliferation grounds, or on controlling the spread of missile technology are directed at friendly or even allied countries. This fact sometimes poses significant political difficulties. Finally, the remaining criterion which the Commerce Department uses to regulate exports is *Short Supply*.[5] Briefly, this authority permits the government to impose export controls when it has been demonstrated that some commodity or technology is in sufficiently short supply in the United States that there is danger of an "excessive drain on scarce materials" or a "serious inflationary impact of foreign demand."

GEOPOLITICAL TRANSFORMATION

During the latter parts of the 1980s the United States saw still more dramatic changes in the economic and geopolitical under-pinnings of its technology transfer policies. The most dramatic changes, of course, are those which reflect or portend the fundamental realignment of friends and adversaries on the international stage. We have seen the dramatic decline if not disappearance of adversaries, the growth in economic competition with friends and allies, and the movement of countries from one political camp to the other.

The contraction of adversaries for export control purposes might be dated back some two decades to the Nixon-Kissinger rapprochement with the Peoples Republic of China. Those dramatic political steps led to more tangible export control policy results more than a decade later, as the Reagan Administration negotiated a significantly liberalized COCOM export control regime for the Peoples Republic of China. This process resulted in the raising of various technology thresholds for permitted exports across the list of COCOM-controlled technologies—the so-called "China Green Line." What was noteworthy in this exercise is that the "Green Line" was also extended across the munitions list, formalizing COCOM's decision to permit the export of some defense articles and services to the Peoples Republic. Before this action, the munitions list had effectively been an embargo list for countries proscribed by COCOM agreement. This could well be a prototype for how we deal with

Eastern European countries in the not too-distant future, and perhaps even with the Soviet Union itself, eventually.

The reaction to the Tienanmen Square massacre included a halt to the process of export control liberalization for the PRC, but barring more of the same on the part of the Chinese government, a rollback on export controls would continue to seem implausible. Over time, in fact, a return to a continued relaxation would appear to be more likely.

In the latter half of the 1980s fundamental changes began to manifest themselves in the Soviet bloc and various of its members including the Soviet Union itself. These changes culminated in events variously referred to as the Revolutions of 1989 and the end of the Cold War. The results included the disappearance of East Germany into a reunified democratic Germany, the clear emergence of democracies in Poland, Hungary and Czechoslovakia, and the substantial movement in similar directions in Romania and Bulgaria, clearly signifying the disappearance of the Warsaw Pact as a serious military organization and the removal of any remaining Soviet military threat hundreds of kilometers to the East. Beyond these consequences, the Soviet Union itself has entered an apparently open-ended period of political and social turmoil.

In parallel with these internal changes, Soviet foreign policy has undergone dramatic transformation as well. From the Soviet withdrawal from Afghanistan, to Soviet cooperation with the United States and the West, at least in the United Nations Security Council, in the campaign to reverse the Iraqi invasion of Kuwait, there has been growing evidence of fundamental change in the adversary relationship upon which the Cold-War was based. In short, the end of the 1980s and beginning of the 1990s have provided powerful reasons to reassess policies which were consistent with that relationship. Some have concluded that the rationale for COCOM-based "National Security" export controls is virtually eliminated. Others have argued that prudence is in order, as long as there remains the combination of powerful Soviet military forces in existence and substantial uncertainty about the long-term political shape of the Soviet Union.[6] While this issue remains open to debate, these geopolitical changes have in fact already provoked substantial policy changes.

The reunification of Germany immediately resulted in the elimination of export controls on what had once been a member country of the Warsaw Pact and a COCOM-proscribed destination. Obviously the elimination of all internal economic and customs barriers in reunified Germany necessitated the elimination of export controls directed at what had formerly been East Germany, by other members of COCOM since they would no longer have been enforceable.

More generally, the so-called policy of "differentiation," under which the U.S. Government has sought to encourage some degree of independence from Moscow on the part of other members of the Warsaw Pact, has taken on new content. Prior to 1989 that policy was largely one of appearances. The United States would treat Warsaw Pact countries somewhat differently, in response to the degree of "independence" which they demonstrated in their foreign policy. This policy of differentiation could even go so far as to include selective granting of most-favored-nation treatment but not so far as to differentiate in export control policy. This was so because notwithstanding occasional political or foreign policy differences between the Soviets and one or another Warsaw Pact Ally, there was little doubt in the U.S. Government that technologies sold to a Poland or Romania, for example, could not be kept from the Soviets, should the Soviets desire access. Since the 1989 changes of government in the countries of the Warsaw Pact, and in fact its official dissolution, it is not unreasonable to believe that undertakings by those democratically elected governments to protect COCOM origin technology, would be carried out. In fact, since 1990 the United States has been involved in technical discussions with several former Warsaw Pact governments on the subject of establishing export controls and related safeguard regimes. Thus, in the wake of the

"Revolutions of 1989" the policy of differentiation may well acquire more substantive content.

Perhaps the most dramatic response to the Revolutions of 1989 in the area of export controls was the top-level political decision, taken in 1990, to substantially reduce the COCOM industrial list.[7] That decision consisted of several elements. One was an immediate reduction in the control list of roughly 30 items. A second was a near-term effort to reduce controls further in the areas of computers, telecommunication and machine tools. A third initiative was to undertake to replace the remaining COCOM industrial list with a new and further reduced "core list," agreement upon which was announced in May of 1991.

This latter goal is important because it has produced an additional and dramatic reduction in COCOM export controls. The idea of a "core list" is contrary to the general tendency of regulatory agencies to produce comprehensive lists and then establish differing control standards for the various components of such lists. Comprehensive lists in turn provide a basis for broader controls. The importance of a "core list" is that it is limited to only those categories of sufficient strategic importance to be worth controlling, implying that what is not listed is not controlled.

Establishing that positive requirement as the principle governing export control list-making helps to reduce the length of the control lists over time, and establishes a useful barrier to the automatic expansion of controls. However, the principle is by no means self-enforcing, and regulatory bureaucracies, particularly where regulatory criteria are related to national security, will always tend to err on the side of caution.

On the other side of the coin, the continued existence of large and competent Soviet military forces, and continued uncertainty about the risks of a Soviet regime emerging which once again takes on a primarily adversarial coloration, will reenforce institutional resistance to the decline of national security export controls for the foreseeable future. That decline, therefore, may well prove less rapid than some would anticipate.

NEW CHALLENGES

If national security controls continue to decline in scope, no matter how gradually, are they likely to be supplanted by an offsetting expansion in other kinds of export controls? If one were to consider the controversy raised over U.S. and other COCOM country exports to Iraq in the wake of the invasion of Kuwait and the War in the Persian Gulf, it would not be difficult to conclude that "Foreign Policy Controls", which cover all U.S. exports to Iraq (a number of other countries actually exported munitions, the United States did not) would certainly expand substantially.

As alluded to earlier, Foreign Policy Controls refer to export controls established in support of human rights and anti-terrorism policies, embargoes on trade with a number of legally proscribed countries, and policies aimed against the proliferation of nuclear weapons, chemical and biological weapons, and nuclear-capable missiles.[8]

The nuclear non-proliferation controls date back conceptually to the Baruch Plan for international controls of nuclear technology proposed by the United States in 1946. Legally the authorities currently reside in the Export Administration Act and the Nuclear Non-Proliferation Act of 1978. The objective is to restrict the spread of technologies and commodities useful in the design or development of nuclear weapons or in the enrichment of uranium or reprocessing of plutonium. The difficulty has always resided in the dual-use character of the latter two capabilities, both being normal elements of a complete nuclear fuel-cycle, and necessary elements of an independent nuclear power capability.

On the positive side, it is worth noting that in the nearly half-decade of the nuclear age, only a half dozen or so nations have chosen to demonstrate a nuclear weapons capability. By contrast, based upon technical capabilities alone, there is little doubt that number could have been three or four times as large. Thus, the phenomenon that bears explaining is probably why so few rather than why so many. Part of the explanation may result from the international non-proliferation regime of which U.S. export controls are a part—the collaboration on exports in the Nuclear Suppliers Group, the international inspection regime run by the International Atomic Energy Agency, and the near-universal adherence to the Nuclear Non-Proliferation Treaty. In any case, there would seem to be little reason to expect the rate of spread of nuclear weapons capability to alter significantly from historical tendencies. If anything, a number of developments on the international scene would seem to auger well for a decline in the rate of nuclear spread. Thus, export controls associated with nuclear non-proliferation policy are unlikely to produce a significantly expanding regulatory workload.

A greater potential for expanded export controls would appear to exist in the area of chemical warfare, where the so-called Australia Group[9] of countries has been the focus of international efforts to expand controls on both chemicals which can be used in chemical weapons and industrial facilities and associated technologies related to chemical weapons production. The greatest difficulty here is that the overlap between proscribed activities and capabilities and normal civilian applications is even more extensive. Fertilizer manufacture, pharmaceutical production, even facilities for brewing beer can be modified to produce militarily usable products. Furthermore, there is no scarcity at all of the knowledge of chemistry needed to produce chemical weapons.

Yet chemical weapons are of sufficiently modest military utility, and are sufficiently widely-proscribed, that there would not appear to be a strong "demand" to produce them. Only a handful of "pariah countries" have historically shown any interest, and there is little reason to expect this to change significantly for the worse in the foreseeable future. Thus, here also there would appear to be as much reason for optimism as for pessimism with respect to prospective demand for the significant expansion of export controls.

Finally, the third potential candidate for the substantial expansion of foreign policy export controls would be the Missile Technology Control Regime, formally established in July 1987, after five years of negotiation. The objective of this regime is to inhibit the spread of technologies related to the development and production of nuclear-capable missiles. Here again, the control problem is technically difficult, the potential benefits of export controls are limited, and an overlap with legitimate activities exists. Specifically, space launch vehicles are functionally the equivalent of ballistic missiles. Thus, countries which have or are acquiring the capability to launch payloads of any consequence into space, such as Israel, India, or Brazil, are by definition also capable of delivering those payloads at substantial ranges to targets on the earth's surface. The significance of this capability should, however, not be overstated. There are, for example, a number of countries not in possession of space launch capabilities which have nonetheless acquired ballistic missiles upon which they could eventually mount some kind of nuclear weapon. Furthermore, there are a number of countries which remain potential suppliers. Beyond this of course, one need not be in possession of ballistic missiles to deliver a nuclear weapon. Jet passenger or cargo aircraft would serve more than adequately, and these exist in the commercial airlines of nearly ever country in the world.

In any event, here again, the number of countries "of concern" is unlikely to grow, and if anything, more likely to remain small or even shrink. Thus, the real, long-term prospect for an increasing export control workload resulting from the spread of nuclear-capable missile programs is likely to remain modest.

More generally, the disappearance of the Cold War, the emergence of democratic governments in many key countries, and the growing focus upon the demand for economic growth are likely to remain the dominant tendencies reducing the list of "pariah countries" over the longer run, and it is this phenomenon which will ultimately determine the foreign policy controls workload. So here also, the longer-term trend is likely to be downward.

CONCLUSIONS

If national security controls are a diminishing phenomenon and foreign policy controls, over the longer run, may well move in the same direction, do other policy objectives exist which can affect the scope of export controls? Quite possibly, our relations with friends and allies may undergo changes in ways that affect technology transfer policies and export controls, just as have our relations with adversaries in the case of national security controls, and our fluctuating relations with still other countries in the case of foreign policy controls. The issue at the heart of this possibility is a familiar one, and that is economic competitiveness. Its more recent manifestations include the controversy over defense industrial collaboration in the development and procurement of weapons systems, other forms of offsets in defense procurement, the foreign acquisition of U.S. defense firms, and so on. Other, somewhat older manifestations include political pressures to "buy American."

Debates over such issues are likely to result from multiple motives on the part of multiple constituencies. But it is likely that protectionist forces will make increasing use of the technology transfer issue in an effort to keep production at home. In short, it is entirely possible that technology transfer policy and export control practices could become dominated by domestic political forces.

Perhaps the most common motivation in issues of this type is a straightforward concern about jobs... buy American in order to employ Americans. Another concern is to preserve a capability viewed as important to future defense production, either by preventing the foreign acquisition of a defense company or by procuring from that company, the economics of the procurement notwithstanding. Such policies and motivations need not necessarily influence technology transfer policy or export control practice directly, and are more likely to be manifested in U.S. government procurement policy and practice, arms transfer offset policy, or positions on potential foreign acquisition of U.S. companies.   There are, however, manifestations of this issue from time to time that portend a more direct impact upon technology transfer policy and practice.

At the end of the Reagan Administration, the United States had completed the negotiation of a Memorandum of Understanding with the government of Japan outlining the collaborative development of a new combat aircraft, the FSX. This agreement was a compromise that was not the preferred outcome for some on the U.S. side, who preferred that Japan simply purchase an off-the-shelf U.S. aircraft, nor was it the preferred outcome for some on the Japanese side who preferred that Japan develop and build a fighter aircraft independently.

This project arose as a subject of substantial political controversy early in the Bush Administration, and as a result came close to being politically de-railed in the United States. Much of the debate was about the "fairness" or "balance" of the exchange in terms of the contributions of technology and prospective workshares of the two sides. At bottom, however, there was strong concern expressed on the U.S. side about whether too much U.S. technology would be released to Japan in the course of this project. "To much" in this instance meant specifically technology which could be employed by Japan to improve its commercial competitiveness vis a vis the United States in the aerospace industry. This example is not idiosyncratic. There are a number of trends emerging in international economic and technological affairs that suggest that the issue of competitiveness will, over time, come to occupy a larger and more controversial role in the technology transfer policy area.

The likely global decline in defense budgets, coupled with the continuing rise in real costs of major weapons systems, generates continuing pressures toward greater collaboration. The advantages of shared research and development costs and the advantages of larger, combined production runs need no elaborate explanation. And, while declining defense budgets will also generate countervailing protectionist pressures, on balance, the net effect is likely to be in the direction of collaboration. That means a more frequent opportunity for technology transfer to be a subject of controversy.

The substantial and perhaps growing overlap between technologies with military and those with civilian applications, such as computers, jet engines, advanced materials, telecommunications, and so on, will generate both traditional sensitivities with respect to national security considerations, and growing sensitivities about commercial spinoffs and competition such as those which have characterized the FSX debate.

In short, our technology transfer policies and export control practices will in all likelihood become focused upon the non-traditional considerations of economic competitiveness with friends, and decreasingly upon the more traditional concerns of keeping sensitive technologies out of the hands of adversaries, as our technology cooperation and technology control policies come to overlap almost completely.

NOTES

1. These terms refer to policies and practices that facilitate the ability of allied military forces to fight effectively together by, for example, explicit division of labor (rationalization) and measures such as agreement on common weapons calibers, communications frequencies, tactics, operational procedures and so on (standardization and interoperability).

2. Michael Mastanduno, "What is COCOM and how does it work?" Robert Cullen, ed., *The Post-Containment Handbook: Key Issues in US-Soviet Economic Relations* (Boulder, Colo.: Westview Press, 1990), p. 75.

3. Ibid.

4. Section 5(k) of the Export Administration Act states:

   Negotiations with other Countries.-The Secretary of State, in consultation with
   the Secretary of Defense the Secretary of Commerce, and the heads of other
   appropriate departments and agencies shall be responsible for conducting
   negotiations with other countries including those countries not participating in
   the group known as the Coordinating Committee, regarding their cooperation
   in restricting the export of goods and technology in order to carry out the
   policy set forth in section 3(g) of this Act, as authorized by subsection (a) of
   this section, including negotiations with respect to which goods and technology
   should be subject to multilaterally agreed export restrictions and what
   conditions should apply for exceptions for those restrictions comparable in
   practice to those maintained by the Coordinating Committee, the Secretary
   shall treat exports, whether by individual or multiple licenses, to countries
   party to such agreements in the same manner as exports to members of the
   Coordinating Committee are treated, including the same manner as exports are
   treated under subsection (b)(2) of this section and Section 10(o) of this Act.

5. Sections 7 and 3(2)(c) of the Export Administration Act as amended.

6. Stephen D. Bryen, "Don't sell the Patriot to Moscow," *Wall Street Journal*,
February 26, 1991, p. H-4.

7. See, for example, "COCOOM Adapts Strategic Trade Rules," *Bulletin of the
Atlantic Council of the United States* 1 (July 1990).

8. Section 6 of the Export Administration Act of 1979 as amended in 1981, 1985,
and 1988.

9. An informal group of 20 industrialized countries which meet periodically to
consider ways to coordinate exports of sensitive chemicals and related commodities.
See for example "White House sets rules to halt spread of chemical, biological,
nuclear arms," *The Wall Street Journal*, March 8, 1991, p. A7A.

Conclusions
and
Policy Recommendations

Ethan B. Kapstein

As the chapters in this volume make clear, the policy issues associated with the globalization of the defense industrial base in general, and international armaments collaboration in particular, pose a series of vexing dilemmas for public officials and defense industry executives. In this chapter I try to analyze some of those dilemmas, and to suggest areas for future research.

WHY COLLABORATE?

Why do countries collaborate in the production of advanced weaponry? As I argued in my chapter, arms collaboration appears to represent a "second-best" response to the political economy of arms production. In the first-best world of the laissez-faire economist, arms would be provided like any other commodity, product, or service; that is, according to the principle of comparative advantage. Those countries with a comparative advantage in arms production would export final products to countries lacking the requisite technology, capital, and labor.

There are two prominent reasons for the divergence between theory and practice in arms production and trade, though the relative weighing which should be assigned to each reason remains unclear. First, of course, is *national security*. In an anarchic international environment, states must look to their own wherewithal for survival. All other things being equal, states would prefer to be autarkic in the production and deployment of advanced weaponry. Given that no country today can achieve the desired condition of self-sufficiency at politically acceptable costs, governments will still do what they can to maintain at least some defense production at home. This enables them to retain indigenous "know-how" in the event that domestic industry must turn to weapons manufacture on a larger scale at some future date.

The second reason, however, concerns *economics*, and more specifically, jobs. In Joel Johnson's felicitous phrase, many countries have "defense jobs policies" instead of "defense procurement policies." He reminds us that defense expenditures are made with funds provided by taxpayers, who generally like to see their money spent at home. Even if the costs of building armaments in a domestic plant are greater, there are few countries in which citizens would be willing to see all their defense procurement budget used to purchase goods from abroad.

The economic reasoning, however, goes beyond job creation. Today, fewer and fewer countries or industries are willing to invest the risk capital needed to perform up-front R&D and then to engage in the production of advanced weaponry, especially in light of the fact that foreign markets may be closed to off-the-shelf export sales owing to government policies. In this environment, countries or firms may seek foreign partners to share the risks, and to ensure that the final product can be sold in more than one defense market.

International arms collaboration thus exists *between* economics and national security. It keeps jobs, defense spending, and industrial capability at home, while accessing capital and technology from abroad.   It would thus seem like the ideal solution to the contemporary problems that face procurement officials and industry executives; but appearances are often deceiving, and as this book has demonstrated, arms collaboration brings with it a host of economic and security challenges.

BARRIERS TO COLLABORATION

History shows that arms collaboration is difficult to achieve in practice. This study has identified several factors that mitigate against project success:

1. **Harmonization of Requirements**. Collaboration can only succeed when the parties to an arms project agree on the military requirement to be fulfilled and the appropriate response. This would seem straightforward, but both the assessment of need and determination of response are fraught with uncertainty; further, both processes are dynamic, in that new information is constantly being received over the life of a weapons program that may take ten years or more from blueprint to deployment. Of course, this uncertainty has only grown since 1989, with the dissolution of the Warsaw Pact.

One policy response that has been suggested in light of this harmonization problem is to provide NATO with something like a supranational procurement authority. These officials would determine *for* the member states the alliance requirements that must be met and the weapons that should be deployed. They would even be responsible for running procurement competitions.

While it would be easy to dismiss this supranational idea as "pie in the sky" on the alliance-level, it is altogether conceivable that such a development will occur within the context of an evolving European Community. The European defense industries have undergone a feverish period of mergers and acquisitions over the past five years, and now several of the continent's large defense firms (e.g. British Aerospace and Deutsche Aerospace) rival in size their American counterparts. European weapons *will* be built collaboratively; isn't it possible that the procurement process, through the vehicle of the Independent European Programme Group (IEPG), will become community-wide as well?

2. **Technology Transfer**.   Every collaborative arms program generates debate within American administrations about the transfer of technology.   To some officials, the transfer of defense-related technology to friends and allies only represents the first step toward a global diffusion process that will inevitably come back to hurt our national security interests.   To others, the transfer of such technology will rebound in the form of heightened economic competition from such countries as Japan, which seem to be better than the United States at making commercial use of whatever new products and processes enter their factories.   In both cases, the technology transfer argument gives adversaries of arms collaboration a powerful trump card.

Traditionally, the export control debate has occurred largely within the foreign policy and defense communities.   But as Stan Sienkiewicz points out in his chapter, it may be that domestic political actors will make increasing use of it in an effort to protect industries and jobs.   This would be an important new twist, and provide an added challenge to those officials and executives who seek to pursue international arrangements for weapons production.   Going through Congress, domestic actors can seek to stop a foreign project on the basis of technology transfer considerations, when their foremost concern is with keeping the defense factories operating at home.

3. **Arms Control**.   With the end of the Cold War, many observers expected the export control regime to evaporate.   Saddam Hussein's brutal invasion of Kuwait certainly ended that speculation.   During the Iraq war, President George Bush declared his intention to seek controls on global arms proliferation, and during the summer of 1991 the members of the United Nations Security Council opened talks with such an objective in mind.   While this suggests that the focus of arms control concerns will take on more of a north/south perspective, that in itself may only *add* to the debate over armaments collaboration.   After all, with rare exceptions, no allied nation sold defense-technology directly to the Soviet Union, but the allies have

all vigorously pursued arms sales and coproduction deals in the third world. Indeed, some claim that it was this aggressive marketing that made it possible for a Saddam Hussein to amass such a huge military-industrial complex. In the future, it will become increasingly difficult to dissociate debates on technology transfer from those on arms control, and this development can only work against international collaboration.

POLICY RECOMMENDATIONS

Armaments collaboration provides an example of a public policy issue area in which the programmatic logic seems compelling on the one hand, while the actual impediments to execution are almost overwhelming on the other. This would imply that either the logic is wrong, or that the process must be reformed. I would argue some of each, and as a result the following policy recommendations emerge:

1. **Off-the-Shelf Sales Are Preferable to Collaboration.** In those cases where arms sales are deemed to be in the national interest, I would assert that off-the-shelf sales should generally be pursued rather than arms collaboration. That is to say, in economic terminology, a "first-best" approach. It might be argued that such a policy would only lead to greater arms proliferation. While recognizing the need for continued export and technology transfer controls, the counter-argument could be made that what is most dangerous for the security environment is the sale of *processes and capabilities* rather than end-items. Indeed, when arms are sold off-the-shelf the buyer must usually purchase an array of services and spare parts that result in continued reliance—one could say dependence—on the seller. When a seller, in contrast, provides the buyer with a complete industry, as was the case when General Dynamics sold the F-16 to Turkey, providing that country with an advanced aerospace production facility, then the problems of control are greatly multiplied.

2. Change the Government-Industry Relationship. Arms collaboration projects have been most successful in those cases when industry rather than government took the lead; that is, when the collaborative arrangements had a market logic to them. Again, contrast the many postwar coproduction arrangements (the Starfighter, the Harrier, the F-16) that succeeded, versus the "Nunn amendment" programs (e.g. the NATO frigate) that have largely failed. In the former case, industry initiated and executed the deal; in the latter, the program was directed by a government office, usually responding to some perceived political need (such as "strengthening the alliance").

This, of course, does not imply that government has no role to play in collaborative projects. On the contrary, government officials are ultimately responsible for approving such projects and agreeing to the types of technologies that can be released; indeed, governments will probably strengthen their policies in these areas. But I remain unconvinced that governments can "make" collaboration succeed when their industrial partners fail to find some mutual interests.

3. Educate Procurement Executives. As Michael Farr points out in his chapter, European respondents to a survey regarding trans-Atlantic arms collaboration expressed enormous frustration with their American counterparts. The Americans rarely spoke a foreign language, failed to understand the culture in which they were operating, and were victimized by high job turnover. Clearly, this is no way to run an international program!

Unfortunately, Farr's results mirror similar findings for American business as a whole. The decline of America's industrial competitiveness has, of course, manifold macro- and micro-economic roots, but almost all commentators have pointed to the nation's "education gap." Furthermore, with rare exceptions, American firms themselves have done little in the way of worker advancement.

To its credit, the Department of Defense has begun to remedy the problem. It now offers a one-week course on international armaments collaboration at the Defense Systems Management College in Fort

Belvoir, Virginia. But this is hardly enough, and we urge the Pentagon to bolster its efforts with regard to the education of procurement executives.

FUTURE RESEARCH REQUIREMENTS

Every good academic study ends with a call for more research. In the case a hand, such a call would appear entirely justified. Indeed, it should be emphasized that several members of our project's study group, some of whom have been associated with defense procurement for twenty years or more, expressed the view that in recent years the Department of Defense has seemingly lost touch with academic research into weapons acquisition. Whereas a veritable cottage industry existed during the Kennedy and Johnson administrations, when substantial support was given to such think tanks as RAND in an effort to improve procurement practices, more recently there has been a "disconnect" between the Pentagon and the academic community. Thus, one of our hopes is that this study, along with others produced by the Economics and National Security Program and its counterpart institutes elsewhere, will cause the Pentagon and defense ministries abroad to establish a renewed dialogue with the academic community, an effort that may pay needed dividends at a time of significant adjustment to their procurement budgets.

1. **Economic Analysis.** As Jacques Gansler points out in his chapter, we have few data points concerning collaborative programs. In short, we need greater project *transparency*. We have no illusions about getting access to such data. Under the guise of national security, Pentagon officials will make it difficult for scholars to assess the costs and benefits associated with major weapons systems. Nor is the Pentagon alone in this regard. Anyone who has tried to conduct research in international organizations knows that the

problems are greatly compounded overseas. Few countries have a "freedom of information act" or release nearly as much information about defense programs as does the United States. Still, the paucity of data makes economic analysis next to impossible.

2. **Technology Transfer.** A second area for research concerns the effectiveness of alliance technology transfer policies. As Sienkiewicz points out in his chapter, many of our policies in this area date back to the end of World War II, and obviously need updating. Should technology transfer focus on individual products, or should it focus on industrial processes? There are numerous issues associated with export controls and technology transfer policies that would benefit from academic scrutiny.

3. **Comparative Procurement Policies.** Finally, more work is needed in the area of comparative procurement policies. In the process of writing this book, the members of the study group discovered that they knew relatively little about how arms procurement decisions are actually made in foreign capitals; indeed, the process in Washington remains a mystery! Clearly, a number of useful studies could be conducted that compared the procurement policies and practices of different countries, with one possible objective being the formulation of objective performance measures. It is not always possible to transplant government or industry techniques and operations from one country to another, but analysis of differing approaches can always be useful in understanding the strengths and weaknesses of domestic systems, and in promoting reforms of existing procedures.

In sum, this book notwithstanding, we still know relatively little about the globalization of the defense industrial base, and its implications for the economic and security environments. We do know, however, that issues at the interface of economics and national security will remain at the forefront of public debate, both in the United States and abroad. Further, we know that officials charged with policy formulation in these areas take on a tremendous responsibility, to this and to future generations. If our work contributes to public understanding of the policy dilemmas involved, and points toward some useful recommendations, we will have largely achieved our objectives.

Index